UNLOCKING OUR SHARED VALUE

Corporate Sustainability Strategies in the West African Mining Industry

ROBERT NDONG

FOREWORD BY MINISTER SOPHIE GLADIMA

FriesenPress

Suite 300 - 990 Fort St
Victoria, BC, V8V 3K2
Canada

www.friesenpress.com

ISBN
978-1-03-911489-0 (Hardcover)
978-1-03-911488-3 (Paperback)
978-1-03-911490-6 (eBook)

1. Business & Economics, Industries, Natural Resource Extraction

Distributed to the trade by The Ingram Book Company

TABLE OF CONTENTS

ACKNOWLEDGEMENTS

*"The most powerful way to create change
is to create a model for others to
critique, imitate or iterate on."*

Jeffrey Hollender

To Detto, Théa, Youngar, and to all
sustainability professionals within the extractive industry

My sincere thanks to Minister Sophie Gladima for
the foreword, and to Aziz Sy, Adama Barry, Aminata Ly Faye,
and Michel Thioyine Mbodji for their sound advice.

FOREWORD BY MINISTER SOPHIE GLADIMA

Africa's subsoil is rich in hydrocarbons, precious and base metals, and rare metals that are particularly strategic for the global transition to a low-carbon economy. In this context, the continent's beautiful, serious and pressing challenge is to ensure that the exploitation of its immense natural resources takes place in compliance with the best international standards in terms of sustainable development and transparent management, so that the wealth created can contribute to the significant improvement of living conditions for the populations of the host countries, while ensuring the attractiveness and competitiveness vis-à-vis other major mining regions. The mining industry obviously has a central role to play in this dynamic, and this is what, in my opinion, provides all the meaning and relevance of this book, which has the merit of focusing on the issues of the West African sub-region whose mineral potential is no longer to be demonstrated.

The West African mining world is in the midst of change and full of vitality, with a breath of youthfulness that is eager to make its voice heard in order to expose and propose its new vision of sustainable, modern mining in line with major global issues such as good governance, equity, protection of biodiversity, the fight against climate change, and the decarbonization of the world economy. This new dynamic is embodied by new sustainable development leaders who are dynamic, well-trained, experienced, and lucid, such as Robert Ndong, a credible and authorized voice for sustainable development in the West African mining industry.

In the 2000s, Robert was my student in geology for his bachelor's degree in natural sciences at the Faculty of Science and Technology of the Cheikh

Anta DIOP University in Dakar, Senegal. About fifteen years later, after completing his training and gaining solid professional experience in the field of sustainable development in France, Canada, and the Democratic Republic of Congo, Robert returned to Senegal as Environmental Manager in a gold mine in the Kédougou region in the east of the country. We had frequent interactions, since during this period, I was the Minister of Mines and Geology of Senegal, and issues related to environmental protection and sustainable development, in general, were at the heart of my concerns. Our exchanges therefore naturally focused on issues related to the cohabitation between gold panning and industrial mining, the conservation of biodiversity, and the financing of income-generating activities for women in rural areas, but also on the rehabilitation of mining sites and the post-closure use of these sites at the end of mining operations. A few years later, it is with renewed pleasure that we find ourselves, through this book, continuing the conversation on this more-than-ever-topical subject of corporate sustainable development strategies in the West African mining industry.

Through this book, the author attempts to adapt the main principles of sustainable development and social sciences in a perspective compatible with the context and realities of the mining industry in the sub-region. In contrast to those who predict the spectre of the curse of natural resources, the author demonstrates with lucidity and realism that the sustainable exploitation of African mining resources can and must be a powerful lever for development that will help lift millions of Africans out of extreme poverty and thus enable them to resolutely embark on the path of emergence. Such a perspective is, obviously, only conceivable insofar as we accept to change the paradigm in which we perceive sustainable development in the mining industry as an optional, superficial dimension that would be limited to sporadic philanthropic gestures in a perspective of public relations, or temporarily obtaining the social license to operate. Such an approach would neither meet the strong and legitimate aspirations of local populations and host countries, nor the expectations of investors and shareholders who increasingly demand that their money be invested with full consideration of the environmental, social, and governance dimensions of sustainable development.

In contrast, in this book, the author addresses sustainable development in its strategic and business case perspective, which will be of greater interest to decision-makers, investors, members of the boards of directors and managers of mining companies, as well as to the governments of host countries. It is in this strategic perspective with an African flavour that the chapters of this book, all equally relevant, demonstrate the business case for sustainable development, both in its financial and non-technical risk management dimension, and as a competitive advantage in the race to obtain concessions for the exploitation of natural resources that are increasingly prized in West Africa, along with obtaining and securing the significant financing required. From the formalization of gold panning and its harmonious cohabitation with industrial mining, the use of local content to promote capacity building and employability of the local workforce, strategies for stakeholder engagement to community development programs, the author courageously addresses and positions himself on these major issues of the West African mining industry. Issues related to biodiversity conservation, the valorization of traditional knowledge and know-how as well as those associated with the preservation of cultural heritage are also well-documented and the author presents tools, standards, and best practices for sustainable mining.

The question of local valorization of mining resources is increasingly raised from an international equity perspective. It is in this perspective that the author highlights the immense assets of the sub-region, particularly in terms of high-grade iron ore reserves, to envisage the future positioning of West Africa as a new continental and global hub in terms of production of high-grade iron ore and its local processing into steel to meet the continent's needs, as well as part of global demand. Obviously, this transformation will have to be done in a perspective of progressive de-carbonization of the mining and steel industries in connection with the global problem of climate change, the negative consequences of which are already severely affecting vulnerable populations in West Africa. This new global movement towards the decarbonization of the world economy provides excellent momentum for the West African sub-region, which must already take advantage of it to strongly position itself as a hub of the green economy, and thus attract the billions of dollars that will soon be invested in low-carbon projects. Once again, the West African mining industry will have a crucial role to play in the success or failure of this positioning. All in all, it is with great pleasure and interest that I read this rich document, which I will keep as a bedside book, and I sincerely hope that it will be the same for all other readers.

Mrs. Sophie Gladima
Minister of Oil and Energy of the Republic of Senegal,
Former Minister of Mines and Geology
Dakar, February 22nd, 2021

LIST OF ABBREVIATIONS

AfCFTA	African Continental Free Trade Area
ASM	Artisanal & Small-Scale Mining
BF-BOF	Blast-Furnace-Basic Oxygen Furnace
BFFI	Biodiversity Footprint Financial Institutions
BIA	Biodiversity Impact Analytics
BIF	Bounded Iron ore
BSR	Business for Social Responsibility
CAPEX	Capital expenditure
CAPP	Central African Power Pool
CBF	Corporate Biodiversity Footprint
CDB	Convention on Biological Diversity
CDP	Carbon Disclosure Project
CEOs	Chief Executive Officers
CITES	Convention on the International Trade in Endangered Species of Flaura and Fauna
CIM	Canadian Institute of Mining, Metallurgy and Petroleum
CO_2eq	CO_2 equivalent
COMELEC	Comité Maghrébin de l'Électricité
CRD	Community Relations and Development
CSR	Corporate Social Responsibility
CSB	Center for Sustainable Business
CSV	Creation of Shared Value
CSM	Critical and Strategic Minerals

DRI	Direct Reduced Iron
DSD	Driving Sustainable Decision
EAF	Electric Arc Furnace
EAPP	East African Power Pool
ECOWAS	Economic Commission of West Africa
E&Y	Ernst & Young
EI	Extractive Industry
EITI	Extractive Industry Transparency Initiative
ENCORE	Exploring Natural Capital Opportunities, Risks and Exposure
ESG	Environmental, Social, Governance
ESIA	Environmental & Social Impact Assessment
ESMS	Environment & Social Management System
FIs	Financial Institutions
FMG	Fortescue Metals Group
GBSFI	Global Biodiversity Score for Financial Institutions
GDP	Gross Domestic Product
GHG	Greenhouse Gas
GMI	Global Mining Initiative
GRI	Global Reporting Initiative
HDI	Human Development Index
HFO	Heavy Fuel oil
HR	Human Resources
ICMM	International Council on Mining & Metals
ICT	Information and Communication Technologies
IFC	International Finance Corporations
IGF	Intergovernmental Forum on Mining, Minerals, Metals and Sustainable Development
IISD	International Institute for Sustainable Development

INSD	Institut National de la Statistique et de la Démographie
IP	Indigenous People
IPIECA	International Petroleum Industry Environmental Conservation Association
IRMA	Initiative for Responsible Mining Assurance
IUCN	International Union for the Conservation of Nature
JORC	Joint Ore Reserve Committee
LFO	Light Fuel Oil
LNG	Liquefied Natural Gas
LSM	Large-Scale Mining
LTO	License To Operate
LULUCF	Land Use Land Use Change and Forestry
MAC	Mining Association of Canada
MDGs	Millennium Development Goals
MIFERSO	Société des Mines de Fer du Sénégal Oriental
MMSD	Mining Minerals & Sustainable Development
Mt	Million tons
NGO	Non-Governmental Organization
NTRs	Non-Technical Risks
OHF	Open Hearth Furnace
PDAC	Prospectors & Developers Association of Canada
R4I	Resource for Infrastructure
REDD+	Reducing Emissions from Deforestation and Forest Degradation
RSI. M.	Robert's Sustain Invest Matrix
SASB	Sustainability Accounting Standard Board
SMB	Société Minière de Boké
SMFG	Société des Mines de Fer de Guinée
SNIM	Société Nationale Industrielle et Minière

SDGs	Sustainable Development Goals
SI	Social Investment
SRI	Sustainable Responsible Investing
STAR	Species Threat Abatement and Restoration metric
SVI	Shared Value Initiative
TCFD	Task Force on Climate Finance Disclosure
TEK	Traditional Ecological Knowledge
TSF	Tailings Storage Facility
TSM	Toward Sustainable Mining
TwH	Terawatt-Hour
UN	United Nations
UNECA	United Nations Economic Commission for Africa
UNPRI	United Nations Principles for Responsible Investment
USD	United States Dollar
UNFCCC	United Nations Framework Convention on Climate Change
WABiCC	West Africa Biodiversity and Climate Change
WAPP	West African Power Pool
WGC	World Gold Council

INTRODUCTION

From Guinea to Burkina Faso and Nigeria, from Democratic Republic of Congo to Mali, Angola, Côte d'Ivoire, and Senegal, the African continent is rich in mineral resources, and the continent's potential remains under-explored. Nevertheless, around the world, the huge economic output of the extractives sectors, valued at $35 trillion in 2012, has not always translated into improved social and environmental outcomes for countries and communities where these companies operate (Shared Value Initiative, 2014). Among nations that depend most heavily on mineral and fuels, only two rank among the top 50 countries globally in the United Nations Development Program's Human Development Index (HDI). At the same time, extractives companies are losing billions to community strife despite extensive community relations programs (Shared Value Initiative, 2014). The challenges related to sustainable development are particularly critical in the mining sector, especially in Africa. "Africa is standing on the edge of enormous opportunities" stated Kofi Annan in the Africa Progress Panel Report 2013 (Equity in Extractives—Stewarding Africa Natural Resources for All). Annan also highlighted that Africa loses twice as much in illicit financial outflows as it receives in international financial aid. In this context, the core critical question is: "*Does or will African resources wealth ensure better life for local communities in host countries and future generation*"?

Extractive industry has emerged as a powerful engine of economic growth, and Africa's petroleum, gas and mineral resources have become a powerful magnet for foreign investments. With new explorations revealing much larger reserves than were previously known, Africa stands to reap a natural resources windfall (Africa Progress Panel, 2013). And this happens

1

in a context of three big trends around the world: depletion of natural resources, radical transparency, and high expectations. So, the obvious challenges facing the region's governments is to convert the temporary windfall to a breakthrough in human development, and this could be leveraged though the score for United Nations Sustainable Development Goals (SDGs) from now to 2030. The SDGs and the UN Sustainable Agenda for 2030 represents the world's action plan for social inclusion, environmental sustainability, and economic development (UNDP et al., 2016). Obviously, the mining industry has both a negative and positive impacts on the SDGs, especially in the least developed countries where all the SDGs are urgent and essential to achieve for the survival of local populations and the fight against extreme poverty. Therefore, the momentum is still perfect for the mining industry to better demonstrate that it can mainstream sustainability and be a key player in achieving or at least robustly implementing the SDGs in Africa. As highlighted by the Africa Progress Panel, the reality is that "[…] well-managed mineral resources wealth has the potential to lift millions of African out of poverty in the next decades while giving hope to future generations". This challenge is a shared responsibility mainly between governments, corporations, and western countries, as "[…] we all stand to win from an Africa that is truly prosperous, stable, and fair" (Africa Progress Panel, 2013, p. 7 & 8).

The extractive industry has an unprecedented opportunity to contribute to achieving the SDGs, through strong corporate sustainability strategies deeply embedded in corporate culture, and the creation of shared value principles. Furthermore, the business case for sustainability has shown that only this approach could ensure long-term total shareholder returns while maximizing the total social impacts of the extractive industry. The relevancy of this business case is widely understood and claimed by extractive industries' executives and investors, and more and more foreign investors show that they can make healthy profits, while also adhering to the highest international standards of social and environmental protection. Western countries are also supporting this trend through regulatory tools such as the Dodd Frank Act in the USA and comparable legislation in the European Union, and voluntary initiatives such as the Extractive Industry Transparency Initiative (EITI). It is also becoming more and more demonstrated that unsustainable corporate practices or Environment, Social, and Governance (ESG) incidents could have direct and dire consequences on corporate reputation, share price, company valuation, and on access to natural resources.

Despite the acknowledgment of the business case of sustainability, the demonstrated consequences of unsustainable corporate practices, and the positive trend of significant progress on countries' Gross Domestic Product (GDP), we are still facing mixed progress on poverty reduction and human development in Africa. In theory, it is expected that natural resources wealth should strengthen economic growth, provide governments with an opportunity to support human development, and create employment. Unfortunately, in practice, in several of Africa's resource rich countries, it has often led to poverty, inequality, and violent conflicts. These are the symptoms that have been widely attributed to a resources curse, or to the mineral-based poverty trap (Africa Progress Panel, 2013). In summary, translating African resources into revenues, and those revenues into development outcomes is not straightforward (Oxfam, 2016). This currently results in mixed progress on poverty reduction and human development, as shown by the Human Development index (HDI) rank of resource rich countries in Africa, where economic wealth does not translate into the improved health and education indicators that might have been anticipated. "This failure to build human capital creates real business costs, some obvious (e.g., conflicts with local communities that see no benefits from resources extraction), and some subtler (e.g., the added cost of sourcing goods and services from uncompetitive local suppliers, employing an expatriate workforce at a premium due to lack of local talent). [...] Moreover, as technology becomes less of a differentiator between companies, demonstrating the ability to address social issues to host governments and communities will be critical to securing concessions (Shared Value Initiative, 2014, p.6)".

In this context it is critical to have a deep understanding of the business case of sustainability within the mining industry. This will help organizations embedding sustainability strategies in their core business to create shared value, improve risks management, gain and maintain license to operate and competitive advantage.

For the specific case of West Africa, increased interest is noticed for its extractive resources, from minerals to oil and gas. Several companies of all sizes are competing to secure these resources (explorations companies, juniors, independents, mid-tiers, majors, super-majors, etc.). It is therefore truly relevant to take a deep look at the business case, challenges, opportunities, and outcomes of the corporate sustainability strategies of the extractive industry in this region.

The chapters of this essay cover wide sustainability-related topics.

The first chapter (*Corporate sustainability: the role of business in society*) will be to provide an overview of the two main theories of corporations' role in society, including a deep explanation of the notion of sustainable value creation, then going through the main corporate sustainability strategies used within the landscape of the mining industry. Chapter two (*Sustainability in the extractive sector*) presents the main steps of the mining industry sustainability journey, and how this industry is continuously responding to the challenges related to sustainable development, while at the same time addressing the increasingly central issue of its non-technical risk management. It also shines a spotlight on the often-disastrous consequences of unsustainable corporate practices. Chapter three (*Business case of corporate sustainability*) demonstrates the business case of sustainability through the results of academic research, then by presenting the notion of materiality as a channel of communication between sustainability and finance professionals, and finally by presenting an approach for the monetization of intangible aspects of sustainability. Chapter four (*Sustainability in West African mining industry*) review the main issues and challenges related to both industrial and artisanal mining in West Africa. It will also try to demonstrate that a better understanding of the local socio-cultural and political context, and a stronger mapping of corporate sustainability strategies with the UN SDGs and host states priorities could help the mining industry improving its local social outcomes and license to operate in West Africa. Chapter five (*Local content and local workforce empowerment*) tries to clarify how incoming expatriation could be used as a trigger for local employment in the extractive sector. Through the local content lens, the continuing relevance of long-term expatriate deployment will be questioned, and alternative solutions proposed if required. This chapter is also mainly intended as an overview of the current state and new trends of local content frameworks with a focus on the local employment pillar within the extractive industry and within host countries. Chapter six (*License to operate and stakeholder engagement*) presents the concept of "social license to operate" through complementary definitions and will also propose indicators to characterize it. It will then focus on stakeholder engagement processes to identify some limitations in the West African context, and then propose a complementary model for continuous improvement. The links between strategies for stakeholder engagement and for business will be also highlighted. Finally, this chapter concludes with the presentation of a tool (*Robert's Sustain Invest Matrix*), designed by the author, to provide the industry with a simple and coherent framework and criteria for the selection, prioritization, and financing of community development initiatives, always from the perspective of creating shared value. Chapter seven (*Land acquisition, cultural heritage, and biodiversity conservation*) begins by highlighting a particularly important but generally neglected local asset: traditional ecological knowledge (TEK). The judicious use of this knowledge could be of great value in the mining industry's efforts to preserve cultural heritage and conserve biodiversity, while at the same time restoring the rightful recognition and respect of the holders of this knowledge. This chapter will then discuss the issues of biodiversity conservation, cultural heritage preservation, land acquisition, and involuntary displacement detail. For each of these issues, the international standards most commonly used in the mining industry are presented. Based on the premise that we develop by creating value and wealth, Chapter eight (*Mineral beneficiation: West Africa, the next iron ore, and steel hub?*) begins by presenting the concept of mineral beneficiation and its potential for creating greater local value-added. Then the example of steel is used to present the value chain and the global market for a product that can play a leading role in the transition to a green economy, and on which West Africa could further position itself. Following an overview of the concepts of resources and reserves, this chapter presents some of the major West African iron ore deposits, with a view to recalling its sub-soil wealth and its potential as a hub for the production and local processing of this ore. Finally, given that the mining and metals industry is energy-intensive and requires heavy investment in infrastructure, this chapter concludes with a presentation of the West African's energy potential, as well as the need to develop mining infrastructure with a view to regional integration and infrastructures sharing among the various stakeholders. The last chapter (*Climate change and decarbonization*) deals with a particularly serious, and more than ever current and global topic, climate change and the decarbonization of the mining industry. West Africa is particularly vulnerable to climatic variations, which translate into emerging risks and opportunities for the regional mining industry. The inevitable decarbonization of the global economy to achieve the Paris agreements offers unprecedented opportunities, and the West African mining industry will need to seize these opportunities by positioning itself as a leader in green energy, and low or zero carbon industry. This chapter provides the regional mining industry with a realistic framework for achieving this goal.

As sustainability is a wide topic, this paper is mainly intended as an overview of the current state and new trends of the sustainability journey of the extractive industry, with a particular focus on the mining industry in West Africa. It also confirms that responsibility and profitability are not incompatible, and that it is in the best economic interest for corporate managers and investors to incorporate sustainability considerations into decision-making processes (as previously stated by authors such as Clark et al.). This paper also demonstrates that a deep understanding of the political and socio-cultural context of West Africa is, for the extractive industry, a key success factor for any corporate sustainability strategy in this region.

For corporate executives, operational managers, and sustainability practitioners, this book will provide useful tools, strategies, best practices, and a roadmap to build, strengthen, or realign the sustainability journey of their organization, while helping investors have the whole picture of the risks and opportunities related to sustainability during their investment decisions. Therefore, this work will set a new level of corporate sustainability strategies within the mining sector in West Africa and around the world. We are entering in a new era of sustainability revolution which bring tremendous opportunities and the mining industry will not afford to miss them.

1. CORPORATE SUSTAINABILITY: THE ROLE OF BUSINESS IN SOCIETY

Although sustainable development means different things to different people, the generally accepted definition is from the Brundtland Commission (1987, 41): "Development that meets the needs of the present without compromising the ability of future generations to meet their own needs." It is now often associated with the United Nations Sustainable Development Goals, a set of 17 aspirational goals, with targets set between them (United Nations 2015, 13) (Cameron and Stanley, 2017).

"What is the proper role of business in society? Debates about the private sector's responsibility for its economic, social, and environmental impacts have been raging since the dawn of the capitalism". There is a global emerging consensus that business is the engine of economic growth and international development, and that business can and must play an indispensable role alongside governments and civil society (Heifer International, 2014, p.2).

The focus of this first chapter will be to provide an overview of the two main theories of corporations' role in society, including a deep explanation of the notion of sustainable value creation, then going through the main corporate sustainability strategies used within the landscape of the mining industry.

1.1 THEORIES OF CORPORATIONS' ROLE IN SOCIETY

In an article issued in June 2017 by the *Harvard Business Review and* entitled "Managing for the long term; the error at the earth of the corporate leadership," the authors brilliantly summarize the two main models of corporate governance: the "Agency Based Model" and the "Company Centered Model" (Bower and Paine, 2017).

1.1.1 THE AGENCY THEORY

The Agency Theory is relatively recent, as it was put forth by academic economists. It's underlying idea is that corporate social responsibility should be rejected. In a 1970 New York Times Magazine article, the economist and Nobel Prize winner Milton Friedman ignited a debate about the obligation of business to address social problems. He wrote: "There is one and only one social responsibility of business – to use its resources and engage in activities designed to increase its profits so long as it stays within the rules of the game, which is to say, engages in open and free competition without deception or fraud" (Mattesson & Metivier 2021; Heifer International, 2014).

Bower and Paine highlighted that at the core of this theory is the assertion that shareholders own the corporations and by the virtue of their status as owners, have ultimate authority over its business, and may legitimately demand that its activities be conducted in accordance with their wishes. And all corporate managers should care about is maximizing shareholder value. First, Friedman writes that shareholders generally want managers to make as much money as possible, while conforming to the basic rules of society, both those embodied in laws and those embodied in ethical custom. Later, he suggests that shareholders simply want managers to use resources and pursue profit by engaging in open and free competition without deception or fraud. "Yet practitioners continue to embrace the Agency Theory's doctrine, regulators continue to embed it in policies, boards and managers are under increasing pressure to deliver short term results, and legal experts forecast that trend toward greater shareholder empowerment will persist" (Bower and Paine, 2017).

1.1.2 THE COMPANY CENTERED MODEL

At the opposite of the "Agency Theory" is the "Company Centered Model," which has at its core the health of the enterprise, rather than near term returns to its shareholders (Bower and Paine, 2017).

Authors emphasize that the Company Centered Model recognizes that corporations are independent entities endowed by law with potential indefinite life. With the right leadership, they must be managed to serve markets and society over a long time. They also stressed that another key pillar of this model is that corporations perform many functions in society. One of them is providing investment opportunities and generating wealth, but corporations also produce goods and services, provide employment, develop technologies, pay taxes, and make other contributions to the communities in which they operate. It is also highlighted that the choices made by corporate decision makers today can transform society and touch the lives of millions, if not billions, of people across the globe (Bower and Paine, 2017)

The Company Centered Model is becoming the new norm, as almost all mining companies and extractive industry associations strongly support it, especially through their mission, vision and value statements, where there is a strong commitment to creating and sharing value for all stakeholders. Nevertheless, the definition of value creation needs to be clarified, as it raises the fact that much of what is called "value creation" is more accurately described as "value transfer."

Despite these differences, we believe that Friedman's maximizing shareholder value view is compatible with the Company Centered Model. As emphasized by Chris Lazslo, in the new global business environment, companies can pursue both simultaneously. Indeed, they must if they want to succeed. Companies that deliver profits to shareholders while destroying value for society are incurring hidden liabilities. Those that offer solutions to environmental and social challenges are discovering huge profit opportunities. The corporate path to doing well by doing good has become the smart way to do business, if you have the knowledge and competencies required for it (Lazslo, 2008).

1.1.3   WHAT IS SUSTAINABLE VALUE?

At the center of corporate sustainability strategies is a core question: *What is the role and purpose of business in society* (Laszlo, 2003)? And when it comes to the essence of the matter, there is strong agreement among parties: "Business is there to create value." But the meaning of the word "value" can have different definitions that will have direct influence on the sustainability agendas in the extractive sector. In summary, there are three main definitions of value creation within the business sphere, the first two are: creating value for shareholders and creating solutions for internal and or external clients. In the third and less visible definition, value is defined as a set of end benefits and outcomes for customers, consumers, employees, and other key constituencies.

The answers given to the following questions will define in which category companies could be classified regarding a sustainability strategy perspective.

- *If this decision is taken, for whom is value created? destroyed?*
- *Who is harmed and who benefits by this decision?*
- *Whose rights are enabled?*
- *and whose values are realized by this decision (Moore 1903 in Freeman et al. 2010)?*

All this discussion about value creation and sustainability in the extractive industry happens in the context of three big trends as highlighted by Laszlo: *declining natural resources, radical transparency, and increased expectations* from stakeholders. In this context, the meaning of sustainable value is defined "[…] as a dynamic state that occurs when a company creates ongoing value for its shareholders and stakeholders" (Lazslo, 2003). The Laszlo matrix presented in Figure 1 clearly defines where to spot sustainable value within the sets of company's strategies.

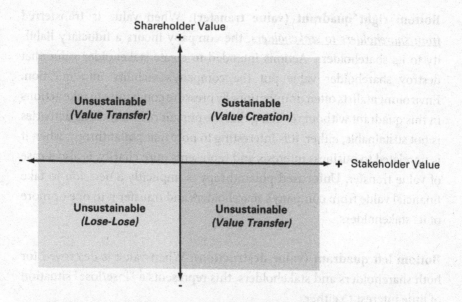

Figure 1: The Sustainable Value Framework. From The Sustainable Company, edited by Chris Laszlo. Copyright © 2003 Chris Laszlo. Reproduced by permission of Island Press, Washington, DC. Published in cooperation with the Sustainable Value Foundation

Figure 1 considers the following four cases of value creation and destruction as explained by Laszlo (2003 and 2005):

Upper left quadrant (value transfer): When value is transferred *from stakeholders to shareholders*, the stakeholders represent a risk to the future of the business. Companies that avoid environmental regulations in their home markets by exporting production to countries with lower regulatory standards create similar risks. In this quadrant are also firms that create shareholder value through a low-cost strategy that tolerates management actions to cut costs through avoiding overtime pay, undertraining on employee safety, or discriminating based on gender and ethnic background. Shareholder value in these cases is created "on the backs" of one or more stakeholder groups, thereby representing a value transfer rather than true value creation.

Bottom right quadrant (value transfer): When value is transferred *from shareholders to stakeholders*, the company incurs a fiduciary liability to its shareholders. Actions intended to create stakeholder value that destroy shareholder value put the company's viability into question. Environmentalists often unintentionally pressure companies to take actions in this quadrant without realizing that the pursuit of loss-making activities is not sustainable, either. It is interesting to note that philanthropy, when it is unrelated to business interests and represents pure charity, is also a case of value transfer. Unfocused philanthropy is implicitly a decision to take financial value from company's shareholders and transfer it to one or more of its stakeholders.

Bottom left quadrant (value destruction): When value is destroyed for both shareholders and stakeholders, this represents a "lose/lose" situation of little interest to either.

Upper right quadrant (sustainable value): When value is created for *stakeholders and shareholders*, stakeholders represent a potential source of hidden value. Sustainable value is created only in this case. An essential aspect of sustainable value is that by doing good for society and environment, the company does even better for its customers and shareholders than it otherwise would.

In summary, stakeholder value, based on a company's economic, environmental, and social performance, is a "new" and largely untapped source of competitive advantage that is likely to grow in the years ahead. A disciplined approach that integrates stakeholder considerations into core business strategy and operations can help senior executives and line managers create above-average returns. By identifying and acting on stakeholder-related business risks and opportunities, companies can reduce costs, differentiate products and services, enter new markets that serve unmet societal needs, enhance corporate reputation, and influence industry "rules of the game." Success in capturing these opportunities requires new leadership and the courage to understand and engage a diverse set of constituencies, including those previously considered adversarial or marginal to the business (Laszlo et al. 2005).

Through the Sustainable Value Framework (Figure 1) it is important to highlight that Friedman's theory of maximizing shareholder value is compatible with the creation of sustainable value. After all, the only way to maximize value sustainably is to satisfy stakeholders' interests (Stakeholders' Theory).

1.2 CORPORATE SUSTAINABILITY STRATEGIES

These are multiple arrows in the corporate quiver that are used to engage in social or sustainability initiatives. Three primary ones are corporate philanthropy, Corporate Social Responsibility (CSR), and Creation of Shared Value (CSV). While there are parameters that define each of these approaches, in reality, companies use varying languages and operationalize them differently. Thus, companies are happy to switch amongst the three approaches based on the task at hand (NCBI, 2018).

1.2.1 PHILANTHROPY AND CORPORATE SOCIAL RESPONSIBILITY (CSR)

Traditionally, corporate philanthropy involves setting an objective, devising a strategy, and then measuring outcomes, all without regard to the interests of the company (NCBI, 2018).

"The modern CSR movement can be traced to Article 23 in the 1948 "United Nations Universal Declaration on Human Rights," which called for the right to employment, favorable work conditions, equal pay for equal work, and the right to join trade unions" (Heifer International, 2014, p.2). CSR could be described as an approach with two goals. The first is serving stakeholders, employees, and communities in which companies operate and have a consumer base. This first goal contributes to the second one, which is to enhance the efficacy and profitability of the company itself.

According to Michael Porter, "CSR is fundamentally about taking resources from the business, and investing those resources in being a good corporate citizen" (Porter, 2012). According to Jane Nelson, "CSR encompasses not only what companies do with their profits, but also how they make them. It goes beyond philanthropy and compliance and addresses how company manage their economic, social, and environmental impacts, as well as their relationships in all key spheres of influence: the workplace, the marketplace, the supply chain, the community yard, and the public realm" (Nelson, *in* Heifer International, 2014, p.3). Nelson also stressed that "[…] what companies do through their philanthropic programs can make a meaningful contribution to achieving community and national development goals, in developed as well as developing countries" (Harvard Kennedy School & Saudi Arabian General Investment Authority , 2008, p.4).

1.2.2 CREATION OF SHARED VALUE & INVESTING WITH PURPOSE

Extractives companies have large community relations groups and sophisticated manuals for stakeholder engagement and impact mitigation; nevertheless, they are losing billions to community strife despite extensive community relations programs. The huge economic output of the extractives sectors, valued at $3.5 trillion in 2012, has not always translated into improved social and environmental outcomes for the countries and communities where these companies operate (SVI & FSG, 2014).

1.2.2.1 CREATION OF SHARED VALUE

The Shared Value Initiative defines Shared Value as "policies and activities that measurably improve socio-economic outcomes and improve related core business performance (e.g., decreased operational costs, enhanced productivity, and/or a predictable and stable business environment)—establishes a framework for identifying opportunities to address societal issues and deliver real business value" (SVI & FSG, 2014, p.6). That is why sustainable businesses are redefining the corporate ecosystem by designing models (Figure 2) that create value for all stakeholders, including employees, shareholders, supply chains, civil society, and the planet. Michel Porter and Mark Kramer pioneered the idea of "creating shared value," arguing that businesses can generate economic value by identifying and addressing social problems that intersect with their business (Whelan, 2016).

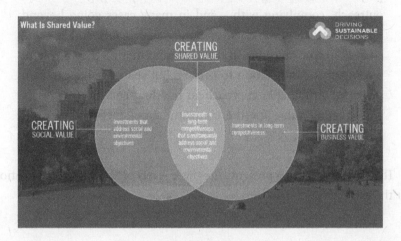

Figure 2: Creation of Shared Value Model (Driving Sustainable Decision (DSD), 2018). With permission.

As stated by the Shared Value Initiative, aligning the business interests of extractives companies with community needs and priorities is the only real solution for companies and communities alike. The root causes of community strife are lack of economic opportunity, poor health, lack of effective local or national governments, and environmental degradation. These issues are fundamental to business success due in part to the very long-time horizons of extractive operations and the deficits in the regions where these companies operate. Companies must tie community prosperity to the present long-term needs of the business in areas such as a qualified labor pool, capable suppliers, and well-functioning community infrastructure. The Shared Value Initiative also added that maintaining the status quo is no longer an option as protests and disruptions mount, companies move into ever more remote locations, and governments seek partners with a shared value mindset with which to develop resources.

Considering the concept of Shared Value in the broader societal engagement agenda, the Shared Value Initiative stated that:

> "Shared value is not the only way in which companies engage with society, nor should it be. Mitigating the social impact of projects, conducting effective community engagement and outreach, complying with - and in many cases going beyond - regulatory requirements, operating sustainably and making charitable contributions in host communities all play a role in a company's contribution to society. But shared value can be a powerful sustainable approach to building societal prosperity and creating value for the company simultaneously" (SVI & FSG, 2014, p.7).

The chart in Figure 3 presents the three levels of Shared Value Creation for the extractive's companies.

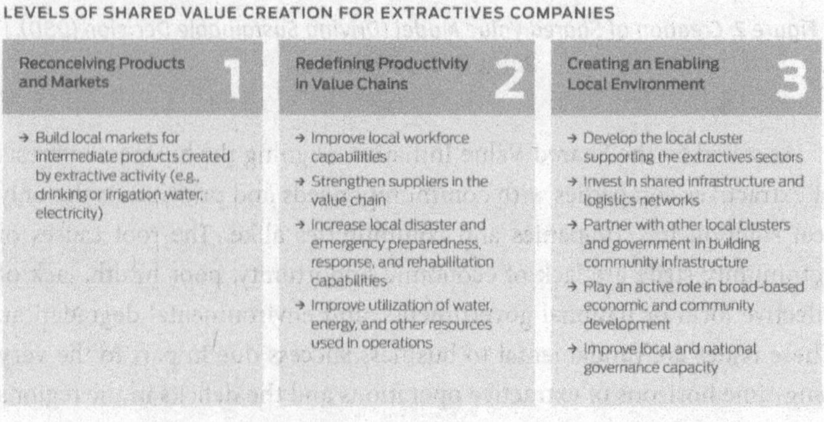
LEVELS OF SHARED VALUE CREATION FOR EXTRACTIVES COMPANIES
Reconceiving Products and Markets
1
→ Build local markets for intermediate products created by extractive activity (e.g., drinking or irrigation water, electricity)
Redefining Productivity in Value Chains
2
→ Improve local workforce capabilities
→ Strengthen suppliers in the value chain
→ Increase local disaster and emergency preparedness, response, and rehabilitation capabilities
→ Improve utilization of water, energy, and other resources used in operations
Creating an Enabling Local Environment
3
→ Develop the local cluster supporting the extractives sectors
→ Invest in shared infrastructure and logistics networks
→ Partner with other local clusters and government in building community infrastructure
→ Play an active role in broad-based economic and community development
→ Improve local and national governance capacity
Few companies, however, are developing company-wide
• Measuring the Opportunity: Companies do not size

Figure 3: Levels of Shared Value Creation for Extractives Companies (SVI & FSG, 2014). With permission.

The extractive industry is strongly moving towards corporate sustainability strategies aligned with the Shared Value principles. Figure 4 provides a framework for a Shared Value Investment pattern over a lifetime of an extractive industry project.

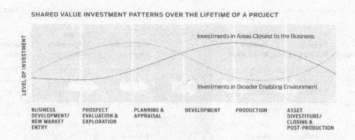

SHARED VALUE INVESTMENT PATTERNS OVER THE LIFETIME OF A PROJECT

Investments in Areas Closest to the Business

LEVEL OF INVESTMENT

Investments in Broader Enabling Environment

| BUSINESS DEVELOPMENT/ NEW MARKET ENTRY | PROSPECT EVALUATION & EXPLORATION | PLANNING & APPRAISAL | DEVELOPMENT | PRODUCTION | ASSET DIVESTITURE/ CLOSING & POST-PRODUCTION |

Figure 4: Shared Value Investment Pattern over a project life cycle
(SVI & FSG, 2014). With permission.

1.2.2.2 INVESTING WITH PURPOSE – IMPACT INVESTING

As currently more and more investors care about sustainability issues and want to direct their investments towards companies supporting long-term sustainability (Manning, 2016), companies that demonstrate corporate sustainability strategies based on the principles of Shared Value Creation will have a real competitive advantage to attract investors (Impact Investing or Investing with purpose). "Impact investing is investing with the intention of achieving financial returns and positive economic, social, or environmental impact that is measurable" (CECP, 2016, p.6). A growing number of investors (fund managers, portfolio managers, etc.) are expressing a desire to "do good while doing well". These are impact investors, who seek opportunities for financial investments that produce significant social or environmental benefits (Figure 5). Investment in such strategies is on the rise and has enormous potential – considering the volume of unmet societal needs, the scale of critical environmental issues and the availability of resources that could be invested (according to an article by *The New York Times*, US$1.9 trillion of liquid assets exists on US corporate balance sheets) (Davidson, 2016).

SOCIAL ←——→ FINANCIAL

Philanthropy	Venture Philanthropy	Program Related Investment	Impact Investing	Sustainable Investing	Socially Responsible Investing	Traditional Investments
Pure charitable giving with no expectation of financial return	Donations used as seed capital for catalytic effect with expectation of operational sustainability over time through earned income models	Loans or equity investments focused on preservation of capital or below-market returns in exchange for social or environmental performance	Investments in companies, organizations, and funds to produce social and environmental impact alongside financial returns	Investments in companies that integrate environmental, social and corporate governance practices into long term strategy	Negatively screened investment portfolios that exclude companies or industries deemed "harmful"	Investments in financial assets for maximum risk-adjusted financial returns

Figure 5: Impact investing (CECP, 2016). With permission.

Environmental, social, governance (ESG) investing, primarily in the form of equity investments in the secondary market; that is, purchasing shares of public companies through stock exchanges, is already in the trillions, as high ESG performers are proving to be high financial performers as well (Manning, 2016).

The themes we have just covered in this first chapter, namely the role of business in society and the notion of shared value creation, are of paramount importance as they form the backbone on which the rest of this book, which focuses on the West African mining industry, will be built. But before going any further, let us review the sustainability journey of the mining industry, which is the subject of Chapter Three.

2. SUSTAINABILITY IN THE MINING SECTOR

It is critical to understand the main steps of the mining industry sustainability journey, and how this industry is continuously responding to the challenges related to sustainable development. This chapter responds to this need, while at the same time addressing the increasingly central issue of non-technical risk management within the mining industry. It also shines a spotlight on the often-disastrous consequences of unsustainable corporate practices.

The mining sector can therefore have major adverse environmental and social impacts and the challenges of sustainability arise at all stages of extractive operations. As highlighted by Cameron and Stanley, in the past, these issues have not always been well recognized or addressed by governments, but good practice has improved greatly since the end of the 20th century. As more and more extractive industry companies sign on to international environmental and social standards or implement their own, the challenge for many governments is to ensure that local communities, indigenous peoples, and other affected citizens are able to participate in decisions relating to the exploitation of the resources and benefit from their development. As stated previously, the generally accepted definition of sustainable development is "Development that meets the needs of the present without compromising the ability of future generations to meet their own needs." The implementation of sustainable development (the process of getting to the common goal of sustainability) is less well-defined, and more a series of optional tracks. There are various ways of contributing to sustainability, and the way that exploitation of nonrenewable natural capital contributes is known as *nonrenewable natural capital conversion*. Essentially, extractive-led investment is a transformation of one class of assets—finite, nonrenewable natural capital in the form of oil, gas, or minerals—into financial, human, social, manufactured, or other forms of capital. The capital conversion in the extractive sector must contribute to the creation of more sustainable opportunities and livelihoods if the sector is to have any legitimacy in the sustainable development agenda (Cameron and Stanley, 2017). The critical challenge of the extractive industry will be to design and implement corporate sustainability strategies that will be at the level of these issues and expectations. The future of the extractive industry is strongly linked to this new business reality as more and more stakeholders suggest that where there is much doubt about the potential to achieve sustainability goals from an investment, the resource should be left in the ground, meaning that sustainability is really becoming the next competitive advantage within the industry (Forbes, 2018).

2.1 THE MINING INDUSTRY SUSTAINABILITY JOURNEY

In the UNU WIDER book (Extractive Industries - The Management of Resources as a Driver of Sustainable Development), Addison and Roe highlighted that in the 1990s, the environmental and social impacts of the extractive industries on communities increasingly became debated in various forums, and extractive companies faced mounting criticism in the media and from Non-Governmental Organizations (NGOs), academics, and wider civil society. Authors added that in the mining sector, there were cases such as the tailings dam failure of BHO's OK Tedi mine in Papua New Guinea (1984); Placer Dome's Marcopper mine in the Philippines (1996), and the subsequent ongoing pollution; and the conflict in Bougainville sparked by Rio Tinto's mining operations (1989), which drew the most attention and criticism (Addison and Roe, 2018). Figure 6 presents a relevant overview of sustainability issues and opportunities.

In responding to this pressure, Addison and Roe added that several chief executive officers (CEOs) of international mining companies decided to form the Global Mining Initiative (GMI), to spur a major study of mining and sustainability entitled "Mining, Minerals, and Sustainable Development" (MMSD). The GMI eventually led to the creation of the International Council on Mining and Metals (ICMM), which was founded in 2001 to improve sustainable development performance in the mining and metals industry. The ICMM was set up as a CEO-led industry association with a mandate based on the core recommendations of the MMSD project, and over the years it helped both to standardize the mining industry's approach to social and environmental issues, and to promote good practice norms through the development of industry standards and good practice guidance (Addison and Roe, 2018).

In summary, during the last three decades, sustainability within the mining industry has "progressed from a general neglect of the issue coupled with ad hoc philanthropy, to a risk management approach modelled on specific international standards. Today, the principles of social and environmental management in the extractive industries can be broadly summarized as "do no harm," and "provide benefits" at the local community level, and a number of tools and approaches have been developed and are variously implemented across the industry to address these two high-level aims" (Addison and Roe, 2018, p. 423 et 424). The current trend is the creation of shared value and net positive impacts through more embedded sustainability strategies, and several new approaches and important initiatives have played a leading role in moving the mining industry to think about new approaches, including: Extractive Industries Transparency Initiative, International Finance Corporation Performance Standards, PDAC Guidelines e3Plus and Early Stakeholders Engagement Guide, Mining Association of Canada Towards Sustainable Mining, Africa Mining Vision, Voluntary Principles on Security and Human Rights, Global Reporting Initiative Mining and Metal Sector Supplement, Responsible Mineral Development Initiative of the World Economic Forum (UNDP et al., 2016).

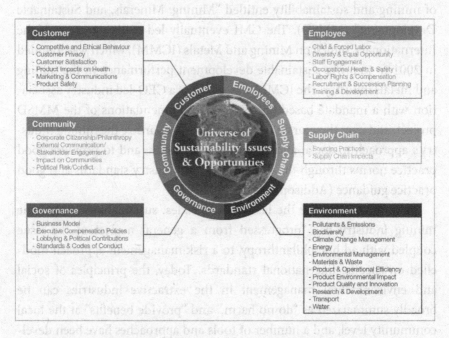

Customer
- Competitive and Ethical Behaviour
- Customer Privacy
- Customer Satisfaction
- Product Impacts on Health
- Marketing & Communications
- Product Safety

Employee
- Child & Forced Labor
- Diversity & Equal Opportunity
- Staff Engagement
- Occupational Health & Safety
- Labor Rights & Compensation
- Recruitment & Succession Planning
- Training & Development

Community
- Corporate Citizenship/Philanthropy
- External Communication/
  Stakeholder Engagement
- Impact on Communities
- Political Risk/Conflict

Supply Chain
- Sourcing Practices
- Supply Chain Impacts

Governance
- Business Model
- Executive Compensation Policies
- Lobbying & Political Contributions
- Standards & Codes of Conduct

Environment
- Pollutants & Emissions
- Biodiversity
- Climate Change Management
- Energy
- Environmental Management
- Materials & Waste
- Product & Operational Efficiency
- Product Environmental Impact
- Product Quality and Innovation
- Research & Development
- Transport
- Water

Universe of Sustainability Issues & Opportunities

Figure 6: Universe of ESG issues and opportunities (Lydenberg et al., 2012).
With permission.

2.2 CORPORATE SUSTAINABILITY AND THE MANAGEMENT OF NON-TECHNICAL RISKS

Neglecting sustainability issues can have a substantial impact on a company's business operations over the medium to longer term, or suddenly jeopardize the survival of a firm altogether (tail-risks). Risk reduction is a major outcome of successfully internalizing sustainability into a company's strategy and culture. The result is a lower volatility of a company's cashflows as the impact of negative effects can be avoided or mitigated. Sustainability activities, therefore, play an important role in a firm's risk management strategy (Clark et al, 2015).

Extractive industry exploration and operation activities have progressively shifted to more challenging geographies across the world, and in a context dominated by the big three trends of declining natural resources, radical transparency, and high expectation from stakeholders. Therefore, Non-Technical Risks (NTRs) issues are becoming more and more complex, and the industry needs to pay closer attention to how it is managed (Adekoya and Ekpenyong, 2016).

NTRs (Figure 7) refer to "all risks and opportunities that arise from interactions of a business with its broad range of external stakeholders. Interactions that could potentially result in stakeholders discontent represent the downside risks dimension, while interactions that could potentially result in stakeholder's satisfaction represent the upside opportunity dimension" (Adekoya and Ekpenyong, 2016, p.1).

Figure 7: Main sources of Non-Technical Risks in the extractive industry (Adekoya and Ekpenyong, 2016). With permission.

The extractive industry is faced with significant NTRs due to complex operating environments and challenging stakeholder interfaces in regions and geographies where natural resources reserves are found (Adekoya and Ekpenyong, 2016). This trend is confirmed by an Ernst & Young (EY) report, published in December 2018, that has named the License To Operate (LTO) as the leading risk facing the mining and metals industries over the next two years (Figure 8). In its "Top 10 business risks facing mining and metals in 2019-20 report," EY surveyed 250 mining and metals industry executives across various topics, with 54 percent of respondents citing LTO as the top risk to the end of 2020. This was up from seventh place in EY's 2017-18 edition and it is the first time the category has led the way in the report's 11-year history (Ernst & Young, 2018; Australia Mining, 2018). The report stated that LTO had "evolved beyond the narrow focus on social and environmental issues," and that there were now increased expectations from stakeholders. These expectations include increased societal participation beyond tax and employment opportunities, technological advancement, and improved disclosure of both positive and negative impacts of projects, among others. The authors highlighted that the issue of LTO is now a broad issue with far-reaching implications and, should be at the top of the agenda of CEOs, their executive teams, and boards.

EY also suggested that LTO should become a greater priority for miners, with commitments spanning beyond the life of the mine. They added that, in the same way as safety, LTO needs to become part of a mining company's DNA. As the stakeholder landscape is shifting, there is more information, bigger platforms, and more at stake than ever before. Underestimating the power of each single stakeholder would be a mistake. It is also important to notice that the increase in nationalization may lead to an expectation that there are true shared value outcomes from mining. Society sees its role as granting access to resources and expects more than just tax and employment opportunities in return (Ernst & Young, 2018). This high and critical importance of the LTO is confirmed in the paper titled "Spinning Gold: The financial returns to external stakeholders engagement," in which the authors estimated the value of cooperative relationship with external stakeholders as twice the market value of the company's gold in the ground (Henish et al., 2011).

Top 10 business risks

New World commodities
Fraud
Disruption
Future of workforce
Energy mix
Rising costs
Cyber
Maximizing portfolio returns
Digital effectiveness
License to operate

2019-20   Ranking in 2018

↟ Up from 2018   ↡ Down from 2018   ━ Same as 2018   ★ New to the radar

*Figure 8: Top 10 business risks facing mining and metals in 2019-2020
(Ernst & Young, 2018). With permission.*

In order to preempt and avoid LTO risks in the future, EY offers seven key takeaways that mining companies should consider:

- Think global and act global
- Identify the leading indicators of license to operate to pre-empt and avoid issues—provide a single source of truth—what we promised, what we delivered and how we measured it
- Make an objective, detailed assessment of your activities— be purpose-led
- Do not just listen to the loudest voices, listen to the important voices
- Empower the business to make decisions that consider more than just financial returns, and give them the tools to better value the broader returns
- Make social development decisions that deliver lasting outcomes
- Improve the collaboration and branding of the sector

While the COVID-19 outbreak has been a truly disruptive event for the mining industry and has reshuffled rankings, LTO remains the number one risks for miners in 2020/2021 and EY provided additional detail in its comment (EY, 2020):

"We expect the issue to become even more important as stakeholders broaden and develop a stronger voice. As effective engagement becomes even more critical, we believe miners should consider three tiers of community:

- Local communities will have greater expectations around how miners respect indigenous rights and native title.
- National communities may push for a return to resource nationalism, with increased debate around who miners sell to and for what purpose.
- Broader community commitment will come into focus as socioeconomic issues are highlighted post-COVID-19. We may see pressure build to provide ownership of assets to communities."

It is well known that many developing countries across the world where oil and gas and solid minerals are found suffer from weak governance, insecurity and high incidence of criminal activities, poor transparency, weak or absent regulatory framework, human right abuses, and a host of other structural weaknesses (Ernst & Young, 2018). Table 1 presents key detailed NTRs mapped to stakeholder segments.

Table 1: Non-Technical Risks mapped to stakeholder segments (Adekoya and Ekpenyong, 2016). With permission.

Dimensions	Socio-economic	Security	Environmental	Regulatory/Political	Health	Commercial
				NTR classification		
Global	Poverty/unequality, HDI, refugee/migration	Arms proliferation, cross border conflicts, terrorism	Emissions, global warming, waste management	Government aspiration, increasing capacity of NOCs, increasing stakeholder scrutiny	Epidemics and communicable diseases - MERS, Zika, safety	Low oil prices, Iran - prospect for increased supply, global economic slow down
Country	Poverty/inequality, unemployment, acces to energy, resource control, corruption	Violent crimes, conflicts, armed insurgency	Government regulation, discharges pollution, Waste pond, increasing environmental activism, Biodiversity	Election and government policy changes, local content, Acreage bid rounds, changes to regulation	Epidemic, Communicable diseases, road safety	National government approvals, Joint venture arrangements
Company	High community expectation, Legacy issues, community disruptions	Armed conflicts, War, ethnic clashes	Flooding, Environmental. footprint, biodiversity	Local content, acreage bidding, Permits and Consents, changing regulation	Community health and safety, communicable diseases, occupational health, road safety	National government approvals, Joint venture arrangements
Stakeholder/Parties to engage	Local communities, CBOs, NGOs, Government	National government, security agencies	regulatory agencies, Environmental activists, local communities	National government, national oil company, regulatory agencies	Ministry of Health, National immigration, Health and Safety agency	National Oil company, Major contractors, National government

These NTRs are the most common causes of project delay. As highlighted by McKeeman and Brewer, NTR are likely to be underestimated and over-looked, but have the potential to cause significant erosion of project value when they manifest at the project level, and in extreme cases, significant portfolio value decreases when they manifest at corporate or industrial levels. It is documented that NTRs could account for up to 70-75% of cost and schedule failures in projects in the form of schedule delays and cost overruns, local deal opportunities, and a host of stakeholder-related issues. For example, as mining is a water-dependent industry, water-related risks threaten to strand billions of dollars for mining, oil, and gas companies (i.e. assets that lose value prematurely due to environmental, social, or other external factors). For example, social conflict related to disruptions to water supplies in Peru has resulted in the indefinite suspension of $21.5 billion in mining projects since 2010 (McKeeman and Brewer, 2012).

Also, costs often overlooked by companies were indirect costs resulting from staff time being diverted to managing conflicts, particularly senior management time, including, in some cases, that of C-suite executives (McKeeman and Brewer, 2012). In his paper "Managing human rights impacts in a world of converging expectations," John Ruggie (2011) illus-trated how failure to develop cross-functional strategic responses to NTRs related to social impact can have devastating effects. Ruggie gives the example of a company in the extractive industry that suffered 6.5 billion USD value erosion over 24 months due to NTRs including community opposition and delays in regulatory approval. Indeed, the management of NTRs can be considered as a key component of the corporate sustainability function, as these risks can have a direct impact on the total shareholder returns. It is therefore obvious that unsustainable corporate practices, mismanagement of NTRs or ESG incidents can have significant adverse impacts on the extractive industry. To cite just a handful of well-known examples with financial, reputational, political and regulatory impacts such as the British Petroleum's Deepwater Horizon 2010 oil spill in the Gulf of Mexico (The *Economist* estimates $42bn in clean-up and compensation costs, whereas the *Financial Times* estimates that the clean-up costs alone may amount to $90bn. BP's share price lost 50% between 20 April 2010 and 29 June 2010 as the catastrophe unfolded), and the global indignation following the Rio Tinto blasting of 46,000-year-old Aboriginal site in the Pilbara region of Western Australia, or allegations of human rights violations by mining companies that put the sector under scrutiny and lead to more stringent regulations, and tailings dams failure with dire human and environmental consequences such as the Vale dam collapses in Brazil and the Mount-Polley dam breach in British Columbia Canada (Clark et al, 2015; Rio Tinto, 2020; Vale, 2019; Government of British Columbia, 2014). In Nigeria, community disruptions to pipelines lowered oil production by 18 percent between 2005 and 2008. Strikes at platinum mines in South Africa in 2012 caused production to drop by 12 percent of the total annual global supply (SVI & FSG, 2014).

These examples demonstrate that sustainability challenges are putting pressure upon the metals and mining, and that responsible management of environmental and social impacts has the potential to affect important business drivers. Hence the need to have a deep and definitive understanding of the business case of sustainability to confirm again that sustainability is the right way of doing good business. This central theme in corporate strategies is discussed in Chapter 4.

3. BUSINESS CASE OF CORPORATE SUSTAINABILITY

Sustainability, as highlighted by Clark, has been one of the most significant trends in financial markets for decades. Whether in the form of investors' desire for sustainable responsible investing (SRI), or corporate management's focus on CSR, the focus on sustainability and ESG issues is the same. The growth of the UN Global Compact, the United Nations-backed Principles for Responsible Investment (UN PRI), the Global Reporting Initiative (GRI), the Carbon Disclosure Project (CDP), the Sustainability Accounting Standards Board (SASB), the American and European SRI markets, and the fact that more than 20% of global assets are now managed in a sustainable and responsible manner all bear strong testament to sustainability concerns. However, it is imperative that the inclusion of sustainability in strategic corporate management is based on business performance (Clark et al., 2015). Businesses increasingly understand that their long-term success is linked to addressing the most pressing development challenges of our time, from poverty and disease to climate change. Solving these problems is good business, solving them well in an environmentally and socially sustainable manner is better business. A recent study of IFC's equity portfolio across emerging markets showed that companies do better financially when they do right by their communities and environment (IFC, 2018).

Even if the business case of sustainability is becoming more and more understood within the mining industry, the conversation between sustainability peoples and corporate finance teams is not always straightforward. Indeed, since the issues related to sustainable development are often intangible, it becomes crucial to have a language that allows the financial world to understand the value created or destroyed by this issue. This chapter will attempt to provide a solution to this problem, first by demonstrating the business case of sustainability through the results of academic research, then by presenting the notion of materiality as a channel of communication between sustainability and finance professionals, and finally by presenting an approach for the monetization of intangible aspects of sustainability.

3.1 BUSINESS CASE OF SUSTAINABILITY: ACADEMIC RESEARCH AND BUSINESS EXPERIENCE

Academic research and business experience suggest that embedded sustainability efforts clearly result in a positive impact on business performance (Whelan & Fink, 2016). In 2013, Accenture conducted a survey of 1,000 CEOs in 103 countries and 27 industries. They found that 80% of CEOs view sustainability as a way to gain competitive advantages, relative to their peers (Accenture, 2013). Mounting evidence shows that sustainable companies deliver significantly positive financial performance, and investors are beginning to value them more highly. The Arabesque Group and the University of Oxford reviewed the academic literature on sustainability and corporate performance and found that 90% of the 200 studies analyzed conclude that good ESG standards lower the cost of capital, 88% show that good ESG practices result in better operational performance, and 80% show that stock price performance is positively correlated with good sustainability practices (Clark et al., 2015). An analysis by the Boston Consulting Group found that top performers in ESG enjoy valuation multiples 3 percent to 19 percent higher, all else being equal, than median performers, and margins up to 12.4 percent higher (Forbes, 2018).

According to the 2015 EY Global Institutional Investor Survey, investors are increasingly using companies' nonfinancial disclosures to inform their investment decisions. In its survey of over 200 institutional investors, 59.1% of respondents view nonfinancial disclosures as "essential" or "important" to investment decisions, up from 34.8% in 2014. Some 62.4% of investors are concerned about the risk of stranded assets and over one-third of respondents reported cutting their holdings of a company in the past year because of this risk (Whelan, 2015).

Corporate sustainability initiatives aimed at improving ESG performance and proving value to society can increase employee loyalty, efficiency, and productivity, and improve human resources (HR) statistics related to recruitment, retention, and morale. Research is finding that 21st century employees are focusing more on mission, purpose, and work life balance. Companies that invest in sustainability initiatives tend to create sought-after culture and engagement due to company strategy focusing more on purpose and providing value to society. In addition, companies who embed sustainability in their core business strategy treat employees as critical stakeholders, just as important as shareholders. Employees are proud to work in these companies, and feel part of a broader effort (Whelan, 2015).

> "One study found that morale was 55% better in companies with strong sustainability programs, compared to those with poor ones, and employee loyalty was 38% better. Better morale and motivation translate into reduced absenteeism and improved productivity. Firms that adopted environmental standards have seen a 16% increase in productivity over firms that did not adopt sustainability practices. Corporate sustainability performance also positively impacts turnover and recruitment. Studies show that firms with greater corporate responsibility performance can reduce average employee turnover over time by 25-50%. It can also reduce annual quit rates by 3-3.5%, saving replacement costs of up to 90%-200% of an employee's annual salary for each retained position" (Whelan & Fink, 2016).

When players in a value chain embed sustainability in their core strategy and practices, they consistently drive more innovation, higher operational efficiency, improved sales and marketing, and other positive outcomes. These provide tangible financial benefits such as lower cost of capital, greater profitability, and higher corporate valuation (CSB, 2018). In an article in the *Harvard Business Review*, Michael Porter and Claas van der Linde claim that pollution translates to inefficiency. They argue that "when scrap, harmful substances, or energy forms are discharged into the environment as pollution, it is a sign that resources have been used incompletely, inefficiently, or ineffectively." In one example, they examine 181 ways of preventing waste generation in chemical plants, and find that only one of them "resulted in a net cost increase" (Porter and Van der Linde, 1995). In other words, process innovation more than offsets costs in 180 out of 181 cases.

Thus, it is more and more demonstrated that a sound management of material sustainability issues is a strong lever for business value creation. The materiality assessment of ESG issues is therefore a key step in the demonstration of the business case of sustainability.

3.2 MATERIALITY OF SUSTAINABILITY ISSUES

Companies use the concept of materiality to guide their sustainability strategic planning process, including their social investment strategies (CSB, 2018). It is important to draw a distinction between the concept of materiality as it refers to financial reporting, and the concept of materiality as it refers to sustainability reporting. With respect to financial reporting, information is deemed material if its omission or misstatement could influence the economic decision of users taken, based on the financial statement (DSD, 2018).

According to the Sustainability Accounting Standard Board (SASB) "For the purpose of SASB's standard-setting process, information is financially material if omitting, misstating, or obscuring it could reasonably be expected to influence investment or lending decisions that users make on the basis of their assessments of short-, medium-, and long-term financial performance and enterprise value"(SASB, 2020 p. 7). For the Global Reporting Initiative (GRI) Standards the Materiality principle was stated as, "The report should cover Aspects that:

- Reflect the organization's significant economic, environmental, and social impacts; or
- Substantively influence the assessments and decisions of stakeholders

[...] Relevant topics are those that may reasonably be considered important for reflecting the organization's economic, environmental and social impacts, or influencing the decisions of stakeholders" (GRI, 2021). In the GRI Standards, unless otherwise stated, 'impact' refers to the effect an organization has on the economy, the environment, and/or society, which in turn can indicate its contribution (positive or negative) to sustainable development. It does not refer to an effect upon an organization, such as a change to its reputation" (GRI, 2021).

The European Commission recently introduced the concept of double materiality (Financial materiality, Environment & Social materiality, figure 9) for the reporting of climate related information (European Commission, 2019, p. 6 and 7):

- The reference to the company's "development, performance [and] position" indicates financial materiality, in the broad sense of affecting the value of the company. Climate-related information should be reported if it is necessary for an understanding of the development, performance and position of the company. This perspective is typically of most interest to investors.
- The reference to "impact of [the company's] activities" indicates environmental and social materiality. Climate-related information should be reported if it is necessary for an understanding of the external impacts of the company. This perspective is typically of most interest to citizens, consumers, employees, business partners, communities and civil society organisations. However, an increasing number of investors also need to know about the climate impacts of investee companies in order to better understand and measure the climate impacts of their investment portfolios.

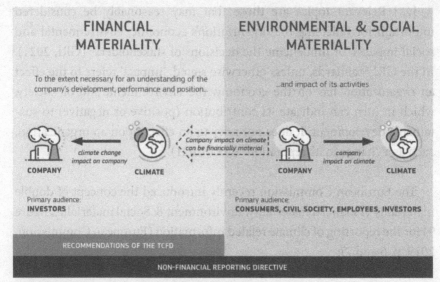

Figure 9: The double materiality perspective of the Non-Financial Reporting Directive in the context of reporting climate-related information (European Commission, 2019)

Firms are more and more required by shareholders, regulatory bodies, and other stakeholders to implement sustainable management strategies that improve business performance. To achieve this, companies are required first to identify the specific sustainability issues that are material to them. Table 2 shows a selection of ESG issues that, depending on the individual company in question, can have a material impact.

Table 2: *Selection of material ESG factors (Clark et al., 2015). With permission.

ENVIRONMENTAL ("E")	SOCIAL ("S")	GOVERNANCE ("G")
Biodiversity/land use	Community relations	Accountability
Carbon emissions	Controversial business	Anti-takeover measures
Climate change risks	Customer relations/product	Board structure/size
Energy usage	Diversity issues	Bribery and corruption
Raw material sourcing	Employee relations	CEO duality
Regulatory/legal risks	Health and safety	Executive compensation schemes
Supply chain management	Human capital management	Ownership structure
Waste and recycling	Human rights	Shareholder rights
Water management	Responsible marketing and R&D	Transparency
Weather events	Union relationships	Voting procedures

*Note: The data has been synthesized by Clark et al. from several sources, including MSCI (2013), UBS (2013), Bonini and Goerner (2011), Sustainability Accounting Standards Board (2013), Global Reporting Initiative (2013a), and the academic papers reviewed by the authors. Table in alphabetical order.

The understanding of the material ESG factors will be an important step for any future sustainability investment strategies to deliver positive impacts with demonstrated shared value for stakeholders and for the business. A roadmap is essential to a productive strategy. After identifying ESG risks and opportunities material to their business, companies will want to focus on the two or three that are most strategically significant. These will vary from one enterprise to the next. In companies competing based on differentiation and strong brands, for example, boards may find their time best spent monitoring issues that impact brand value. Companies competing on price may wish to focus on factors that affect cost structure (Forbes, 2018). A study in 2016 by Khan, Serafeim, and Yoon shows that companies with strong performance on material ESG topics outperform companies with poor performance on material topics. Interestingly, after controlling for high performance in material issues, a portfolio of companies scoring low on immaterial issues generated higher alpha than the portfolio of high performance on immaterial issues. In other words, spending resources on immaterial issues appears to have been value detracting (Russell, 2018). This further supports the view that differentiating between material and immaterial issues matters from an investment perspective.

3.3 THE CHALLENGE OF MONETIZING SUSTAINABILITY—TANGIBLE AND INTANGIBLE BENEFITS

As demonstrated by academic research and business experience presented previously, sustainability investments could create strong business value, including intangibles. According to the author Andrew Winston, intangibles are indirect and unpriced value creators or destroyers, and include the ability to gain support from community, gain and maintain social license to operate, and improve talent recruitment and retention. And obviously, company sustainability performance can enhance or diminish all these assets (DSD, 2018). Many people believe that there are things that just cannot be measured. But in his book, *How to measure anything*, Douglas Hubbard said this is a myth, and explained that "anything can be measured and when we fail to quantify and monetize intangibles such as the value of quality, employees' moral, and environmental conditions, we are missing critical information when we make decisions". In this context, a measurement is defined as a quantitatively expressed reduction of uncertainty based on one or more observations, or simply put, observations that quantitatively reduce uncertainty (Hubbard, 2014)

Figure 10 presents the three principal ways of business value creation with sustainability investments. In other words, this graphic shows that there are many ways to assess business value creation (DSD, 2018):

- **Protect**: Activities that result in risk reduction and cost avoidance
- **Strengthen**: Improvement of efficiency and production or other activities that help improve margins and profits
- **Advance**: Activities that help company grow, either through new or expanded revenue, or in ways that increase the valuation multiple of the company.

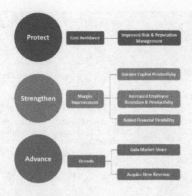

Figure 10: Business value creation through the Creation of Shared Value (DSD, 2018). With permission.

Unfortunately, many companies do not assess or realize all the positive business impacts a sustainability investment might have. Also, often, sustainability people are not speaking the same language as the financial and strategic planning people. The first thing we must understand is what creates value in a sustainability investment. Sustainability teams will then need to identify all the different areas for value creation to build a better business case of sustainability, first to convince themselves of the value they are adding, and then being able to communicate that value to shareholders, to investors, and to other stakeholders (DSD, 2018). This should be achieved through the monetization process that will help the companies in making intangibles more tangible, thus building a more effective business case. The detailed way to monetization requires asking and answering ten critical questions arising from the three steps above (see Figure 11 and Figure 12).

Figure 11: Three steps of the monetization process (DSD, 2018).
With permission.

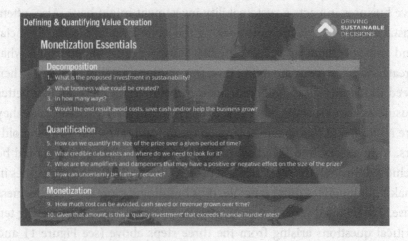

Figure 12: Detailed monetization process for the quantification of value creation
(DSD, 2018). With permission.

3.4 OUTLOOK

Companies face a big challenge when integrating sustainability into
business strategy; namely, how to quantify the expected benefits, and
the increase in the value of a business as a result of implementing more

sustainable practices, including those aimed at reducing energy consumption and carbon emissions (Eckerle et al., 2020).

> "Sustainable decisions are the leadership choices, initiatives, or investments that create business value and positive environmental and/or social impacts, simultaneously. These decisions are not based on concepts such as "the right thing to do" or "social license to operate," but on a translation of sustainability's benefits into tangible terms business leaders can understand. They are also applicable throughout entire business lifecycle, from acquisition, integration, operation, and decommissioning, through divestiture planning and ultimate investment exit, and must take into consideration the immense pressures, expectations, and requirements coming from different stakeholders" (Alo Advisors, 2020).

Executives can no longer afford to approach sustainability as a "nice to have," or as solid function separated from the "real" business. Those companies that proactively make sustainability core to their business strategy will drive innovation, and engender enthusiasm and loyalty from employees, customers, suppliers, communities, and investors (Whelan & Fink, 2016). When a company embeds sustainability in its strategy and practice, it improves customer loyalty, employee relations, innovation, media coverage, operational efficiency, risk management, sales and marketing, supplier relations, and stakeholder engagement. This drives greater profitability, higher corporate valuation, and lower cost of capital, delivering short and long-term value for both shareholders and society (Sustainable brand, 2018). Having said that, in the next chapter, we will put the spotlight on the West African mining landscape and discuss its main sustainability challenges.

4. SUSTAINABILITY IN WEST AFRICAN EXTRACTIVE INDUSTRY

Briefly, the importance of natural resources to Africa's economy is set to increase. Africa's natural resource wealth is largely unexplored, so its reserves are likely to be heavily underestimated. On a per square kilometer basis, Africa spends less than one tenth of the amount that major mineral producers such as Australia and Canada spend on exploration (Africa Progress Panel, 2013). With investment in exploration increasing, new technologies lowering the cost of discovery, and demand rising, the level of known reserves has been rising. Major discoveries and the development of existing facilities are changing the resource map of Africa and the region's place in global markets, with potentially far-reaching consequences for national budgets (Fig. 13).

The African picture is more or less the same as the West African region, which is generally considered a "Gold Mine" for the mining industry. Ghana, originally and appropriately named "The Gold Coast," has traditionally been the gold hub of West Africa, but recent years have seen a huge boom in gold exploration and production in many other West African states (GCA, 2018). Western Africa has surpassed Southern Africa as the continent's gold-mining hub. Numerous new gold-mining projects are being developed in West Africa, particularly in Ghana, Burkina Faso, Mali, Senegal, and Côte d'Ivoire (Money Web, 2018).

Through the lens of the value creation model, there is no doubt that the West African mining industry could be a strong lever to lift millions of people out of poverty, and a strong pillar for the economic development of host countries. Nevertheless, the current results are mixed on the ground, despite the efforts of the mining industry for stronger local benefits. This chapter will therefore review the main issues and challenges related to both industrial and artisanal mining in West Africa. It will also try to demonstrate that a better understanding of the local socio-cultural and political context, and a stronger mapping of corporate sustainability strategies with the UN SDGs and host states priorities could help the mining industry, improving its local social outcomes and license to operate in West Africa.

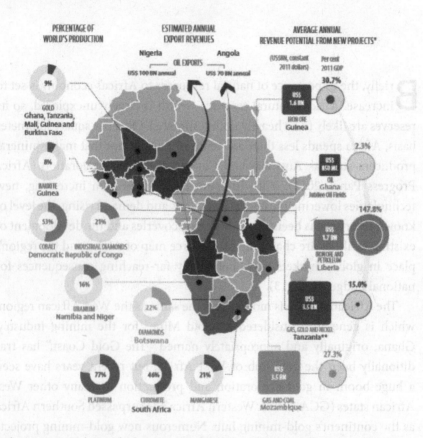

Figure 13: Mapping Africa's natural resources wealth—Selected countries and commodities (Africa Progress Panel, 2013). Free reproduction authorized.
This map is without prejudice to the status of or sovereignty over any territory, to the delimitation of international frontiers and boundaries and to the name of any territory, city or area.

4.1 LARGE SCALE EXTRACTIVE INDUSTRY IN WEST AFRICA

There is an extensive established mining industry in West Africa (Fig. 14), with the region supplying 9% of the world's bauxite (dominated by Guinea), and 9% of the world's gold, (primarily by Ghana and Mali). West Africa also produces significant volumes of uranium, diamonds, manganese, lead, phosphates, and iron ore, with top producing countries also including Mauritania (iron ore) and Senegal (phosphates). Strong growth in mining activity is expected, with large iron ore projects planned in Guinea, Liberia, Senegal, Côte d'Ivoire, Sierra Leone, Mauritania, and possibly in Ghana and Togo. There is planned expansion in uranium mining in Niger, and several new gold mine developments or expansions across West Africa including Burkina Faso, Senegal, Mauritania, and Côte d'Ivoire. Furthermore, there are significant volumes of unexploited mineral resources across the region, including iron ore, gold, and uranium (World Bank, 2012).

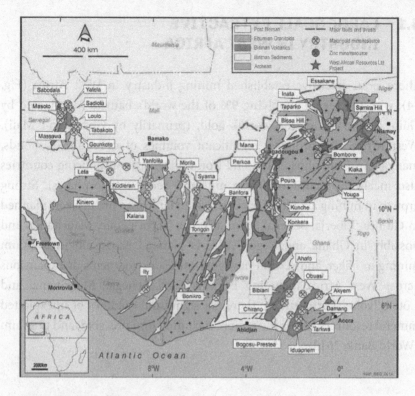

Figure 14: West African Greenstone Belts and Gold deposits
(West African Resources, n.d.). With permission.

With mining investment expanding rapidly in West Africa, the mining sector has been identified as a potential catalyst for economic development. This is supported by a range of strategy and policy frameworks, including the African Mining Vision 2050, which identifies a resource-based industrialization and development strategy for Africa, based on developing downstream, upstream, and side-stream linkages.

Businesses in the region are faced with a multitude of different pressures, and are increasingly recognizing that long-term success will mean effectively managing relations with communities where they operate. Companies that can do business in a way that provides opportunities for benefits sharing, community participation and local procurement, and can generate decent work and jobs, respect human rights, and protect the environment can better manage risks and seize opportunities. They can also help build more resilient communities and create and foster sustainable livelihoods. Almost all of the mining companies operating in West Africa are committed to responsible mining and to sharing benefits with all stakeholders (Iamgold, Barrick Gold, B2gold, Torogold, Anglogold Ashanti, Compagnie des Bauxites de Guinée, Endeavour mining, Guinea Aluminae Corporation, Eramet, etc.) and have initiated extensive sustainability strategies, ranging from philanthropy, to community investment through traditional CSR, to new approaches such as the Creation of Shared Value.

4.2   ARTISANAL AND SMALL-SCALE MINING IN WEST AFRICA

A significant feature of the mining industry is the prevalence of large numbers of artisanal miners. As outlined by Cameron and Stanley, this is a common feature of many developing countries in Africa, Asia, and Latin America. The diversity of artisanal and small-scale mining (ASM) should not be underestimated. The category embraces any mining that is conducted with little machinery and by miners who possess few if any legal rights. Such mining is often the only means of survival for the miners and their dependents, thus having a close correlation with poverty. It is notorious for its negative environmental impacts, lack of safety, and social impacts. Previously, the dominant policy approach was to criminalize ASM activities, but increasingly, they are seen as important in the overall development of a country's mining sector (Cameron and Stanley, 2017).

Much of the international debate on extractive industries tends to focus on foreign investment. The firms at the center of these debates tend to be highly capital-intensive and employ few workers. By contrast, artisanal and small-scale mining (ASM) is one of Africa's fastest-growing industries and sources of employment. Many of these miners are involved in the production of gold. In the specific case of West Africa, artisanal miners are extensively involved in production across the Sahelian "gold belt." Estimates put the number of artisanal gold miners in Mali between 100,000 and 200,000. These miners produce around four tons of gold a year—8 per cent of national output—valued at US$240 million in 2011 prices (Africa Progress Panel, 2013). In Burkina Faso, a national survey of the gold panning sector was carried out in 2017 by the national institute of statistics and demography (INSD). According to the more precise results of this exercise, gold production from gold panning in 2016 was estimated at 9.5 tons, generating 232.2 billion FCFA (US$434 million) in terms of income from this activity, while the number of jobs in this sector would be 140,196 (INSD, 2017). In 2000, artisanal mining contributed 9 per cent of Ghana's gold production. By 2010, that figure had risen to 23 per cent, with over a million Ghanaians directly dependent on artisanal mining for their livelihoods (Africa Progress Panel, 2013).

According to an Organisation for Economic Co-operation and Development (OECD) report published in October 2018, the cumulative ASM gold production of Mali, Burkina Faso, and Niger is around 50 tons per year, a volume that represents more than 50% of the legally registered industrial production for the year 2017. Entitled "Gold at the Crossroads: An Assessment Study of Gold Supply Chains Produced in Burkina Faso, Mali and Niger," the study, prepared by Roberto Sollazzo based on research conducted in 2018, indicates that, using the average gold price in 2017, this production, the vast majority of which is exported illegally, represented a value of 2.02 billion dollars.

The development of the phenomenon in these countries is also manifested by the increase in the number of gold ASM sites—in Burkina Faso, between 500 and 700, while in Mali there are 300 to 350 sites (Ecofin, 2018). This OECD report also notes a number of instances of interference by non-state armed and terrorist groups in the production and trade of gold in these border countries and calls on the Sahel Alliance to acknowledge artisanal mining in its programs to improve regional security. Artisanal mining is an important source of employment and income for a vulnerable workforce, many of whom are migrants or from local rural populations working on a seasonal basis. Most artisanal miners, however, receive incomes too low to provide an escape from poverty, and many work in dangerous conditions, and face acute risks of human rights violations security (Africa intelligence, 2018). In the face of all these threats, the organization recommends sensitization and involvement of actors on the ground, including intelligence and peacekeeping forces operating in the region. The involvement of all, according to the OECD, could prove useful to support the governments of the region, and thus refine the understanding of the permeability of the local chain of production and marketing of gold at risk of infiltration by terrorist groups. Several West African countries seem to be aware that it is better to regulate gold panning than to discourage it. Attempts to supervise and formalize ASM activities and the artisanal gold marketing chain are underway in Mali, Burkina Faso, Niger, and Senegal, but the results are currently inconclusive.

ASM and Large-Scale Mining (LSM) often operate side by side. Large mining companies have been engaging with ASM and their dependents through general community development programs for some time. However, the sustainable development challenges of ASM, including security, human rights, pollution, deforestation, relocation programs, and regulatory frameworks, need specific consideration (ICMM IFC, World Bank, CommDev, and ASM, 2010).

"The fact that most ASM activities occur outside the regulatory framework, whether illegal or not, can also present significant challenges for mining companies and regulators. There can be significant tension between ASM and their host governments, with mining companies caught in the middle. In recent years, there has been increasing interaction between mining companies and ASM operators, and it has not been always positive. [...] The relationship between LSM companies and the ASM sector is often poorly understood and has been troubled by a general mismatch of expectations, which has led to mistrust and conflict, in some cases. In the absence of effective engagement, LSM companies can find themselves facing delays in project development or impacts on production as they respond to ASM concerns or actions. These could include potential competition for the same mineralization, impact on livelihood if access to resources is limited, and changing social conditions, including conflicts between ASM, host communities, and LSM companies" (ICMM IFC, World Bank, CommDev, and ASM, 2010, p.1 and 2).

In the paper entitled "Mapping Artisanal and Small-Scale Mining to the Sustainable Development Goals," De Haan and his co-authors emphasized that:

> "ASM, low-tech, labor-intensive mineral processing and extraction constitute an essential livelihood for more than 40 million people living in rural and typically impoverished areas in lower-income countries across the developing world. [...] Altogether, the > 40 million miners could support up to another 280 million indirect livelihoods" (De Haan et al., 2020, p. 7 and 14), meaning almost 90 million in Sub-Saharan Africa, as around 13 million ASM are based in this region as stressed by the authors.

They also made the point that several frameworks, including the Yaounde Vision on ASM adopted at the Seminar on Artisanal and Small-Scale Mining held in Yaounde, Cameroon, in 2002 and the Africa Mining Vision of February 2009, recognized ASM as both a poverty-driven and a poverty alleviation sector, with a potential to improve rural livelihoods and foster entrepreneurship. As such, the Yaounde Vision called for ASM to be integrated into poverty reduction strategies and in rural community development programmes, for example. This report clearly demonstrated that, even in its informal state, the ASM sector makes positive contributions to almost all of the 17 SDGs, but also impacts negatively on most of them. Rudimentary, inefficient, and linear production models contribute to environmental degradation, chemical pollution, wasteful practices, and high-grading, leading to the sterilization of ore deposits. Child labor remains a challenge. Therefore, ASM formalization is an essential pathway if we are to mitigate the sector's negative impacts and realise its full development potential—thus sustaining livelihoods, engendering local development, and fostering employment creation. Without formalization, the negative impacts will be aggravated, deepening the sector's marginalization and association with human rights abuses and (armed) conflict. In essence, formalization can be understood as a long-term process of progressively building the capacity of government and ASM actors (understood as miners, traders, and all other participants along the mineral supply chain) to enable the latter to comply with applicable regulations, and ultimately access and equitably benefit from participation in formal local and global commodity markets (De Haan et al., 2020). Six key components of the formalization process are outlined in Figure 15.

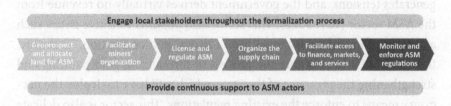

Engage local stakeholders throughout the formalization process

Geoprospect and allocate land for ASM | Facilitate miners' organization | License and regulate ASM | Organize the supply chain | Facilitate access to finance, markets, and services | Monitor and enforce ASM regulations

Provide continuous support to ASM actors

Figure 15: Key components of the ASM formalization process (De Haan et al., 2020). With permission.

In the West-African context, Senegal has recently set up a legal framework for ASM formalization. As outlined by the Intergovernmental Forum on Mining, Minerals, Metals and Sustainable Development (IGF), artisanal and small-scale mining is governed by the Mining Code and the Mining Policy Statement, and significant efforts are underway to formalize these activities through gold panning maps, defined corridors for traditional gold panning, and shops for the sale of artisanal gold. Artisanal miners organizations and associations have been established throughout the Kédougou region of southeastern Senegal, and the Senegalese government is seeking to strengthen transparency, legalization, and regulation/formalization of the collection and management of artisanal mining revenues. Conflicts between artisanal miners and large-scale mining companies are declining, and training programs for miners have been put in place to reduce the social and environmental impact of artisanal mining (IGF, 2016).

Despite these encouraging initiatives, in the field, the process of formalizing gold panning presents major challenges. IGF also emphasized that the artisanal mining sector remains largely informal, and migrants from neighboring countries continue to flock in and operate illegally, outside defined corridors, and using cheap techniques that are disastrous for the local environment. The use of mercury in the gold processing remains widespread, and it is used without gold processing equipment or adequate protection. Child labor remains widespread in artisanal mining even though it is prohibited under the mining code. Women's health is compromised, as many women are involved in the mercury treatment processes. Finally, national operators have the feeling that the interests of large companies take precedence over livelihoods and rights of the premises, which generates tensions, and the government derives virtually no revenue from the ASM sector (IGF, 2016). This sector also presents sensitive issues such as prostitution, the widespread use of drugs, and corruption. Therefore, there is a need to continue the process of formalizing gold panning and strengthening the presence of the State, which will have to deploy the necessary means to enforce the existing regulations. This sector is also delicate on the social and societal level, in the sense that it constitutes a social valve for these thousands of young people, generally without training, who earn their living there, some of whom would not hesitate to attempt the disastrous illegal immigration to Europe. Thus, any attempt at formalization should also go in the direction of improving working conditions and increasing the capacity to create decent jobs for young West Africans.

"ASM is not only a poverty-driven livelihood for millions of people worldwide, but also a vibrant, dynamic and emerging economy—although its linkage to development imperatives is systematically understated in global metrics" (De Haan et al., 2020).

4.3 MINING INDUSTRY IMPACT IN WEST AFRICA: A MIXED BLESSING FOR COMMUNITIES

For countries in Africa, and particularly in West Africa, mining has the potential to contribute significantly to economic growth, and to help lift millions of people out of poverty. However, there have been concerns that the benefits of the resource boom are not widely shared and do not always translate into local development. Large scale mining investments have not always led to the generation of local employment opportunities, nor have they contributed significantly to poverty alleviation, which can leave communities feeling excluded from the benefits and the wealth made by extractive industries.

Challenges such as poor governance and non-transparency are key issues hindering growth and development in the region. Large scale mining companies are also faced with potential conflicts with artisanal miners which can lead to a loss of production. Governments are increasingly recognizing the importance of ensuring an enabling environment for mining that supports development, boosts the economy, and reduces social tensions (IFC, 2014). Despite the positive trend of significant progress on countries' GDPs, we are still facing mixed progress on poverty reduction and human development in West Africa. In theory, it is expected that natural resources wealth should strengthen economic growth, provide governments with an opportunity to support human development and create employment. Unfortunately, in practice, in several African resource-rich countries, it has often led to poverty, inequality, and violent conflicts. These are the symptoms that have been widely attributed to a resources curse, or mineral-based poverty trap (Africa Progress Panel, 2013).

In summary, translating African resources into revenues, and those revenues into development outcomes, is not straightforward (Oxfam, 2016). This currently results in mixed progress on poverty reduction and human development, as shown by the Human Development index (HDI) ranking of resource-rich countries in Africa—economic wealth does not translate into the health and education indicators that might have been anticipated. As stated in a report drafted by the Shared Value Initiative, this failure to build human capital creates real business costs, some obvious (e.g., conflicts with local communities that see no benefits from resources extraction), and some subtler (e.g., the added cost of sourcing goods and services from uncompetitive local suppliers, employing an expatriate workforce at a premium due to lack of local talent) (SVI & FSG, 2014).

In this context, as elsewhere, mining companies operate in complex environments where many decisions involve tradeoffs among competing interests. They understand the importance of relations with host governments and communities (SVI & FSG, 2014; Teranga Gold, 2018; Iamgold, 2018; Randgold, 2018).

> Many extractive companies around the world "[…] have invested in gaining a better understanding of the negative impact of their

operations, and improving both their own and the host governments' abilities to address societal issues. They have invested in social and environmental engagement, developing toolkits, guidance, and processes to help improve societal outcomes, prevent human rights violations, and improve accountability and revenue transparency. They have adopted performance standards on social and environmental issues with the aim of preventing harm in communities and countries with extractives operations. Despite these investments, the relationships between extractive companies and host nations and communities where companies extract subsoil assets is often transactional, if not adversarial" (SVI & FSG, 2014, p.6).

In this global context, one of the critical challenges of the West African extractive industry will be to thoroughly understand the local ESG issues and context to rethink and redesign embedded corporate sustainability strategies that will translate African resources into revenues, and those revenues into large scale development outcomes that will raise host communities out of poverty.

4.4 CORPORATE SUSTAINABILITY AND SOCIAL INVESTMENTS IN THE WEST AFRICAN CONTEXT

4.4.1 UNDERSTANDING THE SOCIO-POLITICAL AND CULTURAL CONTEXT OF WEST AFRICA

The African people have a rich culture of giving, sharing, and mutual support, especially in West Africa. In this region, philanthropy is shaped by community and social values. It is also true that philanthropy as a set of values and practices is a mirror of social values, visions, and norms. The African type of philanthropy is not tied to times of boom or prosperity. It is daily. In hard times, people will probably give less in other societies, for example. In Africa, hard times are also moments of sharing and togetherness. It is important to highlight that West African philanthropy is not generally supported by formal foundations but by individuals, groups, and communities. However, corporate, individual, religious, and public foundations do exist, and they perform essential roles that serve society at large (Sy & Hathie, n.d.)

The design and the smooth and successful implementation of any sustainability strategy in this region will require a sound understanding of this local socio-political and cultural context. In their paper entitled "Institutional Forms of Philanthropy in West Africa," the authors provided a great overview of this context (Sy & Hathie, n.d.). Indeed, throughout the 1980s and 1990s, the region has suffered interstate armed conflicts and civil wars, with negative spill-over effects for neighboring countries. Therefore, many states became fragile and were hardly able to assume the basic demands of the populations. Earlier, in the 1960s, most states assumed a central development role, but failed to deliver and became increasingly oppressive and corrupt. A conjunction of negative factors such as misman-agement; the deteriorating international environment, with the first oil shock in the 1970s; and cyclical droughts contributed to a deep economic and financial crisis, which precipitated the calls for IMF and World Bank intervention. These institutions prescribed painful remedies based on a market-oriented model of economic development that confined the state to limited functions. As a result, key sectors such as education and health were almost abandoned, and the poorest populations were left unassisted.

In many areas, local solidarity and Non-Governmental Organizations' involvement and supply of services for potable water, sanitation, health, and education alleviated the situations of many people, and offered a way out for the most vulnerable. The fragile states of the 1980s and the 1990s were often incapable of meeting the basic needs of their populations and delivering essential social services. Finally, Sy and Hathie stated that the beginning of this new century has witnessed remarkable changes, with extensive poverty reduction programs initiated by states. The emergence of worldwide programs such as the Millennium Development Goals (MDGs) and the SDGs are also showing encouraging results on the ground, and are providing positive perspectives for the future (Sy & Hathie, n.d.).

Nevertheless, despite these positive results and trends, some remote areas where the extractive industry is usually found still lacking essential social services and live in concerning poverty and where all the SDGs could be considered as critical. For these communities, the mining industry is seen as a unique opportunity to solve all the issues related to the lack of basic needs and social services. In that context of high expectations, communities usually expect the mining industry to play the role of the State, the role of the NGOs, and the traditional CSR role of corporations. The failure to effectively manage these expectations at the early stage of the project can lead to massive disappointment that could threaten the social license to operate of the mining industry.

4.4.2 MAPPING MINING SUSTAINABILITY INVESTMENTS TO THE SUSTAINABLE DEVELOPMENT GOALS

In September 2015, the 193 United Nations (UN) member states adopted the resolution, "Transforming our world: the 2030 Agenda for Sustainable Development," which includes a set of Sustainable Development Goals (SDGs) for 2015-2030. The agenda provides a successor framework for the Millennium Declaration and the MDGs that covered the period from 2000-2015. "The 17 SDGs represent the world's comprehensive action plan for social inclusion, environmental sustainability, and economic development. Meeting the SDGs by 2030 will require unprecedented cooperation and collaboration among governments, non-governmental organizations, development partners, the private sector, and communities" (UNDP et al., 2016). The SDGs are underpinned by three key principles that have implications for how to address and achieve the goals.

- The goals are integrated and indivisible.
- The goals are universal, which means that they are relevant to all countries and all societal actors.
- The goals cannot leave anyone behind. The goals and targets should be met for all people and segments of society, including the most vulnerable.

The mining industry has the opportunity and potential to positively contribute to all 17 SDGs. Mining is a global industry and is often located in remote, ecologically sensitive, and less-developed areas that include many indigenous lands and territories. When managed appropriately, it can create jobs, spur innovation, and bring investment and infrastructure at a game-changing scale over long time horizons. However, if poorly managed, mining can contribute to many of the problems that SDGs are trying to address. Mining companies are therefore encouraged to look first at how their business operations can be leveraged for positive impacts rather than focusing primarily on social investment or philanthropy. In this sustainability journey, the most important will be the ability for companies to integrate contributions to the SDGs into the core business. Core business refers to the range of activities and functions required to conduct primary business activities (UNDP et al., 2016).

For companies seeking to align their operations with the SDGs, the goals relating to social inclusion, environmental sustainability, and economic development are a useful starting point:

- **Environmental Sustainability**
    - SDG6 – Clean Water and Sanitation
    - SDG15 – Life on Land
    - SDG7 – Energy Access and Sustainability
    - SDG13 – Climate Action

- **Social inclusion**
    - SDG1 – End Poverty
    - SDG5 – Gender Equality
    - SDG10 – Reduced Inequalities
    - SDG16 – Peace, Justice, and Strong Institutions

- **Economic development**
    - SDG8 – Decent Work and Economic Growth
    - SDG9 – Infrastructure, Innovation, and Industrialization
    - SDG12 – Responsible Consumption, and Production

A company's specific actions and opportunities will depend on the local social, political, and economic context, the mineral resource, the phase of mining activities (exploration, development, extraction, or closure), and the input received from local communities and other stakeholders through formal dialogue and engagement. In this context, "sustainable" investment (SI) is defined as investment that continues to make positive impacts well beyond the end of company involvement, for example, by enabling people to take control of, and improve, their own lives without having to depend on corporate resources (IPIECA, 2017). Figures 16 and 17 provide guidance about the focus areas and typical geographical level of social investments.

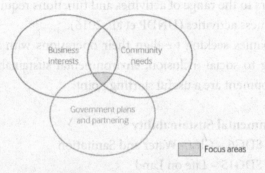

Figure 16: Identifying focus area for social investments (IPIECA, 2017). With permission.

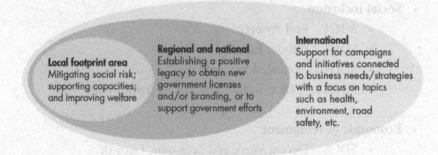

Figure 17: Typical geographical levels for social investment (IPIECA, 2017). With permission.

Some companies define SI to encompass a broad range of activities which are not separated out, including: philanthropy, community projects not related to core corporate activities (e.g. micro-credit and medical programs), those related to core corporate activities (e.g. local hiring or contracting, or waste management); and social impact mitigation. Indeed, one single blueprint of the ideal approach towards social investment does not exist (IPIECA, 2017).

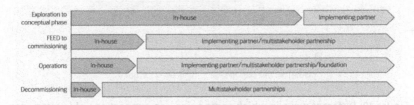

Figure 18: Evolution of the social investment models across the oil and gas project life cycle (IPIECA 2017). With permission.

Figures 18 and 19 were developed for an oil and gas project life cycle (IPIECA, 2017). It could be relevant for the mining industry, or modified by interested mining companies to better align with their particular context. The first figure presents a set of mixed social investment implementation models during a project life cycle, while the second figure presents different ways in which companies can support social investments through the project life cycle.

FEED = Front End Engineering and Design

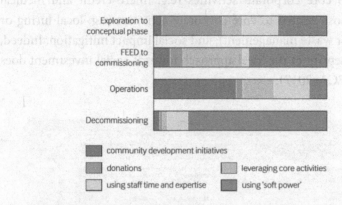

Figure 19: Different ways in which companies can support social investments throughout the project life cycle. (IPIECA 2017). With permission.

These two models clearly highlight the importance of designing a clear exit strategy for any social investment in order to be able to close a project in a responsible way while "hand overing" a sustainable post-closure activity for the remaining stakeholders. It is unrealistic to think that a company can exit an area and leave a positive legacy without having planned for it long in advance. The development of a company's exit strategy cannot be left until decommissioning starts. Community ownership of the post-closure goals should be built from the earliest project phases. Until recently, closure planning was a technical subject and focused predominantly on environmental aspects. However, it is becoming increasingly recognized that closure planning needs to take an integrated approach, with stakeholder engagement and SI as key elements (IPIECA, 2017).

The content of this chapter clearly shows the powerful role that the West African mining industry can and must play in contributing to the continuous improvement of the living conditions of the populations of the host countries. One of the strongest and most durable levers for achieving this objective is capacity-building and empowerment of the local workforce through skills transfer, particularly via expatriates, in addition to technical and managerial training that will enable West Africa to have human resources commensurate with its potential. The next chapter deals with this central issue for West Africa.

5. LOCAL CONTENT & LOCAL WORKFORCE EMPOWERMENT

In an article about How to invest responsibly in Africa's human capital, Soraya Narfeldt provided this statement particularly relevant for the subject on this chapter:

> "For many developing countries, building a skilled workforce is one of the greatest challenges. In a digital age where an increasing number of traditional jobs are being replaced with technology, it is crucial for emerging markets to build a knowledge economy where their citizens can contribute to their nations' sustainable development. However, history shows that in many countries, international companies and expatriates have often gone in, done the work, reaped the rewards, and left" (Narfeldt, 2017).

In their report tiled Local content policies in the mining sector: Stimulating direct local employment, the International Institute for Sustainable Development (IISD) and the Intergovernmental Forum on Mining, Minerals, Metals and Sustainable Development (IGF) outlined that when a mining company arrives in an area, the promise of local employment is central to public debate in least developed, developing, and developed countries alike. For local communities, decent mining company jobs that are safe, stable, and compensated, allow employees and their families to plan to improve their livelihoods and financial security. For host governments, local employment in the mining sector supports national priorities and political promises for job creation, human capital development, and inclusive economic growth. For mining companies, employing local people drives cost efficiencies and helps in the ongoing process of gaining and maintaining a social licence to operate (IISD & IGF, 2018). Regarding the data on global mining sector employment, authors stressed that current estimates are that the sector contributes around 1-2 percent of total direct employment in a country. When indirect (e.g., contract) and induced employment (i.e., resulting from spending by mining employees) is included, the contribution can jump to 3-15 percent (IISD & IGF, 2018).

History shows that an abundance of natural resources does not necessarily improve a country's human development. Most governments have expressed a commitment to turn revenues from new natural resource discoveries into outcomes that matter for their citizens: better health, better education, and access to quality social services. They also want to make sure the discovery of extractives translates into more and better jobs and business opportunities. According to the World Bank, local employment is consistently the top concern of communities located near extractive projects (AfDB & BMGF, 2015 a, b). Work that is safe, stable, and fairly compensated allows workers to extend the benefits of a steady income and new skillsets to their families and communities. Therefore, creating sustainable jobs for the local population is seen as "investing in [a state's] own future" (IISD & IGF, 2018).

This chapter tries to clarify how incoming expatriation could be used as a trigger for local employment in the extractive sector. Through the local content lens, the continuing relevance of long-term expatriate deployment will be questioned, and alternative solutions proposed if required. This chapter is also mainly intended as an overview of the current state and new trends of local content frameworks with a focus on the local employment pillar within the mining industry and within host countries. It will provide useful tools, and a roadmap for building, strengthening, or realigning the sustainability journey of the West African mining sector to be positioned as a trusted partner of choice that gains and maintains its license to operate.

5.1 EXPATRIATION & WORKFORCE NATIONALIZATION IN THE WEST-AFRICAN EXTRACTIVE INDUSTRY

When analyzing the employment effects of a large extractive project, three types of effects are usually distinguished: direct, indirect, and induced employment (AfDB & BMGF, 2015b).

- **Direct employment** refers to those who are employed by the company that owns and operates the extraction site. Contractor staff are usually included if their regular workplace is at the site.
- **Indirect employment** concerns those working with other companies that supply goods (such as machinery and raw materials) and services to the extractive project in question, or that use its outputs. These employees are part of the supply chain.
- **Induced employment** includes those who are employed as a result of the in-country spending of those who receive income from the extractives sector (i.e. government, in the form of taxes and salaries, and the wages and dividends of those employed and contracted by the company).

This chapter deals mainly with the direct employment, focusing on the various government policies and regulations and the corporate strategies of mining companies to strengthen the capacity of the local workforce and promote the employment of nationals at all levels of responsibility within the industry.

5.1.1 BUSINESS NARRATIVES FOR LONG TERM EXPATRIATION

Hocking (2007) investigated how expatriates contribute to the transnational firm's strategic objectives of global efficiency, national ("local") responsiveness, and worldwide learning and found that the reasons most often mentioned for the application of income expatriate employees are allocation and coordination between headquarters and international subsidiaries, the transfer of technological and managerial know-how, the implementation of strategies, organizational development, and the aim to influence the corporate culture. Expatriates implement elements of the headquarters' base of knowledge by establishing routines and processes in the subsidiaries abroad and training their colleagues there. What all these aims have in common is that expatriation is first used in the attempt to achieve unification in form of a unified worldwide strategy, the application of the same technology in all plants at home and abroad, the development of a cadre of junior managers across national boundaries (Hocking, 2007). Hocking also found that expatriate knowledge applications result from frequent knowledge access and communication with the corporate headquarters and other global units of the firm. In contrast, their experiential learning derives from frequent access to host country (local) knowledge that is subsequently adapted to the global corporate context. From a practical perspective, he concluded that experiential learning is an invaluable resource for both present and future corporate assignments (Hocking, 2007). Consequently, expatriation, if well framed, with clear objectives and performance indicators, can be a powerful lever for the transfer of technical and managerial skills to the benefit of the local workforce, and this must be done within a realistic timeframe.

5.1.2 LOCAL CONTENT POLICIES & EMPLOYMENT IN AFRICA'S EXTRACTIVE INDUSTRY

According to the Extractive Industries Transparency Initiative (EITI), it is estimated that 90% of resource-rich countries have adopted a form of local content policy, and increasing local content is a high priority among these governments. EITI also highlighted that Several African countries, such as Nigeria, Ghana, Mali, Burkina Faso, Senegal, and Liberia, have local content policies or provisions, either in laws or contracts. These countries have adopted different definitions or approaches to local content, through requirements in laws or individual contracts, or as policy. The policies and provisions are generally aimed at supporting more jobs for the local population, boosting the economy, facilitating technology transfer, and building skills among the local workforces. They are often directed at increasing local employment and training for local staff, providing subcontracting or service provision opportunities for extractive projects to national companies, or sourcing of local products used in extractive operations (EITI, 2018). Under certain conditions, local content policies can play a pivotal role in setting the structural framework for in-country value retention in the mining sector. Government policies and strategies promoting local employment in the mining sector are generally seeking to achieve one or more of the following objectives (IISD & IGF, 2018):

- Responding to national priorities and political pressures for job creation from constituents,
- Gaining and maintaining a "social license to operate" for mining projects,
- Growing and developing the skills of the national labor force,
- Supporting efforts to progress gender equality and social inclusion,
- Minimizing project costs (through localizing labor) to maximize company profits and fiscal revenues.

According to the IISD and IFG, there is no "one-size-fits-all" approach to promoting direct local employment in the mining sector. Policy settings and strategies must be context-specific, reflecting the needs and capacities of a host country at a given stage of development, as shown by Figure 20.

Figure 20: Key stages for developing a local employment policy for the mining sector (IISD & IGF, 2018). With permission.

There are two main approaches used by host governments to enhance local employment (Figure 21), namely:

- **Regulatory approaches**, which typically result in mandatory, "stick"-based policies that rely on strong compliance mechanisms, with the prospect of financial sanctions or loss of licenses,
- **Facilitative approaches**, which typically result in incentive-based, "carrot" policies that offer support and incentives for the development and employment of local workers (IISD & IGF, 2018).

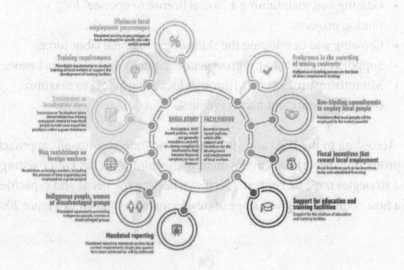

Figure 21: Regulatory and facilitative approaches to local employment in the mining sector (IISD & IGF, 2018). With permission.

5.2 COUNTRY-SPECIFIC LOCAL CONTENT POLICIES & EMPLOYMENT STRATEGIES

In sub-Saharan Africa, the region with the world's youngest and fastest growing population, investing in human capital is imperative if millions are to gain employment and build better lives for themselves and their families. The good news is that for many organizations doing business in African countries, hiring a proportion of local people is now a legal requirement as part of "nationalization" strategies (Narfeldt, 2017). From an economic security and a social inclusion perspective, establishing a skilled local workforce is one of the most critical challenges facing countries with emerging extractive industries. Therefore, the integration of local skilled workforces and the replacement of expatriate workers have been on the top of agendas for such countries (Paydar, 2014).

Several West-African countries have initiated local content programs with a strong focus on workforce nationalization. Nigeria and Burkina Faso are presented below as examples.

5.2.1 NIGERIA

Nigeria is Africa's largest producer of oil, and the 13th largest oil producing country in the world. Most of the oil and gas activities are found in the Niger Delta, in the southern part of the country. Nigeria is richly endowed with various types of mineral resources (EITI, 2020). As outlined by the Columbia Center on Sustainable Investment (2014), Nigeria requires operators to submit an employment plan that includes the hiring and training needs of the operator and its contractors, a breakdown of required skills, and the anticipated training requirements and expenditure for such training. Reports on the progress of the implementation of the plan are to be submitted on a quarterly basis. A maximum of 5 percent of expatriates may be maintained by an operator for management positions in respect of each project, and where foreign workers are hired, a succession plan for the "Nigerianization" of expatriate positions must be approved by the local authorities. Table 3 provides an overview of Nigeria's local content system.

Table 3: Overview of the Nigerian local content system
(Columbia Center on Sustainable Investment, 2014). With permission.

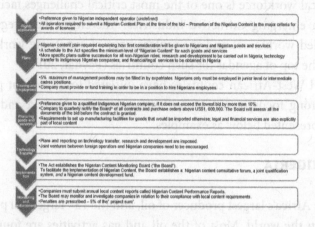

The Nigerian Content plan submitted by any operator or project promoter for any project shall contain an Employment and Training Plan, which, among its requirements, shall include (Columbia Center on Sustainable Investment, 2014):

A time frame for employment opportunities for each phase of project development and operations, to enable members of the Nigerian workforce to prepare themselves for such opportunities.

For each of its operations, the operator must submit to the Board a succession plan for any position not held by Nigerians that provides for Nigerians to understudy each incumbent expatriate for a maximum period of four years; at the end of the four years, the position will become "Nigerianized."

5.2.2 BURKINA FASO

The mining sector in Burkina Faso is considered one of the most dynamic in West Africa. The development of the mining sector was made possible through intensified investment, the opening of industrial mines and an evolution of the legal and regulatory framework for the sector. The main resources are gold, zinc, copper, manganese, phosphate, and limestone (EITI, 2020). Table 4 provides an overview of this country's local content system.

Table 4: Overview of Burkina's local content system
(Columbia Center on Sustainable Investment, 2019). With permission.

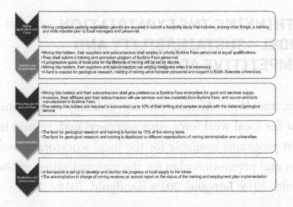

In Burkina Faso, mining title holders, their suppliers, and their sub-contractors shall employ, in priority, national executives at equal qualifications and without distinction of gender. They shall train and promote them for the gradual replacement of expatriate personnel. They are required to respect the quota of local employment that will be set by a decree taken by the Board of Ministers (Columbia Center on Sustainable Investment, 2014).

In each of these countries' local content framework, there is a strong focus on enhancing the training and employment of nationals by extractive companies. This includes the implementation of committees in charge of monitoring and enforcing the implementation of the relevant requirements within the extractive industry. The comparison between Nigeria and Burkina Faso shows that the former seems to have a clearer and stronger local content framework, especially in the training and employment sides. By including clear targets of nationals within the top management of extractive industries, Nigeria put a bigger focus on the local workforce empowerment side of the local content system by having more national representatives within the high level and strategic decision-making process. Nevertheless, it must be stressed that despite good intentions, one of the weak links in all these policies is the limited capacity of local governments to enforce the applicable rules. By making exceptions on a case-by-case basis, host countries often end up diluting the substance of the regulatory requirements and negating the expected benefits.

5.3 RETHINKING THE EXPATRIATION MODEL—SUSTAINABILITY AND COMPETITIVE ADVANTAGE

At a glance, the West African mining industry is responding to the requirement for local workforce empowerment with several learning and development programs available for the local workforce, associated with progressions and promotion plan for the nationalization of the workforce (Teranga Gold, 2019; Iamgold, 2019; Randgold, 2018…).

5.3.1 BUSINESS CASE FOR LOCAL WORFORCE EMPOWERMENT

The International Labor Organization (ILO) highlighted that heavy reliance on expatriates has several consequences for nationals, including unemployment. ILO also outlined that many companies are grappling with the challenge of reducing the high cost of maintaining an international workforce. They recognize the increasing importance of recruiting local talent with local knowledge and experience to join their workforce and to move into business leadership roles. This change in emphasis is important, not just for cost reduction reasons, but for companies to benefit from the best local talent, culture and knowledge (International Labor Organization, 2012).

The business case for hiring a local workforce includes tangible benefits such as cost saving in wages and transportation costs (*fly in fly out*: FIFO). More importantly, the intangible benefit related to the social license to operate and community engagement must be evaluated and understood at all levels of the organization, including managers, HR, and C-suite executives.

"Local employment in the mining sector is a way for governments to develop competencies, address skills shortages, and facilitate knowledge transfer within their national labor force. Particularly for developing or nascent producing states, building

68

the capacity of the national labor force represents an opportunity to increase the productivity as well as the competitiveness of the mining. A trained mining workforce can also help reduce dependence on foreign aid. For instance, a skilled mining workforce can contribute to the export of labor to other countries, which in turn can result in remittances from diaspora mining populations. Provided that the competencies developed by those working in the mining industry are transferable, skills developed in and for the mining sector can be passed on to other industries, such as the construction and manufacturing sectors. This is a vital element of a national strategy to diversify economic activities away from natural resource extraction or to prepare for post-mining transitions" (IISD & IGF, 2018, p.6).

The recent COVID-19 pandemic with its resulting international travel restriction that significantly reduced the availability of expats workforce on the ground is also a strong reminder about the critical of having skilled local workforce to ensure business continuity during such kind of global or regional crisis. In this case it is just about sound business risk management to prevent operation stoppage and care and maintenance costs related with expatriate staff shortage. It is just about ensuring business resilience to deal with these types of crises.

5.3.2 OUTLOOK FOR SUSTAINABLE WORKFORCE MANAGEMENT

In contrast to artisanal & small-scale mining, Large-scale mining have an unusually high capital to labor ratio compared with other industries. This means that they hire fewer employees per investment dollar than most businesses. Though there may be very high expectations for the extraction site itself to employ many individuals, the nature of the business is to have few employees (NRGI, 2015). Therefore, the challenge for miners and host country governments will be to avoid overestimating the job creation capacity of mining projects; instead, miners and politics should avoid overestimating the capacity for job creation of mining projects to prevent the creation of unrealistic expectations that would subsequently lead to disappointment and a breakdown of trust that would threaten the license to operate over the long term.

Sometimes there are weak incentives for expats to commit to and actively support their organization's diversity management policies due to current compensation packages. In addition, the scarcity of resources in the HR departments does not facilitate robust monitoring of implementation of these programs (Scheible, 2017).

"If decisions about international assignments were based on the individual contribution an assignee could make to the team in the foreign subsidiary, the role of expats would surely change. They would no longer be considered representatives of the headquarters who are expected to align the foreigners with the central doctrine, but they would be regarded as teammates who are appreciated for their special abilities, and who appreciate the abilities of the other team members on site" (Scheible, 2017, p.94).

Repositioning expats as trainers, coaches, and mentors with SMART (Specific, Measurable, Achievable, Realistic, and Time bound) key performance indicators and a timescale to transfer the permanent role to the local trainees could be a good option to be considered by mining companies. Then each job will need to have a clear skill matrix detailing technical and managerial skill and competencies required for the position. Usually, depending on the complexity and risk related to the tasks to be performed, a development plan including coaching, mentoring, in class, and on-the-job training from few months to two or three years in length might be enough to fulfill the requirements.

The implementation of local high-quality education programs within host states of extractive industries is also a key factor for the success of local employment programs. It seems that institutions that deliver top quality education are those that have been co-hosted or co-organized through a partnership between government and industry. An example is Nigeria's Institute of Petroleum Studies. This is sponsored by Total Exploration and

Production Nigeria and the state-owned Nigerian National Petroleum Corporation (Odon, 2015). With ongoing training and investment in skills development, companies operating in Africa can contribute enormously to the development of a skilled workforce. This developmental curve adds incredible value to the industry and, most importantly, means that organizations can leave the communities where they work significantly richer in skills (Narfeldt, 2017). Initiatives such as scholarships and internship programs for students could also help improve the employability of local workforce.

Working in West Africa requires people with a high level of soft skills, and the ability to adapt to social codes that are more complex and different than they appear to be, from one country to another in a sub-region or even within the same country (Hazoume, 2020). People in the African diaspora looking for opportunities in their home countries ("Repats") in Africa could be an interesting option to consider. The advantages of "Repats" are well known—they wish to settle in Africa for the long term, often driven by an ideal of contributing to the continent's development. They can sometimes speak several local languages, and can master social codes that could determine the failure or success of a key commercial negotiation or a relationship with an institution. Since it is true that a large proportion of African MBA students do indeed want to relocate to Africa (nearly 70 percent, according to some studies), the use of "Repats" could be an excellent compromise for both mining companies and host countries (Hazoume, 2020). Great progress is shown within the mining industry where, for example, 95 percent of the workforce of Teranga Gold Corporation in Senegal are local, and more than 50 percent are from surrounding areas (Teranga Gold, 2019). Subsidiaries of multinationals were made up of more than 70 percent expatriates 20 to 25 years ago in Africa; currently this ratio has more than reversed—70-30 percent (Hazoume, 2020).

When a mining company arrives in an area, the promise of local employment is central to public debate in developing, and developed countries alike. For local communities, decent mining company jobs that are safe, stable, and well-compensated allow employees and their families to plan to improve their livelihoods and financial security. (IISD & IGF, 2018). The recent development and implementation of local content frameworks in several mineral-rich countries in West Africa have significantly improved the training, nationalization, and empowerment of the local workforce. Beyond the "mandatory requirement" point of view, the business case for training and hiring local staff is becoming better understood by the mining industry, both with respect to financial benefits associated with these cost savings, and the social license to operate. Obviously, expatriate workers have a critical role to play within the West African extractive industry, but the scope and timescale of their assignments could be refocused and aligned with host countries' local content policies, and local communities' expectations.

Despite the importance of transparency when it comes to implementing local content strategies, there is limited data available to fully allow stakeholders to understand how the impact of local content in the extractive sector can be improved. Increased transparency in local content could incentivize companies to hire and buy more services and goods locally (EITI, 2018). This chapter focused on the employment side of local content, but deeper investigation will need to be done to assess the efficient implementation of these policies, and how they really boost the local economies of host countries. Of course, any successful community development initiative, including for the purpose of developing local content, must be embedded in a solid stakeholder engagement process to listen, understand, and manage the concerns and expectations of all parties, including the silent voices of most vulnerable and marginalized communities. Such an approach will enable the West African mining industry to gain and maintain its license to operate, which is the subject of the next chapter.

6. LICENSE TO OPERATE & STAKEHOLDER ENGAGEMENT

Mining activity has, and will continue to have, effects on the land, territories, resources, and ways of life of indigenous peoples (International Council on Mining and Metals (ICMM), 2010). There is, therefore, a need to build constructive relationships between indigenous peoples and the mining and metals industry. These relationships must be based on respect, constructive engagement, and mutual benefit. They must also consider the specific and historical situations of indigenous peoples (ICMM, 2010). Such an approach could be of interest to West African mining companies in gaining and maintaining their "social license" through a harmonious and continuous engagement with their stakeholders, especially with local communities.

This chapter will present the concept of "social license to operate" through complementary definitions, and will also propose indicators to characterize it. It will then focus on stakeholder engagement processes to identify some limitations in the West African context, and then propose a complementary model for continuous improvement. The links between strategies for stakeholder engagement and for business will be also highlighted. Finally, the chapter will conclude with the presentation of a tool, mainly designed by the author, to provide the industry with a simple and coherent framework and criteria for the selection, prioritization, and financing of community development initiatives, always from the perspective of creating shared value.

6.1 SOCIAL LICENSE TO OPERATE IN THE EXTRACTIVE INDUSTRY

6.1.1 DEFINITION

The notion of social license is widely used in the everyday language of major projects, yet its definitions vary. Nevertheless, the three definitions below seem to be complementary, and they provide a broader understanding of social license:

- "Social license is the result of a process by which the stakeholders together construct the minimum conditions to be put in place, so that a project, programme or policy fits harmoniously, and at a given time, into its natural and human environment" (Pétrin, 2012, p. 49).
- "Social license is the anticipated acceptance of a short and long-term risk that either a project or a situation may have" (Conseil patronal de l'environnement du Québec, 2012, p.2).
- "Social license is a tacit contract between the population on the one hand, and a company or government on the other, which stipulates that a project can go ahead. For even if it obtains all the legal authorizations for a project... a company will have difficulty completing it if the population opposes it" (Castonguay, 2011, p.2).

In her essay entitled "Protection of the environment through social acceptability," Pétrin (2012) clearly demonstrates the complementarity of the three definitions by outlining that the second complements the first by referring to risk management. Consequently, it would be the company's responsibility to sufficiently mitigate and prevent risks, so that stakeholders understand and accept this degree of risk and the consequences that may occur. Such a definition refers more to the creation of a bond of trust between the local population and the company, rather than a partnership for the development of the project. As for the third definition, Pétrin highlighted that it emphasises the fact that the promoter must prove its willingness to work with the local population by going beyond the regulatory requirements (Pétrin, 2012).

The synthesis of these three definitions shows that the role of the social acceptability process boils down to facilitating the social integration of a project into a distinct collective landscape (Pétrin, 2012). The five indicators proposed below can be used by the West African extractive industry.

6.1.2 CONDITIONS FOR BUILDING A STRONG LICENSE TO OPERATE

Most mining industry players are aware of the potential impacts of mining projects and the importance of a calm social climate as a prerequisite for the success of any mining project (ICMM, 2010). Thus, in its best practices guide, entitled "Aboriginal Peoples and Mining," the ICMM recognizes that mining activity has affected and will continue to affect the land, territories, resources, and way of life of aboriginal peoples. The ICMM (International Council on Mining and Metals) is an industry organization, led by business leaders, that addresses key priorities and emerging issues in the mining and metals industry. Its members also emphasize that maintaining a healthy and stable natural environment is essential for supporting communities, especially those that wish to maintain a traditional way of life (ICMM, 2010). Therefore, the ICMM urges the mining industry to build a constructive relationship with indigenous peoples, based on respect, constructive engagement, and mutual benefit, with consideration for the specific and historical situation of indigenous peoples. In other words, mining companies operating in indigenous territories must develop processes to ensure the social acceptability of their projects. Although the term "aboriginal" is not the most appropriate in a West African context, the substance of the ICMM recommendations remains valid and relevant for this sub-region. The sections here describe five proposed indicators for the implementation of a sound social license process in West African mining industry. This list is not exhaustive.

6.1.2.1 CONSULTATION OF STAKEHOLDERS

One of the first steps in establishing a process for the social acceptability of a project in the mining industry is the identification of stakeholders and their respective concerns. To do this, proponents must, from the outset of the project, create meeting spaces where the diverse stakeholders can express their concerns, reveal their dissensions, and forge consensus (Batelier, 2011). Thus, mining project promoters must take advantage of the capacity of individuals, groups, and communities to express their points of view and concerns regarding projects that concern them (MDDEFP, 2012a).

More concretely, the proponent must adopt communication plans for its project, begin the consultation process before or as soon as the project notice is filed, and involve all stakeholders, including individuals, groups, and communities, as well as ministries and other public organizations (MDDEFP, 2012a). It is useful to begin consultation as early as possible in the project planning process so that the opinions of stakeholders can have a real influence on the questions to be studied, the issues to be documented, and the decision-making and choices. The earlier consultation occurs in the process leading up to a decision, the greater the influence of individuals, groups, and communities on the overall project, and the greater the likelihood that the project will be considered socially acceptable (MDDEFP, 2012a). This approach could also defuse conflicts that could have heavy financial, human, and political costs for governments, communities, and companies alike (Batelier, 2011).

In West Africa, this duty to consult stakeholders is generally a legal requirement for environmental and social assessments of projects. However, the regulatory part of the consultation process should only be the tip of the iceberg, as it should be preceded by crucial formal or informal voluntary community engagement work to gain and maintain the social licence to operate. Nevertheless, the quality, inclusiveness, and extent of these exercises vary significantly between countries, projects, promoters, and is influenced by the level of expertise of the consultants coordinating the processes and the level of openness of stakeholders to the project. The level of training, expertise, and independence of local government officials is also an important factor in the smooth running of these processes.

6.1.2.2 COMMUNICATION & TRANSPARENCY

Communication and transparency are solid foundations for the social acceptability process, as they help build a relationship of trust between the promoters and stakeholders of mining projects. It is with this in mind that proponents need to build relationships and consult with stakeholders in a fair, timely and culturally appropriate manner throughout the project life cycle (ICMM, 2010). Thus, the relational approach with local communities must be based on honest and open information, and presented in a way that is accessible to them. Such an approach will ensure that these communities are informed and understand the full range (short, medium, and long term) of social and environmental effects (positive and negative) that may result from mining. This notion of transparency is, according to some, a prerequisite for decision-making and for free, prior, and informed consent (FPIC). In the context of mining activities, FPIC is a process whereby affected communities have the opportunity to decide, with sufficient information about the advantages and disadvantages of the project, whether and when the activity will take place, based on their customary decision-making systems (ICMM, 2010).

The FPIC has been made mandatory or recommended by several national and international political and legal documents, including the United Nations Declaration on the Rights of Indigenous Peoples (United Nations, 2007). The FPIC is also linked to an ethical principle—that those who are likely to be exposed to harm, or risk of harm, should be duly informed and given the opportunity to express their willingness to accept it or not (ICMM, 2010). It should be noted, however, that although there is general agreement that the participation of indigenous peoples in the decision-making process should be free, prior, and informed, there is no consensus as to how this should be effectively applied. Indeed, some reticent people see this as an infringement of the sovereign right of states to make decisions regarding the development of natural resources. In some cases, it is understood as the right of stakeholders to approve or refuse activities, and in others as a principle that should respect decision-making processes such as authorizations issued by the competent levels of government (ICMM, 2010).

6.1.2.3   CIVIL SOCIETY MATURITY

In an article on Citizen Mobilization Against Shale Gas in Quebec Batelier and Sauvé (2011) demonstrates, that populations are thirsty and fighting for a participatory democracy regarding choices concerning the common good, land occupation, and resource use. In other words, the populations have developed a maturity that has not ceased to develop and assert itself in the fruitful interaction between groups of citizens, environmental organizations, the media, and the various other actors in this social struggle. This maturity, understanding of the situation, and capacity for interaction, is based on a body of knowledge and know-how. Instead of being perceived as a threat or risk to projects, promoters of mining projects would benefit from perceiving this civil society maturity as a factor in improving the project, and as an opportunity to reduce risks by building a project on a very solid social foundations. Civil society maturity can be illustrated in different ways (Batelier and Sauvé, 2011):

- Citizens have an objective understanding of the stakes of the project in its political, socio-economic, and environmental dimensions, in the short, medium, and long term,
- Citizens have a clear vision to defend collectively,
- Citizens know how to resist social marketing and misinformation,
- Citizens are open to participate in frameworks for exchange on the project and are willing to contribute to its improvement to achieve the minimum conditions for its social acceptability.

The collective maturity of civil society can therefore contribute to identifying risk situations (Batelier and Sauvé, 2011). The vigilance of the public is therefore an irreplaceable link, and they should be partners rather than opponents of the process of social acceptability of mining projects.

Such an analysis is particularly relevant in the West African context, where local civil society is becoming increasingly dynamic and committed in its role of monitoring, warning, and advocacy on all political and socio-economic, and environmental issues affecting local communities.

6.1.2.4 INDEPENDENT ASSESSMENT

Proponents of mining projects are responsible for conducting their Environmental and Social Impact Assessment (ESIA). In practice, mines entrust the conduct of the ESIA to consultants who are expected to carry out this work independently, firstly to maintain their reputation and credibility, and secondly, because of the personal ethics and codes of conduct that must be adhered to by the professionals in charge of these studies. The independence of the consultant may nevertheless be difficult to believe for some citizens because the consultant is in the pay of the promoter, which could in some cases result in conflicts of interest. Consequently, the involvement of government authorities and bodies in the process of issuing certificates of authorization is the best guarantee of the independent expertise and reliability of the information provided by the project promoter. Indeed, analysts from government agencies and authorities screen all ESIA reports for potential deficiencies and can request the proponent to provide additional information or evidence. These analysts represent the legislator who has been elected by the people and who is supposed to represent their interests. As such, the primary responsibility lies with government authorities to verify and validate the quality of the information contained in the ESIA report, and thus ensure transparency.

Nevertheless, in the West African context, the administrations in charge of environmental issues often lack the minimum requirements for ensuring an optimal evaluation of projects. These include a lack of qualified staff, a lack of equipment, and low exposure to socio-environmental issues associated with the extractive industry. On the other hand, the extractive industry works with seasoned, world-class consultants, which results in an obvious technical asymmetry vis-à-vis local government officials. To reduce this asymmetry, project promoters will sometimes be asked to provide a programme to strengthen the institutional capacities of local administrations (provision of vehicles, equipment for environmental monitoring of projects, scholarships, etc.). These actions, although commendable, seem laughably small compared to the heavy responsibility and the seriousness of the stakes associated with a deficient technical, social, and environmental assessment of mining projects. There is, therefore, an urgent need for the various governments to set up ambitious programmes for recruiting, and strengthening the technical capacities of agents, and providing them with rolling stock and equipment.

6.1.2.5 SOCIAL AND INTERGENERATIONAL EQUITY

According to the conclusions of The Public Conversation on Quebec's Mining Future, organized by the Institut du Nouveau Monde (INM), Quebec citizens are concerned about intergenerational and interregional equity in current and future mining development (INM, 2012). This equity translates into the maximization of positive spin-offs for Quebec, including government equity investments in mining companies and more secondary and tertiary processing of ore in Quebec. Citizens also want these spin-offs to be more visible for the regions and localities concerned, particularly through a redistribution of royalties between the local, regional, and national levels, as well as through local purchasing and investments in research and development. They also want to see forward-looking and careful post-mining or inter-boom planning, through the creation of a Sovereign Fund, for example, diversification of regional economies where the mining sector is important, and active support for entrepreneurship, both mining and non-mining (INM, 2012). Although borrowed from a different context, these strong aspirations expressed by the Quebec population are entirely valid for West African populations who might expect no less from the exploitation of their mining resources.

Furthermore, the ICMM recalls that indigenous peoples have historically been at a disadvantage, discriminated against and deprived of their lands, and that they continue to be at a disadvantage compared to most other classes of society. These people are also often more vulnerable to the negative effects of exploitation, especially those that have a negative impact on culture and natural resources. Addressing these issues requires particular attention to the interests and rights of indigenous groups throughout the life cycle of a mining project (ICMM, 2010). Thus, there is some consensus on the need for social and generational equity for sustainable mining development. Nevertheless, the modalities of implementation of social and intergenerational equity, and the responsibilities of the different actors remain ambiguous.

The fundamental question is, *what is the responsibility of mining companies in the implementation of social and intergenerational equity? Isn't their responsibility limited to complying with the legislation in force, honouring their agreements, paying the taxes and royalties set by the authorities and implementing their corporate social responsibility policy?*

In other words, in implementing a social and intergenerational equity approach, is the responsibility of mining companies not limited to being good corporate citizens? Isn't it the responsibility of government authorities to put in place incentives for secondary or even tertiary processing of minerals and to set up a Sovereign Wealth Fund for future generations? Aren't central and local authorities responsible for the effective and efficient use of revenues from royalties and taxes collected from mining to enable the diversification of local economies, and to ensure active support for entrepreneurship, both mining and non-mining?

Answers to these questions would help to better frame the expectations of local populations regarding the West African extractive industry, and consequently defuse deep disappointment and potential social conflicts.

The five indicators proposed in this chapter are part of a dynamic of sustainable mining development and could contribute to the establishment of a peaceful social climate in mining areas.

6.2 STAKEHOLDER ENGAGEMENT STRATEGIES

Sustainability is a journey of humility, respect, authenticity, and trust, embedded in active learning and partnership for the co-creation of a better present, and a best future for all parties. To be successful, no one must be left behind, from the loudest minorities to the silent and most vulnerable majorities. Through the lens of this definition, which could be used as a roadmap, authenticity must be understood by stakeholders as, saying what you mean, meaning what you say, and above all, sticking to your corporate values and principles.

According to a Business for Social Responsibility (BSR) report:

> "Stakeholder engagement is, and will remain, a core element
> of the sustainability toolkit. It is a fundamental component of
> materiality assessments, which are then used to inform sustain-
> ability strategy, reporting, and disclosure. Corporations need
> strategies to understand and respond to existing and emerging
> societal concerns. Without input from key stakeholder groups,
> any approach to sustainability will be limited by an organiza-
> tion's self-interest and inward focus. [...] Stakeholder engage-
> ment has never come with higher stakes or been more impor-
> tant. Companies need a robust, defensible methodology and
> tools that can account fully for a shifting business environment
> in which social and environmental concerns are increasingly
> prominent" (Business for Social Responsibility , 2019, p.6).

6.2.1 STAKEHOLDER ENGAGEMENT PROCESS

Stakeholder engagement is a two-way process of communication and
interaction within and between a project and each of its stakeholders.
It involves meaningful and multifaceted engagement with both external and internal stakeholders. It is an ongoing process throughout the
life of a project. Table 5 shows the International Association for Public
Participation (IAP2) "Spectrum of Public Participation," with the key elements of stakeholder engagement, ranging from informing stakeholders
to empowering them (IAP2, 2018). This Spectrum was designed to assist
with the selection of the level of participation that defines the public's role
in any public participation process.

Table 5: IAP2 Spectrum of Public Participation (IAP2, 2018). (c) International Association for Public Participation www.iap2.org. With permission.

IAP2 Spectrum of Public Participation

IAP2's Spectrum of Public Participation was designed to assist with the selection of the level of participation that defines the public's role in any public participation process. The Spectrum is used internationally, and it is found in public participation plans around the world.

INCREASING IMPACT ON THE DECISION

	INFORM	CONSULT	INVOLVE	COLLABORATE	EMPOWER
PUBLIC PARTICIPATION GOAL	To provide the public with balanced and objective information to assist them in understanding the problem, alternatives, opportunities and/or solutions.	To obtain public feedback on analysis, alternatives and/or decisions.	To work directly with the public throughout the process to ensure that public concerns and aspirations are consistently understood and considered.	To partner with the public in each aspect of the decision including the development of alternatives and the identification of the preferred solution.	To place final decision making in the hands of the public.
PROMISE TO THE PUBLIC	We will keep you informed.	We will keep you informed, listen to and acknowledge concerns and aspirations, and provide feedback on how public input influenced the decision.	We will work with you to ensure that your concerns and aspirations are directly reflected in the alternatives developed and provide feedback on how public input influenced the decision.	We will look to you for advice and innovation in formulating solutions and incorporate your advice and recommendations into the decisions to the maximum extent possible.	We will implement what you decide.

All stakeholders have interests and concerns about mining projects. These interests are generally political, economic, social, scientific, cultural, and environmental. These concerns may also be considered at a local or regional level, and in the short, medium, or long term (Pelletier, 2012). The objectives and duties of project promoters with respect to these concerns are generally as follows (Drolet, 2012):

- Know the expectations of the main stakeholders and, where appropriate, incorporate them into the project design
- Identify potential conflicts of expectation or interest between stakeholders at the earliest possible stage and find a solution, or an acceptable compromise
- Know what can result from both satisfied and unsatisfied stakeholder expectations

- Determine how best to manage stakeholders according to their degree of power and interest in the project and the actions they are likely to undertake

In general, pre-consultation and information sessions organized by mining project proponents are an excellent means of gathering the various concerns of stakeholders. These sessions are implemented voluntarily by the mining companies in advance of the more formal public hearings and enquiries required by the applicable regulatory requirements. It should also be noted that, depending on the extent to which their concerns have been addressed by the mining proponent, the stakeholders may be more or less categorically in favor of, or opposed to, a particular project. Among the types of opposition, the most frequent are as follows (Pelletier, 2012):

- NIMBY (*Not In My Back Yard*) discourse: such an attitude translates into complete opposition and closure to any project idea.
- Questioning the location: opened to the project provided the location criteria are met.
- Opposition based on the nature of the site: its exceptional character, for example.
- Opposition to the methods of implementation: with or without proposals for change (location, equipment, installation, etc.).
- Opposition in principle.

These more or less virulent, and more or less justified, objections can be paralyzing for the development of a mining project. Thus, taking the concerns of stakeholders into account in the design of a mining project has become an integral part of the risk management strategy within companies. A lack of dialogue or difficult relationships with its stakeholders could, therefore, be a risk for a company. The following figure 22 brilliantly presents the key components of a good stakeholder engagement process (IFC, 2007).

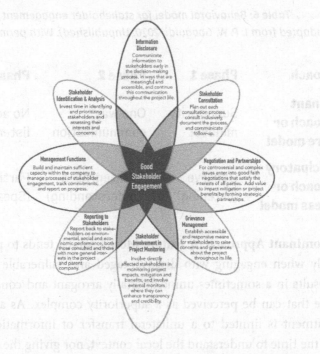

Figure 22: Key component of stakeholder engagement (IFC, 2007).

6.2.2 BEHAVIORAL MODEL FOR STAKEHOLDER ENGAGEMENT

The model below is a generic approach that could be applied to virtually any stakeholder engagement process, particularly in the West African context, where most mining projects are developed in isolated, disadvantaged areas where local communities have not yet developed a strong enough civil society maturity to absorb the important political, socioeconomic, and environmental issues associated with the mining industry. The success or failure of the stakeholder engagement process will therefore depend heavily on the attitude that the leaders of the process have towards the target groups (Table 6).

Table 6: Behavioral model for stakeholder engagement
(adapted from J. P. W. Gbaguidi, 2020. Unpublished). With permission.

Approach	Phase 1	Phase 2	Phase 3
Dominant Approach or Failure model	Superiority mindset	One way communication	No active listening
Participatory Approach or Success model	Observe (listening)	Be integrated (Understanding)	Participate (Speaking)

The Dominant Approach or Failure Model, which tends to prevail particularly when engaging with disadvantaged and vulnerable communities, results in a sometimes unintentionally arrogant and condescending attitude that can be perceived as a superiority complex. As a result, the commitment is limited to a unilateral transfer of information without taking the time to understand the local context, nor giving the other party the opportunity to express itself, or the few bold voices that would have the temerity to express themselves are quickly stifled, and catalogued as opponents and risks for the project. Such an attitude may seem winning in the short term, but often ends in failure due to a revolt of the silent majority, which will sooner or later express itself, particularly with the omnipresence of social networks and the support of civil society, which increasingly plays a role in monitoring, warning, and developing the civil society maturity of the citizens of vulnerable communities.

In West Africa, civil society is becoming increasingly militant and engaged, especially when the stakes are high, such as on extremely sensitive issues related to the extractive industry—land acquisition, involuntary displacement of populations, livelihood restoration processes, protection of cultural heritage, and so on. When anger or revolt erupts as a result of a dominant community engagement approach, it usually becomes too late to repair because the fire will have smouldered for too long and the reaction of the populations and government authorities will generally be passionate, emotional, and spontaneous, and often resulting in popular condemnation and media lynching, rightly or wrongly, of the mining industry. The context will no longer be conducive to a lucid analysis and in-depth diagnosis of the situation. The mining proponent who will have to face such a situation will have no alternative other than to put itself in damage control mode to try to restore credibility, reputation, and licence to operate vis-à-vis local communities, civil society, government authorities, shareholders, investors, their employees, and sometimes even the chancelleries of their home country.

The dominant approach can occur when the timeframes for permitting are very tight and the promoter puts pressure on its consultants and staff to speed up the community engagement process. The other variant would be that the firms responsible for community engagement are so expensive that the project proponent puts pressure on them to remove certain steps from the community engagement process. Indeed, it is often found that project timelines are generally aggressively short, without considering, or through underestimating, the time required to gain and maintain the social licence to operate. It is only after making firm commitments to investors on project delivery timelines that social engineering consultants and internal teams in charge of community relations and permit applications are asked to adjust to the project timing, sometimes set without their knowledge.

The dominant approach may also simply result from a lack of training or insufficient training of the teams in charge of the community engagement process, resulting in inadequate planning and improvisation, but above all, a profound lack of understanding of the risks and opportunities associated with the stakeholder engagement process, and their impact on the achievement of the corporate strategy. Some consultants sometimes make the big mistake of taking Africa as a homogenous entity; they imagine that a winning strategy in Côte d'Ivoire should be systematically applied in Burkina Faso, or vice versa. Selection and training, in terms of skills and competencies of consultants and/or agents in charge of community relations and stakeholder engagement are crucial, but sometimes neglected, steps in planning stakeholder engagement programmes.

The Participatory Approach or Success Model is in line with the following definition: "Sustainability is a journey of humility, respect, authenticity and trust, embedded in active learning and partnership for the co-creation of a better present and a best future for all parties." This approach is based mainly on respect, active listening, and observation, with a view to acquiring a good understanding of the host environment and the social, cultural, historical, and sociological context in which the stakeholders involved evolved. This work, however summary, should be done on the premise that the stakeholders concerned most often evolve in environments that are often uncontrolled, or even unknown and sometimes hostile. It is therefore particularly important to ask basic questions such as: *How do we perceive this new environment? How would we like to be perceived, and what are the sources of power and influence? What are the objectives of this stakeholder engagement process? What are the levers to be used and what are the basic conditions for achieving the objectives?*

Such an approach is inclusive, and considers both the strong voices of communities and the concerns, expressed or not, by silent majorities.

6.3 LINKING STAKEHOLDER ENGAGEMENT STRATEGY TO BUSINESS STRATEGY

6.3.1 BUSINESS STRATEGY AND STAKEHOLDER ENGAGEMENT

The investor community has become significantly more focused on the need for companies to consider environmental, social, and governance issues if they intend to survive and thrive over the longer term. This, in turn, necessitates a strategic shift from an exclusive focus on shareholder value to serving broader stakeholder interests. In 2018, Larry Fink, chief executive officer of BlackRock Inc., the world's largest investment firm, made the bold declaration, "to prosper over time, every company must not only deliver financial performance, but also show how it makes a positive contribution to society." This direct riposte to Milton Friedman's 1970 argument that "the social responsibility of business is to increase its profits" came as a key turning point in mainstream investor thinking on sustainability issues (BSR, 2020).

Over the past two decades, the global mining industry has witnessed the necessity and emergence of community relations and development (CRD) functions, essentially under the rubric of sustainable development and corporate social responsibility (CSR). These functions provide companies with mechanisms through which to engage and manage their relationships with key stakeholder groups, share development benefits, and protect business interests (Kemp and Owen, 2013). The CRD function is typically in charge of operationalizing sustainable development and CSR policy through strategies of engagement, communication, negotiation, conflict resolution, and development programming. On this basis, it can be argued that the extent to which mining companies' value and integrate the CRD function into their core business is a direct representation of their commitment to sustainable development and CSR (Kemp and Owen, 2013). Nevertheless, it is important to remember that, due to the diversity of customs and habits, community involvement can quickly resemble a Tower of Babel, which sometimes translates into a comic succession of blunders that can seriously harm the promoters of mining projects. The example story below illustrates this reality.

6.3.2   EXAMPLE STORY - STAKEHOLDER ENGAGEMENT & SOCIAL RISKS MANAGEMENT IN A WEST-AFRICAN MINE

On the first Thursday in June, consultants from the mining company Youngar Gold Operations, in charge of the community engagement process for the mine extension project, arrived in the village of Detto Salam with gleaming, air-conditioned 4*4 all-terrain vehicles that lifted the fine dust of red laterite throughout the village. The villagers are used to this phenomenon every time a car or even a motorbike crosses the main laterite road in the village. The village nurse claims to have lost the health statistics register when the last rain washed off the roof of the health hut, but confirms that lung diseases are common among children and the elderly. The meeting between the representatives of the mining company and the local population has been scheduled for ten am by the deputy governor, to give the lead consultant time to arrive in the village. Indeed, this consultant has to travel by a chartered plane, which will land on the runway of the old aerodrome of the town of Thiey Yalla, located about twenty kilometres from the village. His plane must then take off again no later than four pm, to avoid being surprised by the rapid nightfall. Indeed, the aerodrome's floodlights have been damaged for almost five years, which prevents night landings and take-offs. During his last visit for the needs of the electoral campaign, the Minister of Transport promised to have them repaired.

For the record, the lead consultant, working for a reputable international firm, collaborates with local consultants, as required by local regulations, which aim to encourage the transfer of skills and the development of local expertise. This international expert in social engineering should travel by road with the national experts, but following the travel risk assessment carried out by the Occupational Health and Safety (OHS) department of this firm, it would not be safe for this consultant to travel by land because of the many potholes in the road. This is why the national consultants travelled by 4*4 on the road, while the lead consultant travelled in a small three-seater plane.

Returning to the planned meeting with the local population, some people are incredibly surprised at the choice of day and time of the meeting. In fact, the weekly market of the rural community that houses the seventeen surrounding villages takes place on Thursdays, and all the men of the village go there to sell or buy cattle, or to sell part of their harvest to buy rice for their families. As for the women, they get up a little earlier on Thursdays because they have to water their market gardens and harvest the fresh vegetables they have to sell at the market, generally to buy condiments, some clothes for their children or notebooks, slates, pens, or books for those with children who go to school. They must then return to the village incredibly early, before noon at the latest, to prepare the meal so that the children can eat before returning to class at three pm. The men stay longer and usually return around five pm, and then go directly to the mosque for prayer.

It was therefore not surprising that at eleven am, there were only three people in the meeting room, in addition to the mining representatives, although there was another reason for the conspicuous absence of the village chief and notables. Indeed, due to a communication problem linked to the late arrival of the deputy governor's notification letter, the village chief only received the official invitation the day before the meeting. Nevertheless, given the importance of this project for the local population, he immediately informed the village notables as well as the president of the village youth association, and asked them to meet him at his house on Thursday morning at nine am, with a view to harmonizing positions, but also to be able to welcome their guests in accordance with the village's legendary tradition of hospitality. Indeed, when guests arrive in the village for any reason, they must first, as a courtesy, go and greet the village chief at his home before continuing their activities afterwards. So, the village chief and his notables had been waiting for the mine consultants since ten am, but at the same time, the representatives of the mine were waiting for them in the village meeting room. It was afterwards that the headmaster whispered in the ear of one of the consultants that they were expected at the chief's house. Obviously, the local consultants known this local custom but this "*Salamalecs*" step was removed the day before the meeting for time optimization purpose. A community relations officer from the mine was asked to inform the village chief. The latter just replied that he was taking note of it.

Arriving at the chief's house at about eleven-thirty am, the delegation was warmly welcomed, and the chief gave them palm wine and cola as a sign of friendship, and introduced the notable guests invited to take part in this meeting with the mining company. At noon, all the guests were all in the meeting room, and the consultant was about to start his PowerPoint presentation after thanking the participants for their availability, but the village chief asked him to give him five minutes for a word of welcome in front of the participants. The village chief's speech ended up lasting more than forty-five minutes because he wanted to recall the remarkably high expectations of the population regarding mining projects, particularly following the latest announcements by the government authorities that this project will radically improve the living conditions of the local population, and that all the young people of the village will now have excellent and well-paid jobs. The chief also took the opportunity to recall the old promises or unfulfilled expectations of the Théa Gold Corp mine, namely the creation of jobs for young people, the asphalting of the road, the granting of a gold panning corridor to the community, the repair and equipping of the village health hut, but above all the repair of the village borehole, which had been broken for three months, to ensure the village's drinking water supply.

The lead social consultant had already worked on similar projects in Congo, Burkina Faso, and Ghana, but this is his first experience in this West African country. He spent the whole week putting together his PowerPoint presentation, but just before he started his presentation, the generator in the meeting room went out due to lack of fuel. The consultant continued his presentation without visual support, but his voice was soon covered by protests from the audience. Indeed, the interpreter only speaks the language of the village chief and there are representatives of two other ethnic groups who demand that the interpretation be done in their own languages to enable them to understand the consultant's message. The village chief was able to calm the situation by promising to organise a restitution meeting soon with an interpreter who speaks the language of the two forgotten groups.

When the consultant addressed the issues related to the protection of cultural heritage, one of the village's notables was keen to recall an unfortunate incident that recently shook the entire population. Indeed, due to an error in taking survey data, the mining company's geologists did not respect the fifty-meter buffer zone around the village's cemeteries, and thus installed a drill in the footprint of the village's sacred wood, where only village elders and insiders are allowed access. This unfortunate incident provoked the anger of the villagers, and some angry youths ransacked the drilling station, and sequestered the geologists' equipment. The drilling campaign was critical for the acquisition of the last data needed to finalise the feasibility study required to finance the project. The continuation of drilling was thus postponed for several months due to the arrival of the rainy season.

Obviously, due to the late start of the meeting and the many questions and interruptions, not all the topics on the agenda were covered, and a second meeting was scheduled at a later date, probably at the end of the rainy season so that the village could be reached by road. It should also be noted that at the end of the meeting, the participants were greeted by a few young people wearing red armbands to protest not being invited to this meeting, which is so important for the future of the region.

The postponement will cause a ripple effect among Youngar Gold's corporate team because its CEO promised his board that the meeting with local communities was taking place today, and that everything should go without a hitch. In fact, communication was planned to inform shareholders that this important step has been successfully completed and to demonstrate the excellent social acceptance that the mine enjoys in the region. The chief financial officer had even anticipated a positive market reaction to this announcement because this project, which is in a high-grade gold sector, will significantly increase the reserves and the life of the mine in this country. Also, due to the particularly high gold prices, the urgent exploitation of this area is considered a priority in the mining plan. This meeting was also critical because the lead investor wanted to be reassured that the non-technical risks associated with this project were being effectively managed.

Of course, this story is completely fictitious, but it has a pedagogical purpose in order to show the subtleties of stakeholder management in community engagement processes in West Africa. Through this example story above, the reader will be able to form his or her own opinion as to whether to use dominant, participatory, or mixed approaches. A similarity with real-life cases from the field would be purely coincidental.

6.4   STAKEHOLDER MAPPING

Stakeholder mapping is a collaborative process of research, analysis, debate, and discussion that draws from multiple perspectives to determine a key list of stakeholders across the entire stakeholder spectrum. Mapping can be broken down into four phases, as shown on Figure 23 (Business for Social Responsability, 2019).

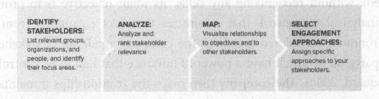

Figure 23: Four phases of stakeholder mapping (BSR, 2019). With permission.

6.4.1 IDENTIFICATION OF STAKEHOLDERS

Stakeholders are individuals or organizations that actively participate in a project and can be affected positively or negatively and have a positive or negative impact on the project (Drolet, 2012). In general, four main stakeholder groups can be distinguished: legislative, political and semi-political, academic and scientific, and populational (Pelletier, 2012).

Mining projects are generally controversial and raise debates that receive some media coverage in the local and regional press. This particularity makes it relatively easy for the promoter to have a good idea of the potential stakeholders of its mining project at an early stage. Furthermore, even if it is not a regulatory requirement, as part of the ESIA process, proponents of mining projects initiate public consultation and information sessions to which all interested parties are generally invited. These meetings are also excellent opportunities to identify more precisely the stakeholders of a mining project.

6.4.2 STAKEHOLDER MAPPING

Depending on their vision of social responsibility and the quality of their relationships with their environment, companies generally adopt two main strategies for managing their stakeholders. The first is firm-centred and positions the company "against" its environment, while the second is socio-centred and positions the company "with" its environment (Pasquero, 2008).

The firm-centred concept relegates stakeholders to the status of permanent applicants, a constraint external to the managers' decision-making system, without recognizing any skills. Its main objective is to provide an analytical framework that minimizes the risks emanating from an environment considered hostile to the company, made up of stakeholders' parts, all of which have a power of nuisance that had to be controlled (Pasquero, 2008). The company then maps the relationships it maintains with its relevant stakeholders, and ranks them according to their foreseeable impact. Such a strategy results in the identification of relevant stakeholders among the almost unlimited number of possibilities, and groups them into categories according to their importance (FAO, n.d.; Pasquero, 2008). The number of stakeholders in a mining project can be extremely high. To optimize the effectiveness and efficiency of the resources allocated to their management, it may be useful to integrate a characterization into the overall stakeholder's management strategy. This characterization can be based on the power and interest of stakeholders for the project (FAO, n.d.; World Bank, IFC and UKaid, 2019) as illustrated in Figure 24. Resources for community engagement are scarce and need to be well targeted. Mapping of community citizens, groups and organizations does not mean that the lower priority ones are ignored or forgotten, but instead that each is given an appropriate amount of attention (World Bank, IFC and UKaid, 2019).

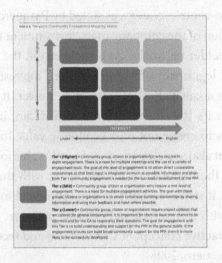

*Figure 24: Template Community Engagement Mapping Matrix
(World Bank, IFC and UKaid, 2019). With permission.*

The stakeholders' degree of power over the project may be more or less high, and is expressed mainly as follows (Drolet, 2012):

- The ability to influence the determination of the project's objectives and the definition of the concept to be implemented,
- The ability to impose constraints,

- The ability to influence the course of the project positively or negatively.

The firm-centred strategy implicitly places the firm in a situation of competition with its stakeholders, within a zero-sum balance of power, where the firm is either dominated (strong stakeholder power) or dominant (weak stakeholder power). The objective is to protect the interests of the company, avoiding unnecessary risks. It is moreover this defensive strategy of stakeholder management that is the most widely used today (Pasquero, 2008). Such a strategy may be the most popular among mining project promoters facing social resistance. This is all the truer as social acceptability is a significant condition for project authorization in almost all countries in West Africa.

As for the socio-centric strategy, as stated by Pasquero, it acknowledges that the socialization of the company in its environment takes place within interacting stakeholder networks. As a social actor, the enterprise recognizes the intrinsic legitimacy of its interlocutors' interests, without having to deduce it from a calculation of interest or power. It co-constructs its environment with its stakeholders, for whom it can, if necessary, show solicitude. It seeks to create not only economic value for its shareholders and employees, but also social or socio-economic value for all its stakeholders. It recognizes the importance of complying with the major universal ethical principles. It strives to limit its environmental footprint, generally in collaboration with its internal and external partners. The socio-centric strategy is an interactive concept of stakeholders and recognizes their four competencies (Pasquero, 2008):

- Stakeholders formulate and carry expectations towards society, the company and the company's role in society,
- Stakeholders experience the consequences of company actions and draw conclusions for their individual and collective behavior,
- Stakeholders define the acceptable limits of corporate action,
- Stakeholders co-construct the systems of relationships that link the company to its environment.

Given the importance of the above-mentioned skills, effective stakeholder management is one of the essential conditions for a peaceful and constructive social climate. Such performance is linked to a fundamental condition: the company's capacity to act as a political actor; that is, to bring together multiple internal and external stakeholders around credible and effective joint projects (Pasquero, 2008).

Many mistakenly view stakeholder engagement primarily as a public relations or communications exercise. They struggle to relate the engagement to their core business activities and find it difficult to build internal awareness and interest in the process. When the time comes to map stakeholders, they talk only to those they already know or to those who speak loudest. Even if they succeed in gathering useful insights from stakeholders, they have difficulty determining what actions to take in response. "Communication takes the company out. Engagement brings the community in" (IFC et al., 2013, p.18).

6.5   COMPLAINTS & GRIEVANCE MANAGEMENT

For projects with environmental and social impacts, grievances are a fact of life. How a company responds (or is perceived to be responding) when such grievances surface is important and can have significant implications for business performance. As highlighted by IFC, a grievance mechanism should be scaled to fit the level of risk and impacts of a project. For affected communities and other stakeholder groups seeking to have their complaints resolved, the perception of transparency and "fairness of process" is important. A good process can enhance outcomes and give people satisfaction that their complaints have been heard, even if the outcome is less than optimal. When designing grievance procedures, think about whether they will be readily understandable, accessible, and culturally appropriate for the local population (IFC, 2007). Mining and other large development projects inevitably raise concerns and complaints from community members and stakeholders affected by these projects. It is now expected practice for mining companies to have in place site-level processes (often referred to as "operational-level grievance mechanisms") for systematically receiving, tracking, resolving, and communicating with local communities and stakeholders, including workers, about their complaints or grievances. Grievance mechanisms should not be considered a substitute for community and stakeholder engagement processes that allow for airing of concerns. The two are complementary and should be mutually reinforcing (IRMA, 2018).

In the West-African context, where mining activities are mainly located in remote areas, the motivations for raising grievances could be very diverse, and could be linked to problems such as livestock or wild animals being killed by mining traffic, dust emissions due to traffic and blasting, noise and vibration, water quality issues due to mine drainage, competition for water usage between the mine and other stakeholders, and damage on farmlands due to mining activities such as exploration and implementation. Grievances could also come from other sensitive issues, such as the destruction of cultural heritage artifacts or lack of respect of buffer zones around identified sacred sites. Also, additional sensitive issues such as sexual abuses, use of drug and alcohol, and prostitution could motivate grievances from local communities. In the case of gold mines, complaints may arise from dissatisfaction with the destruction of gold panning sites by industrial mining activities and the confiscation of gold panners' equipment by mine security services. Complaints related to issues about the transparency and fairness of recruitment and compensation are also common in the West-African mining industry.

It should also be pointed out that in some of these isolated areas, mining companies are the main providers of employment, while at the same time ensuring certain essential needs of the population, especially when the presence of the central state is not very much felt in the improvement of the population's living conditions. Thus, the mines build and equip schools, health huts, wells and boreholes, and millet mills to lighten women's workloads. In this context, the mines are often perceived as enormously powerful and sometimes untouchable entities, and the most vulnerable populations may be afraid to complain when they feel they have been harmed by the activities of mining operations. In those areas where the level of literacy is low, one of the key challenges will also be to build trust with local communities and to faithfully translate any concerns expressed orally.

As stated within the IRMA Standard (IRMA, 2018, p. 32):

"The operating company shall ensure that stakeholders, including affected community members and rights holders (hereafter referred to collectively as "stakeholders") have access to an operational-level mechanism that allows them to raise and seek resolution or remedy for the range of complaints and grievances that may occur in relation to the company and its mining-related activities. [...] The operating company shall consult with stakeholders on the design of culturally appropriate complaints and grievance procedures that address, at minimum:

- The effectiveness criteria outlined in Principle 31 of the United Nations Guiding Principles on Business and Human Rights, which include the need for the mechanism to be legitimate accessible, predictable, equitable, transparent, rights-compatible, a source of continuous learning, and based on engagement and dialogue
- How complaints and grievances will be filed, acknowledged, investigated, and resolved, including general timeframes for each phase
- How confidentiality of a complainant's identity will be respected, if requested
- The ability to file anonymous complaints, if deemed necessary by stakeholders
- The provision of assistance for those who may face barriers to using the operational-level grievance mechanism, including women, children, and marginalized or vulnerable groups
- Options for recourse if an initial process does not result in satisfactory resolution, or if the mechanism is inadequate or inappropriate for handling serious human rights grievances
- How complaints and grievances and their resolutions will be tracked and recorded"

Obviously, policy or process for addressing complaints cannot be effective if nobody knows about it, as outlined by IFC. The latter highlighted that a company's grievance procedure should be put into writing, publicized, and explained to relevant stakeholder groups. Projects that make it easy for people to raise concerns and feel confident that these will be heard and acted upon can reap the benefits of both a good reputation and better community relations. One of the best ways to achieve this is to localize your points of contact. Hire people with the right skills, training, and disposition for community liaison work, and get them into the field as quickly as possible. Maintaining a regular presence in the local communities greatly helps to personalize the relationship with the company, and engenders trust. Talking with a familiar face who comes to the village regularly, or lives nearby, creates an informal atmosphere in which grievances can be aired and sorted out, or referred up the chain of command. This is usually more convenient and less intimidating to people than having to travel distances to the company offices during business hours to file a formal complaint (IFC, 2007). Obviously, not all the complaints expressed will be founded or related to mining activities. Nevertheless, it will be important that the complaints received are dealt with within a reasonable time frame that will be established in the process, and that complainants can receive a response that informs them that their complaint is admissible, and if not, to explain the reasons why it is not.

6.6 COMMUNITY DEVELOPMENT & SOCIAL INVESTMENT: THE RSI MATRIX

"Engaging with communities and contributing towards community development is not only the right thing for companies to do, but also makes good business sense. [...] One of the best ways a company can contribute to community development is by acting as a catalyst for economic and social development opportunities" (Government of Australia, 2016, p. 1 and 10). In the West African context, mining companies are spending millions of dollars annually for community development purposes, but sometimes the criteria for the allocations of these resources are not always clear, even to community development specialists. In the case where criteria exist, they vary significantly within the industry. Therefore, as the requests and expectations for social investments are high, and as the available funds are significant but limited, the need to have a social investments assessment tool adapted to the West African socio-political context and priorities becomes obvious. This kind of tool could help executives, managers, and investors align their investment decision-making process with the business interest and local priorities, and to achieve sustainable outcomes for stakeholders. From that perspective, the author has developed a user-friendly tool that allows a sound assessment of any sustainability investment project using a seven step approach, and scoring each project.

- **Step 1**: Budget allocated for the assessed project
- **Step 2**: Materiality of the project and alignment with SDGs & Government sustainability programs
- **Step 3**: Geographic scale of the project footprint (Local, Regional, National, or Global)
- **Step 4**: Timescale of the project (one shot or less than one year, one to five years, or six to ten years)
- **Step 5**: Partnerships (project developed alone, or with NGOs, Govt agencies or Private entities)
- **Step 6**: Assessment of value creation (Shared Value, Value Transfer, or Value Destruction)
- **Step 7**: Identification of KPI, Metrics, and Goals

This model is called **"RSI Matrix"** or "Robert's Sustain Invest Matrix" is presented in the Table 7. It is also available in a one-page Excel sheet format in the author website.

Table 7: *RSI Matrix – Sustainability Investment Assessment Tool (Ndong, 2021).

*Robert's Sustain Invest Matrix (*RSI Matrix)			
A Seven Steps Assessment Tool for Sustainability Investments Decision-Making			
Date of assessment:			
Assessment team (names):			
Brief description of the statu quo:			
	SCORING MODEL	PROJECT 1	PROJECT 2
TITLE OF THE PROJECT			
PTOJECT MANAGER			
SPONSOR			
1- Budgets (chose one option)	YES		
< 5000 USD	Y=0		
5k to 10k USD	Y=+1		
10k to 20k USD	Y=+2		
20k to 50k USD	Y=+3		
50k to 100k USD	Y=+4		
100k to 1M USD	Y=+5		
2- Materiality & SDGs & Govt program mapping	YES/NO		
Is this project material?	Y=+10, N=-5		
Reason 1:			
Reason 2:			
Is this project aligned with SDGs?	Y=+5, N=0		
SDG:			
SDG:			
SDG:			
Is this project aligned with Govt Programs?	Y=+5, N=0		
Program:			
Program:			
3- Geographic Scales (chose one option)	YES		
Local	Y=0		
Regional	Y=5		
National	Y=10		
Global	Y=20		
4- Timescale (chose one option)	YES		
One shot or < 1year	Y=0		
1 to 5 year	Y=+5		
6 to 10 years	Y=+10		
5- Partnerships	YES		
Alone	Y=0		
With partners (private)	Y=+5		
With partners (Public - Governments)	Y=+5		
With partners (NGOs)	Y=+5		
6- Value Creation (chose one option)			
Shared Value Creation?	YES (+5) + (+5) = +10		
Business value created:			
Stakeholders value created:			
Value Transfer?	YES (+5) + (-5) = 0		
Value created:			
Value transferred:			
Value Destruction?	YES (-5) + (-5) = -10		
Business value destructed:			
Stakeholders value destructed:			
7- KPI - Metrics and Goals	YES/NO		
Is there KPIs for outcomes?	Y=+5, N=0		
Details:			
Details			
Frequence of measure?			
Details:			
Internal measure?	Y=+5, N=0		
Details			
External audit of outcomes?	Y=+10, N=0		
TOTAL SCORE			
Team Leader name		Team Leader signature	
*Robert Ndong - December 2018			

This chapter clearly demonstrates that mining companies can definitively gain and sustainably maintain their license to operate, which is becoming a strong competitive advantage, but only through proper and culturally appropriate stakeholder engagement, and community development strategies linked to the business strategies. Several frameworks and standards exist to support the mining industry in this journey. The question is no longer whether we need to engage, but rather how, and with which mindset and resources do we need to engage?

Obviously, the mining sector needs a certain amount of land for the exploitation of resources that can only be mined where they are found according to the hazards of the geology. Thus, land acquisition is sometimes accompanied by the involuntary displacement vulnerable populations. The quality of the community engagement process takes on particular importance in this context, to respect the best international standards, improve the living conditions of the affected populations, safeguard their cultural heritage, protect environmental biodiversity, and secure the social acceptability of the project in question. The next chapter discusses in detail these issues, which are among the most sensitive in the global mining industry, particularly in the developing world.

7. LAND ACQUISITION, CULTURAL HERITAGE, AND BIODIVERSITY CONSERVATION

"Local communities' relationship with their lands and territories is profound, it constitutes a fundamental part of their identity and is deeply rooted in their culture and history, transcending the material, to become a relationship that is spiritual and sacred in nature. For indigenous populations and communities, land is the source of all life. This relationship extends to, among other things, their natural resources, bodies of water, forests, and biodiversity. In the mindset of indigenous populations and communities, land and territory are "the vital space," and guarantee the existence of present and future generations. [...] Africa's quest for development has largely, if not wholly, been premised on its rich land and natural resources. African countries seem to have redoubled their efforts to explore and extract every natural resource within their jurisdiction with a view to "industrialize and modernize" their economies. Indigenous communities of Africa feel the brunt of this phenomenon the most" (International Work Group for Indigenous Affairs, 2017, p 8 and 28).

In West Africa, where vulnerability to food insecurity and the adverse consequences of climate change are more and more critical (drought, salinization of the soil, etc.), land acquisition for industrial development is becoming a more and more sensitive issue, and no country seems to be spared. Local communities usually depend on these lands for farming, livestock breeding, hunting, fruit picking, honey production, traditional medicine, and other socio-cultural activities. In the specific case of land acquisition for mining purpose, new mines are developed in more and more remote areas that could contain biodiversity hotspots or critical cultural heritage artefacts. Insufficient consideration of these issues could lead to unsustainable corporate decisions that could threaten the project license to operate and the proponent reputation, leading to civil unrest, international media coverage, or destruction of biodiversity hotspots or sensitive cultural heritage sites.

In some cases, involuntary physical or economical resettlement is required to allow the project proponent to access in required land, to be able to develop its project. Obviously, this process is often long, sensitive, and complex, especially with the diversity of stakeholders and studies to be carried out, and the complexity of the issues to be addressed. Nevertheless, processes associated with land acquisition and involuntary resettlement, biodiversity conservation and management, and the preservation of cultural heritage are framed by international conventions, best practices, and standards such as those from the IFC Performance Standards, the ICMM Mining Principles, or IRMA. In addition, a deep understanding and respectful consideration of local traditional ecological knowledge can be a strong driver for smooth land acquisition processes in a peaceful social climate.

This chapter begins by highlighting a particularly important but generally neglected local asset: traditional ecological knowledge (TEK). The judicious use of this knowledge could be of great value in the mining industry's efforts to preserve cultural heritage and conserve biodiversity, while at the same time restoring the rightful recognition and respect of the holders of this knowledge. We will then discuss the issues of biodiversity conservation, cultural heritage preservation, land acquisition, and involuntary displacement detail. For each of these issues, the international standards most commonly used in the mining industry are presented.

7.1 TRADITIONAL ECOLOGICAL KNOWLEDGE AND SUSTAINABLE MINING

There are numerous references to indigenous knowledge, or what is commonly known as traditional ecological knowledge (TEK). "TEK refers to the knowledge base acquired by indigenous and local peoples over many hundreds of years through direct contact with the environment. It includes an intimate and detailed knowledge of plants, animals, and natural phenomena, the development and use of appropriate technologies for hunting, fishing, trapping, agriculture, and forestry, and a holistic knowledge, or "world view" that parallels the scientific discipline of ecology" (Inglis, 1993, p vi). Many scientific and social researchers have begun to recognize the positive role that indigenous knowledge of the local ecosystem can play in the formulation and implementation of sustainable development policies and projects in developing countries. In his paper entitled "African Indigenous Knowledge and its Relevance to Sustainable Development," Lalonde (1993) highlights the positive traditional management practices in rural Africa that have been adapted and passed down over countless generations, in harmony with the short and long-term carrying capacities of the local ecosystem. Some of these positive practices are based on symbolism, and involve spiritual rituals, religious practices, social taboos, and sacred animal totems. Other positive practices are based on the experiential, involving travel to learn from the experiences of other farmers, hunters, gatherers, fishermen, herbal medicine healers, and artisans. The traditional keepers and users of local ecological knowledge and wisdom are typically the key elders from rural African communities. In some of Africa's most ecologically fragile and marginalized regions, knowledge of the local ecosystem simply means survival (Inglis, 1993). The ecosystem view of many indigenous African societies is reflected in the following traditional management practices, which encompass individual and community wisdom and skills (Atteh, 1989):

- indigenous soil taxonomies,
- indigenous knowledge for potential use of local plants and forest products, and animal behavior and acquired hunting skills,
- local knowledge of important tree species for agroforestry, firewood, integrated pest management, the control of soil erosion and soil fertility, and fodder management,
- indigenous agronomic practices such as terracing, contour bunding, fallowing, organic fertilizer application, crop-rotation, and multi-cropping,
- indigenous soil and water conservation and anti-desertification practices.

Many places in Africa testify, in addition, to the harmonious relationship established between man and nature. These are places in which a good environmental and land use planning allow a certain balance between the need for exploitation and the need for renewal and conservation of biodiversity, which is essential for survival. Among these examples, the most remarkable are the environments in which the populations peacefully cohabit with animals that are considered dangerous elsewhere, constituting wonderful examples of the integrated conservation of biodiversity (Craterre-ENSAG / Convention France-UNESCO, 2006). The notion of the totem pole is a very eloquent example of this reality and the importance of TEK. A totem is an animal, a plant, or any other natural object believed to be ancestrally related to a tribe, clan, family, or group of people as a tutelary spirit (Mariko, 1981). Totems are found among different clans and tribes in various African communities. There are ideological, emotional, reverential, and genealogical relationships of social groups or specific persons with animals or natural objects, the so-called totems. For instance, people generally view a totem as a companion, relative, protector, progenitor, or helper, and ascribe to it superhuman powers and abilities. Totems are generally offered some combination of respect, veneration, awe, and fear. Totems are found among different clans and tribes in various African communities. There is usually a prohibition or taboo against killing, eating, or touching the totem. In some African societies, for example, totems were often the basis for laws and regulations, it was a violation of cultural and spiritual life to hunt, kill, or hurt an animal or plant totem (Sambe and Shomkegh, 2013).

7.2   BIODIVERSITY & CULTURAL HERITAGE

7.2.1   BIODIVERSITY

At the 1992 Earth Summit in Rio de Janeiro, the United Nations Convention on Biological Diversity (CBD) was adopted with three main goals, the conservation of biodiversity, the sustainable use of its components, and the fair and equitable sharing of the benefits arising from the use of genetic resources. The CBD defines biodiversity as: "the variability among living organisms from all sources, including inter alia terrestrial, marine and other aquatic ecosystems and the ecological complexes of which they are part; this includes diversity within species, between species and of ecosystems." Biodiversity sustains human livelihoods and life itself. The interdependence between people and biodiversity is most apparent for some indigenous peoples, who lead a subsistence lifestyle and may be critically dependent on biodiversity, or whose culture and history are intimately associated with the natural environment and systems.

At a macro-level, the balancing of atmospheric gases through photosynthesis and carbon sequestration is reliant on biodiversity, while an estimated 40 percent of the global economy is based on biological products and processes (ICMM, 2006). In addition to the essential ecosystem services (classified as "supporting," "provisioning," "and regulating" by the Millennium Ecosystem Assessment), biodiversity is also of value for aesthetic, spiritual, cultural, recreational, and scientific reasons (Figure 25).

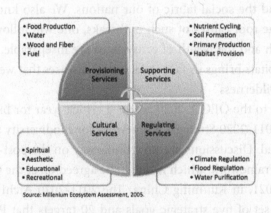

Figure 25: Categories of ecosystem services (Millennium Ecosystem Assessment, 2005).

In a paper published in April 2020 by former presidents Ellen Johnson Sirleaf (Liberia) and Ernest Bai Koroma (Sierra Leone), and entitled, "When biodiversity fails, human health is on the line," the authors strongly highlighted that "human health, and the health of ecosystems are inseparable. Destruction of natural habitats brings us face to face with diseases that were once confined to the wilderness" (African Arguments, 2020). Authors added that "the rapid rise of disease caused by a new coronavirus seems to have caught much of the world by surprise. It should not have. An upsurge in the emergence of new infectious diseases started at least 30 years before this virus appeared. Some of these diseases have been transmitted from wild animals to humans, and the spread of COVID-19 appears to have originated in a market selling dead and living wildlife, including some endangered species. Research also shows that many of the most serious outbreaks—including Ebola, and the Zika and Nipah viruses—have been linked to biodiversity loss, and to deforestation in particular". Both of us governed nations in West Africa through the Ebola crisis of 2014-2016. We served at the helm of the governments of Sierra Leone and Liberia, two countries hit hardest by that crisis which sickened more than 28,600 people and killed more than 11,300. The epidemic also cost our region an estimated $53 billion. Our health systems and economies are still recovering. We know the toll of disease epidemics, the havoc they wreak on lives, economies and the social fabric of our nations. We also know that until we address the root causes of such outbreaks, one will follow another.... Human health and the health of ecosystems are inseparable. Destruction of natural habitats brings us face to face with diseases that were once confined to the wilderness".

According to the OECD, 2020 marks a critical year for biodiversity. It is when the 2011-2020 Strategic Framework for Biodiversity and its Aichi Targets expired. Discussions are now underway on the post-2020 Global Biodiversity Framework, which is due to be agreed on at the CBD COP15 in October 2021, in Kunming China. The 2011-2020 Aichi Biodiversity Targets are a set of five strategic goals and 20 targets that Parties to the UN CBD are intended to use as a guiding framework for their national commitments towards biodiversity conservation, sustainable use, and the equitable sharing of benefits arising from the use of genetic resources. As these Targets expired in 2020, Parties to the CBD will need to adopt a revised suite of targets for the post-2020 Global Biodiversity Framework. Agreement on this is also likely to have implications for two of the SDGs, namely SDG 14, "Life under Water," and SDG 15, "Life on Land," as several of the targets therein come directly from the Aichi Biodiversity Targets, and are therefore also expired in 2020 (OECD, 2019 & 2020).

Mining has the potential to affect biodiversity throughout the life cycle of a project, both directly and indirectly. Direct or primary impacts from mining can result from any activity that involves land clearance (such as access road construction, exploration drilling, overburden stripping, or tailings impoundment construction), direct discharges to water bodies (riverine tailings disposal, for instance, or tailings impoundment releases), or the air (such as dusts or smelter emissions). Direct impacts are usually readily identifiable. Indirect or secondary impacts can result from social or environmental changes induced by mining operations and are often harder to identify immediately. Cumulative impacts occur where mining projects are developed in environments that are influenced by other projects, both mining and non-mining (ICMM, 2006). Therefore, it is not surprising that the mining sector was identified as a high risk ("red zone") sector for bio-diversity risk in the report entitled, "Is Biodiversity a material risk for companies?" published by F&C Asset Management (F&C, 2004). The report defines red-zone sectors as those sectors in which most companies are likely to be exposed to biodiversity risks. Fortunately, most of these risks and impacts are manageable with good practices. However, while parts of the industry have been highly active in managing biodiversity, adoption of good practices has been uneven across the sector, in part because it is so diverse. Nevertheless, for all mining companies, especially when operating in remote areas, the greatest concerns involve less manageable indirect or induced impacts, such as those caused by improved access to an area along roads or other infrastructure corridors. This improved access can facilitate farming, artisanal mining, hunting, or logging operations that can severely impact biodiversity and are extremely hard to control (IFC, n.d.).

As stated in the ICMM's *Good Practice Guidance for Mining and Biodiversity*, "the mining and metals industry's biodiversity conservation performance is under increasing scrutiny from NGOs, commentators, and financial analysts. This is due in part to a growing awareness of the importance of biodiversity conservation, but also because the industry often operates in remote and environmentally sensitive areas of the world. Demonstrating a commitment to biodiversity conservation is now an essential element of sustainable development for the mining and metals industry" (ICMM, 2006, p.5). For the specific case of West Africa, the West Africa Biodiversity and Climate Change program (WA BiCC) shows that the Upper Guinean Forests of this region is a global biodiversity hotspot—a biogeographic region with significant amount of biodiversity that is threatened with destruction. The forests are home to an exceptional concentration of vulnerable, threatened, or endangered species, as defined by the Convention on the International Trade in Endangered Species of Flora and Fauna (CITES) and the Red List of Threatened Species, compiled by the International Union for the Conservation of Nature (IUCN). These species include forest elephants, pygmy hippopotamuses, and rosewood, among many others. The Upper Guinean Forest ecosystem, which once extended across much of the West African region, is now found in fragments and remnants across part of Guinea, Sierra Leone, Liberia, Côte d'Ivoire, southern Ghana, and southwestern Togo (WA BiCC, 2020). According to the WA BiCC, "ninety percent of the Upper Guinean Forest and several of the ecosystem services and functions they provide, such as catchments for sustainable water supplies, have already been lost to human activities including mining, logging, agriculture, and conversion to oil palm and other plantations, at various scales. These drivers are enabled by weak or ineffective governance and law enforcement, inadequate conservation and management support, and a general lack of awareness of the overall values of these areas" (WA BiCC, 2020). Therefore, for mining companies operating in this West African region, biodiversity conservation and management programs, including clear corporate commitments with objectives and clear targets such as No Net Loss of biodiversity or Net Gain should be a key component of sustainability strategies and environment and social management plans. Fortunately, there are currently guidelines, standards, and best practices available for the extractive industry regarding biodiversity conservation and management, such as those from IFC, Initiative for responsible Mining Assurance (IRMA), the Toward Sustainable Mining (TSM) initiative of the Mining Association of Canada (MAC), and the ICMM. If properly embedded within the corporate sustainability strategies, and soundly implemented at the site-level in partnership with stakeholders, these guidelines and standards could significantly improve the overall environmental footprint and the license to operate of the mining industry, in West Africa and globally.

7.2.1.1 TOWARD SUSTAINABLE MINING - MINING ASSOCIATION OF CANADA

Since 2004, the MAC has implemented the TSM initiative. This is an award-winning performance system that helps mining companies evaluate and manage their environmental and social responsibilities. It is a set of tools and indicators to drive performance, and ensure that key mining risks are managed responsibly at participating mining and metallurgical facilities. Participation in TSM is mandatory for MAC's member companies. This involves subscribing to the TSM Guiding Principles, which are backed by specific performance indicators that member companies publicly report on annually in TSM Progress Reports (MAC, 2019). Three performance indicators have been established to assess the performance of MAC members against its Biodiversity Conservation Management Protocol (MAC, 2020):

1. Corporate biodiversity conservation commitment, accountability, and communications,
2. Facility-level biodiversity conservation planning and implementation,
3. Biodiversity conservation reporting.

The purpose of the first indicator is to confirm that corporate commitment and accountabilities are in place and communicated to relevant employees to support the management of biodiversity conservation issues. To get the highest score (AAA) for this indicator, it must be clearly demonstrated that biodiversity conservation commitment includes a stated ambition of No Net Loss, and a commitment to actively partner with other organizations for biodiversity conservation, and roles, responsibilities and resources have been assigned to support this commitment. Facilities with a stated ambition to achieve No Net Loss should consider this objective in the context of the full lifecycle of the facility, and not just at a single point during the operational stages in this lifecycle. It is important to recognize that, at certain stages, biodiversity losses may exceed the sum of impacts avoided, minimized, mitigated, and offset, based on the mitigation hierarchy. Facilities should consider measures to mitigate the heightened risk of long-term biodiversity impacts in their biodiversity action plans, for example, by introducing biodiversity offsets, in advance of certain impacts that cannot be addressed through higher levels of the mitigation hierarchy. The No Net Loss calculation should also consider reclamation and closure planning and rehabilitation activities that will return identified biodiversity values to previously impacted land (MAC, 2020). The mitigation hierarchy is based on a series of essential, sequential steps that must be taken throughout the project's life cycle in order to limit any negative impacts on biodiversity. These steps include:

- Avoidance – Measures taken to avoid creating impacts from the outset,
- Minimization – Measures taken to reduce the duration, intensity and extent of impacts that cannot be completely avoided,
- Rehabilitation and Restoration – Measures taken to improve degraded or removed ecosystems following exposure to impacts that cannot be completely avoided or minimized,
- Offset – Measures taken to compensate for any residual, adverse impacts after full implementation of the previous three steps of the mitigation hierarchy.

The second TSM indicator aims to confirm that effective plans and management systems are implemented at the facility level in order to manage significant biodiversity aspects. The highest score is gained by demonstrating that biodiversity conservation management is integrated into a broader business strategy that includes at least two of the following:

- Investments in research and development that enhance the industry's understanding of, and contribution to, biodiversity conservation, science, and traditional knowledge,

- Contributing to a greater scientific understanding to the protection of biodiversity,
- Contributing to industry or region-specific guidance documents that foster biodiversity conservation,
- Enhancing biodiversity in areas outside of the facility's property,
- Achieving national or regional recognition in biodiversity conservation
- Conducting ecosystem service valuation,
- Encouraging employee volunteerism in community-based biodiversity initiatives.

The purpose of the third indicator is to confirm that biodiversity conservation reporting is in place to inform decision-making and to communicate performance publicly. Biodiversity conservation reporting includes elements such as policy, monitoring, and conservation initiatives. The top score for this indicator is reached when the community of interest feedback on biodiversity conservation reporting is actively sought and reported publicly.

7.2.1.2 THE IFC PERFORMANCE STANDARDS

The IFC Performance Standards apply to private-sector clients of the IFC. However, they are generally regarded as the guiding standard in the extractive sector, with the expectation that companies comply with them or model their own corporate standards on them. Often the standards apply because the financial institutions providing project finance are Equator Principles signatories (ICMM, n.d.). IFC Performance Standard 6, "Biodiversity Conservation and Sustainable Natural Resource Management," recognizes that protecting and conserving biodiversity is fundamental to sustainable development. The objectives of this Standard are to protect and conserve biodiversity and to promote the sustainable management and use of natural resources through the adoption of practices that integrate conservation needs and development priorities. Based on the assessment of risks and impacts, and the vulnerability of the biodiversity and the natural resources present, the requirements of this Performance Standard are applied to projects in all habitats, whether or not those habitats have been previously disturbed and whether or not they are legally protected. The assessment will consider the differing values attached to biodiversity by specific stakeholders and identify impacts on ecosystem services, and will focus on the major threats to biodiversity, which include habitat destruction and invasive alien species (IFC, 2006).

According to IFC, habitat destruction is recognized as the major threat to the maintenance of biodiversity. Habitats can be divided into natural habitats (which are land and water areas where the biological communities are formed, largely by native plant and animal species, and where human activity has not essentially modified the area's primary ecological functions) and modified habitats (where there has been apparent alteration of the natural habitat, often with the introduction of alien species of plants and animals, such as agricultural areas). Both types of habitats can support important biodiversity at all levels, including endemic or threatened species. In areas of modified habitat, the IFC client will exercise care to minimize any conversion or degradation of such habitat, and will, depending on the nature and scale of the project, identify opportunities to enhance habitat and protect and conserve biodiversity as part of their operations. In areas of natural habitat, the client will not significantly convert or degrade such habitat, unless the following conditions are met:

- There are no technically and financially feasible alternatives,
- The overall benefits of the project outweigh the costs, including those to the environment and biodiversity,
- Any conversion or degradation is appropriately mitigated.

Critical habitat is a subset of both natural and modified habitat that deserves particular attention. According to IFC:

"critical habitat includes areas with high biodiversity value, including habitat required for the survival of critically endangered or endangered species, areas having special significance for endemic or restricted-range species, sites that are critical for the survival of migratory species, areas supporting globally significant concentrations or numbers of individuals of congregatory species, areas with unique assemblages of species or which are associated with key evolutionary processes or provide key ecosystem services, and areas having biodiversity of significant social, economic or cultural importance to local communities" (IFC, 2006, p.4).

In areas of critical habitat, the IFC client will not implement any project activities unless the following requirements are met:

- There are no measurable adverse impacts on the ability of the critical habitat to support the established population of species or the functions of the critical habitat described in the paragraph above,
- There is no reduction in the population of any recognized critically endangered or endangered species,
- Any lesser impacts are mitigated.

Mitigation measures will be designed to achieve No Net Loss of biodiversity where feasible, and may include a combination of actions, such as post-operation restoration of habitats, offset of losses through the creation of ecologically comparable area(s) that is managed for biodiversity, and compensation to direct users of biodiversity (IFC, 2006).

7.2.1.3 INITIATIVE FOR RESPONSIBLE MINING ASSURANCE

The Initiative for Responsible Mining Assurance (IRMA) was founded in 2006 by a coalition of NGOs, businesses that purchase minerals and metals for the products they make and sell, organized labor (e.g., trade unions), affected communities, and mining companies (IRMA, 2018). The IRMA Steering Committee set the mission to establish a multi-stakeholder and independently verified responsible mining assurance system that improves social and environmental performance and creates value for leading mine sites. The Standard for Responsible Mining created by IRMA specifies a set of objectives and leading performance requirements for environmentally and socially responsible practice. The Standard serves as the basis of a voluntary system offering independent third-party assessment and certification of environmental and social performance measures at industrial-scale mine sites around the world (IRMA, 2018). IRMA is an answer to global demand for more socially and environmentally responsible mining. Through IRMA:

- Industrial-scale mines can document their leadership and receive value for proven responsible performance.
- Purchasers of metals and minerals can source from mines that meet a full array of leading practices in social and environmental responsibility.
- Communities, workers, and civil society organizations can convey social license with the assurance that a mine operates to leading levels of socially and environmentally responsible performance.

The IRMA Standard is designed to support the achievement of four overarching principles (IRMA, 2018):

- **Business integrity**: Operating companies conduct business in a transparent manner that complies with applicable host country and international laws, respects human rights, and builds trust and credibility with workers, communities, and stakeholders.
- **Planning and managing for positive legacies**: Operating companies engage with stakeholders from the early planning stages and throughout the mine life cycle to ensure that mining projects are planned and managed to deliver positive economic, social, and environmental legacies for companies, workers, and communities.
- **Social responsibility**: Operating companies engage with workers, stakeholders, and rights holders to maintain or enhance the health, safety, cultural values, and quality of life and livelihoods of workers and communities.
- **Environmental Responsibility:** Operating companies engage with stakeholders to ensure that mining is planned and carried out in

a manner that maintains or enhances environmental values and avoids or minimizes impacts to the environment and communities.

The IRMA Standard chapter on "Biodiversity, Ecosystem Services and Protected Areas" puts forward a framework for mines to proactively assess and manage impacts on biodiversity and ecosystem services according to the mitigation hierarchy of avoiding and minimizing impacts early in the project life cycle, and if impacts cannot be avoided, restoring and, if necessary, offsetting or compensating for residual impacts throughout the remainder of the mine's life. IRMA states that, through adherence to the mitigation hierarchy during the most appropriate stages in project development, mining can proceed in a manner that supports global biodiversity, maintains the ecosystem services that communities need to survive and thrive, and leaves behind structurally safe and functioning ecosystems upon closure (IRMA, 2018).

Mitigation measures for new mines are expected to be designed to achieve No Net Loss, and preferably a Net Gain in important biodiversity values and priority ecosystem services. While ideally, existing mines would also seek to achieve No Net Loss in biodiversity and ecosystem services, IRMA recognizes that it may be difficult or impossible to accurately identify the biodiversity values that were present in an area prior to the mine development, which makes it difficult to establish a baseline for calculating a No Net Loss or Net Gain in biodiversity. Instead of requiring No Net Loss/Net Gain at existing mines, IRMA expects them to document, to the best of their abilities, the impacts that their past activities have had on biodiversity and ecosystem services. Where significant impacts have occurred, existing mines will be expected to undertake conservation actions to enhance biodiversity and ecosystem services. Existing mines are also expected to avoid any additional losses of important biodiversity values or priority ecosystem services. This approach enables an existing mine to apply for IRMA certification later in its project life, but ensures that doing so does not allow them to avoid responsibilities that would have been applicable had they applied for IRMA certification at an earlier stage. Although presented in a different format, many of the requirements of the IRMA Standard chapter on "Biodiversity, Ecosystem Services and

Protected Areas" are meant to generally align with the IFC's Performance Standard 6—"Biodiversity Conservation and Sustainable Management of Living Natural Resources," and also the "KBA Partners' Guidelines on Business and Key Biodiversity Areas" (IRMA, 2018).

7.2.1.4 THE INTERNATIONAL COUNCIL ON MINING AND METALS

As highlighted by the International Council on Mining and Metals (ICMM), setting aside any ethical or moral considerations, which are increasingly the subject of corporate policies, it is important for companies to address biodiversity for a variety of sound business reasons. Many mining companies have adopted an increasingly sophisticated approach to managing biodiversity as part of their commitment to establish and maintain a social or functional license to operate. For example, adopting responsible practices with respect to biodiversity management is increasingly viewed as important with respect to (ICMM, 2006):

- Access to land, both at the initial stages of project development, and for ongoing exploration to extend the lifetime of existing projects.
- Reputation, which links to license to operate, an intangible but significant benefit to business, and which can profoundly influence the perceptions of communities, NGOs, and other stakeholders of existing or proposed mining operations.
- Access to capital, particularly where project finance is to be obtained from one of the investment banks that are signatories to the Equator Principles, which apply the Biodiversity Performance Standard of the IFC to all investments in excess of $10 million (recognizing that strengthened commitments to biodiversity assessment and management are likely to be adopted).

In addition, good biodiversity management can bring benefits to mining companies, including (ICMM, 2006):

- Increased investor confidence and loyalty,
- Shorter and less contentious permitting cycles, as a result of better relationships with regulatory agencies,
- Improved community relations,
- Strong supportive partnerships with NGOs,
- Improved employee motivation,
- Reduced risks and liabilities.

As stated earlier, biodiversity is a material risk for the mining industry. The financial sector is also exposed to risks because of biodiversity loss. "Financial institutions (FIs) run reputation and transition risks when they finance companies that have a major negative impact on biodiversity. Therefore, FIs must ensure that they identify the exposure of their portfolios to biodiversity risks in a timely manner, since in-depth understanding of these risks informs adequate risk management" (De Nederlandsche Bank, 2020). Several approaches are being developed and used by FIs for this purpose, and obviously it will become more and more critical for the mining industry to be aware of these initiatives to continue to understand and fulfill investor expectations and requirements, in terms of input data related to biodiversity conservation and impact monitoring.

The following approaches have been selected by the Finance for Biodiversity Pledge in its "Guide on Biodiversity Measurement Approaches;" first, because they are relevant to, and currently explored or used by, the financial sector; second, they include all main drivers of biodiversity loss; and third, they are scientifically robust (Finance for Biodiversity, 2021).

- **STAR - Species Threat Abatement and Restoration metric:** measures the contribution that investments can make to reducing species extinction risk, through abating threats, and restoring habitat. This metric can help the finance industry and investors target their investments to achieve conservation outcomes, and can measure the contributions these investments make to global targets, such as the Sustainable Development Goals.

- **BFFI - Biodiversity Footprint Financial Institutions:** provides a biodiversity footprint for the economic activities in which an FI invests. The methodology allows calculation of the environmental pressures and the biodiversity impact of investments within an investment portfolio, at the level of a portfolio, an asset class, a company, or a project.
- **CBF - Corporate Biodiversity Footprint:** designed to assess the annual impact of corporations, FIs, and sovereign entities on global and local biodiversity. It is based on life-cycle analyses of the impact of their activities, with the goal of correctly capturing the full impact of a product.
- **GBSFI - Global Biodiversity Score for Financial Institutions:** tool that provides an overall and synthetic vision of the biodiversity footprint of economic activities. It is measured by the Mean Species Abundance ratio (the ratio between the observed biodiversity and the biodiversity in its pristine state). Calculation of the Mean Species Abundance is based on PBL Netherlands Environmental Assessment Agency's GLOBIO model of five terrestrial pressures (land use, nitrogen deposition, climate change, fragmentation, and infrastructure/ encroachment), and five aquatic pressures, and their impacts on biodiversity.
- **BIA - Biodiversity Impact Analytics:** an integrated biodiversity impact database developed by Carbon4 Finance and CDC Biodiversity, using the GBSFI methodology. BIA is suitable for calculating the footprint of a financial asset portfolio, and indices composed of listed equity and/or corporate and sovereign bonds.
- **ENCORE - Exploring Natural Capital Opportunities, Risks, and Exposure:** enables users to visualize how the economy potentially depends on and affects nature, and how environmental change creates risks for businesses. It can be used for risk management, communication, and stakeholder engagement, and for biodiversity target setting and portfolio alignment.

All of these initiatives within the mining and financial industry landscape confirm that the global momentum for biodiversity is growing and will continue with the CBD COP15 planned in China in October 2021. The post 2020 Global Biodiversity Framework, to be adopted at that global event, aims to mobilize the world to protect and restore nature. It will serve as an umbrella strategy to governments at all levels, businesses, public and private finance, civil society, and providing coherent guidance and support, with the aim of conserving, restoring, and sustainably using biodiversity and ecosystems (Finance for Biodiversity, 2021).

For all the reasons highlighted above, this is becoming a must for businesses that are likely to have material biodiversity issues, especially within the mining industry, to have a corporate biodiversity management strategy linked to their governance, strategy, and risk management processes. These must including targets and metrics, along with relevant and dedicated financial resources, and trained human resources.

For this purpose, "The Guidelines for planning and monitoring corporate biodiversity performance," published in 2021 by the UICN, could be particularly useful for any mining company that wants to move forward in its sustainability journey. The Guidelines offer an approach for developing a corporate-level biodiversity strategic plan, including measurable goals and objectives and a set of core linked indicators, that will allow companies to measure their biodiversity performance across their operations (Stephenson & Carbone, 2021). These Guidelines are aimed at sustainability teams, managers, and other company staff whose roles include strategic planning and reporting related to biodiversity. They are shaped around four stages (Figure 26) that steer businesses through a series of practical steps to plan biodiversity goals, choose and apply appropriate biodiversity indicators, and to collect, present, and analyse data in a way that facilitates results-based management and corporate biodiversity reporting.

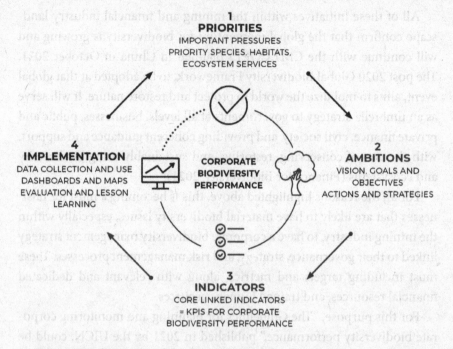

Figure 26: The stages of the UICN Guidelines for planning and monitoring corporate biodiversity performance. With permission.

By following the Guidelines, a company will be able to (Stephenson & Carbone, 2021):

- Identify the species, habitats, and ecosystem services it should focus on.
- Identify the pressures on biodiversity that are most important for the company to address,
- Define a vision, measurable goals and objectives, and a set of strategies to address biodiversity,
- Identify a suite of core biodiversity indicators that will facilitate data aggregation across its operations to the corporate level, thereby allowing the company to assess, report, and communicate its biodiversity performance,
- Develop and use maps and dashboards to visualise information and facilitate data-driven decision-making,

- Mainstream biodiversity data into corporate reporting and adaptive management,
- And, where a company wants to do so, help demonstrate its contribution to international biodiversity goals (such as the Sustainable Development Goals and the post-2020 Global Biodiversity Framework of the Convention on Biological Diversity).

7.2.2 CULTURAL HERITAGE MANAGEMENT

Cultural heritage encompasses properties and sites of archaeological, historical, cultural, artistic, and religious significance. It also refers to unique environmental features and cultural knowledge, and intangible forms of culture embodying traditional lifestyles that should be preserved for current and future generations (IFC, 2012a). "Africa is the cradle of humanity. Its natural and cultural diversity are matched only by its long history […]. Collectively, the rich diversity of African heritage contributes a unique wealth to world heritage […]. Concerns related to the history and heritage, and its valorization were perceived as a luxury compared to development challenges such as hunger, health, and poverty, which were deemed of primary importance. The evolution of people's perceptions, however, indicates that the safeguarding and valorization of heritage can contribute to development, and to combating poverty. The classification, protection and valorization of outstanding natural and cultural sites has a role to play in the development of national or international cultural tourism. There can also be no doubt that it contributes to strengthening the local population's' pride, dignity and feeling of belonging, not to mention the job creation and revenue-making opportunities it offers them" (Craterre-ENSAG / Convention France-UNESCO, 2006, p. 7 & 8).

"In Africa, nature and culture are very closely related. Which territory does not have its tree, its forest, its rock, its hill, its river, its cascade, or its sacred lake? These elements, already present before the appearance of man, are associated to the spirit world, and are usually respected, and sometimes even venerated, in order to ensure a harmonious cohabitation […]. The African continent comprises a great variety of archaeological sites that testify to its history. Next to the most ancient burial sites in the world, and to grand monuments such as the Stone Circles of Senegambia or the walls of Great Zimbabwe, there is a variety of archaeological sites of varying shapes and dimensions (rock shelters, rock paintings and engravings, megaliths, monuments and urban sites, sites linked to iron metallurgy…)[…]. Aside from the already known and excavated sites, there are still many sites that are hidden underground, sometimes covered with abundant vegetation, that are yet to be discovered […]. Archaeological objects can be at risk, due to plundering and to road construction operations that generate digging activities, which may destroy what is underground. Thus, it is particularly important to identify these resources, and then to apply preventive measures in the preparation of large construction works" (Craterre-ENSAG / Convention France-UNESCO, 2006, p. 15 & 23).

As highlighted by the IRMA, over time, mining and other forms of industrial development can both create, and result in profound and irreversible damage to cultural heritage. Most obviously, mining activities can destroy or damage tangible cultural heritage, such as historical buildings, or sites of spiritual significance. But damage to intangible cultural heritage may also occur, for example, as a result of inappropriate visitation of sites or the inappropriate use of traditional knowledge. Increasingly, mining companies are recognizing the importance of protecting, and where possible, promoting cultural heritage to respect the rights of, and strengthen relationships with, communities wherever they operate (IRMA, 2018). In its Resolution 372 passed in 2017, the African Commission on Human and Peoples Rights (ACHPR) highlighted that states, businesses, and civil society must recognize and protect Africa's sacred natural sites and territories in order to guarantee the human rights of her people, and especially the rights of indigenous peoples. Sacred natural sites are recognized internationally as one of the oldest forms of culture-based conservation, defined as "areas of land or water having special spiritual significance to peoples and communities." These sites, and therefore human rights, are under threat globally from the expansion of the extractive industries (ACHPR, 2017). Stating its concern around "the continued growth of environmentally damaging industrial activity," the Resolution urges States, businesses, and civil society groups to "recognize and respect the intrinsic value of sacred natural sites." This is emphasized by a report from the

African Commission, which highlights the impact of the extractive industries on indigenous peoples across Africa (ACHPR, 2017).

IFC Performance Standard 8 aims to guide companies in protecting cultural heritage from adverse impacts of project activities and supporting its preservation. It also promotes the equitable sharing of benefits from the use of cultural heritage (IFC, 2012a). This Performance Standard recognizes the importance of cultural heritage for current and future generations. Consistent with the "Convention Concerning the Protection of the World Cultural and Natural Heritage," this Standard aims to ensure that clients protect cultural heritage in the course of their project activities. In addition, the requirements of this Standard on a project's use of cultural heritage are based in part on standards set by the CBD (IFC, 2012b).

For the purposes of the *IFC's Performance Standard 8*, cultural heritage refers to:

- tangible forms of cultural heritage, such as tangible moveable or immovable objects, property, sites, structures, or groups of structures, having archaeological (prehistoric), paleontological, historical, cultural, artistic, and religious values, unique natural features or
- tangible objects that embody cultural values, such as sacred groves, rocks, lakes, and waterfalls
- and certain instances of intangible forms of culture that are proposed to be used for commercial purposes, such as cultural knowledge, innovations, and practices of communities embodying traditional lifestyles (IFC, 2012a, p. 1).

As highlighted in the *IFC Guidance Note 8* (Cultural Heritage):

When in doubt about whether something is considered cultural heritage, the project proponent should seek the knowledge and advice of local and/or international competent experts, government authorities, and members of local communities. The knowledge of local communities is particularly important for identifying cultural heritage that may be tied to the natural environment, and which may not be evident to outsiders. […] The client should apply internationally recognized practices to site surveys, excavation, preservation and publication, in addition to compliance with national law. An internationally recognized practice is defined as the exercise of professional skill, knowledge, diligence, prudence and foresight that would reasonably be expected from experienced professionals engaged in the same type of undertaking under the same or similar circumstances globally. Where the client is in doubt on what constitutes internationally recognized practice, international peer reviewers are able to provide guidance (IFC, 2012b, p. 3).

The environmental and social risks and impacts identification process should determine whether the proposed location of a project is in areas where cultural heritage is expected to be found, either during construction or during operations. In such cases, as part of its Environment and Social Management System (ESMS), the project proponent will develop provisions for managing chance finds through a "chance find" procedure, which will be applied in the event that cultural heritage is subsequently discovered (…). The "chance find" procedure is a project-specific procedure that outlines what will happen if previously unknown heritage resources, particularly archaeological resources, are encountered during project construction or operation. The procedure includes record keeping and expert verification procedures, chain of custody instructions for movable finds, and clear criteria for potential temporary work stoppages that could be required for rapid disposition of issues related to the finds. It is important that this procedure outlines the roles and responsibilities and the response times required from both project staff and any relevant heritage authority, as well as any agreed consultation procedures. This procedure should be incorporated in the management program and implemented through the mining company's ESMS. As with cultural heritage identified during the ESIA, consideration should be given, where feasible, to alternative siting or design of the project, to avoid significant damage (IFC, 2012b, p. 4).

The IRMA chapter that focuses on the cultural heritage issues uses, as its basis, the IFC Performance Standard 8. In that chapter, IRMA highlights that it will not certify new mines that are developed in, or that adversely affect, the following protected areas if those areas were designated to protect cultural values (IRMA, 2018):

- World Heritage Sites, and areas on a State Party's official Tentative List for World Heritage Site Inscription,
- IUCN protected area management categories I-III, and
- Core areas of UNESCO biosphere reserves.

Also, as required by IRMA:

A cultural heritage management plan, or its equivalent, that outlines the actions and mitigation measures to be implemented to protect cultural heritage shall be developed. [...] If a new or existing mine is in an area where cultural heritage is expected to be found, the operating company must develop procedures for:

- Managing chance finds, including, at minimum, a requirement that employees or contractors shall not further disturb any chance find until an evaluation by competent professionals is made, and actions consistent with the requirements of this chapter are developed
- Managing potential impacts to cultural heritage from contractors and visitors
- Allowing continued access to cultural sites, subject to consultations with affected communities and overriding health, safety, and security considerations, and
- If the mining project affects indigenous peoples' cultural heritage, the operating company shall collaborate with

> indigenous peoples to determine procedures related to the
> sharing of information related to cultural heritage

> The operating company shall ensure that relevant employees receive training with respect to cultural awareness, cultural heritage site recognition and care, and company procedures for cultural heritage management (IRMA, 2018, p. 119).

In summary, the business case for biodiversity conservation and sound cultural heritage management is strongly demonstrated for the extractive industry, and the associated issues are becoming a key topic in boardrooms. For those who are not still convinced, the recent blasting of cultural heritage sites by Rio-Tinto in Australia, and the resulting wave of global indignation, could be seen as a tough reminder and a strong wake-up call for investors, C-suite executives, and asset managers within the mining industry. Obviously, engagement of potentially affected communities and other stakeholders in biodiversity conservation is fundamental to the success of biodiversity initiatives. "Engaging the community and other stakeholders with the objective of developing trust, respect, and partnership, and aimed at keeping the community informed of a mining company's operations, is essential to the success of a sustainable project. It should be recognized that stakeholders may have different, and possibly conflicting, interests in, perspectives on, and priorities for biodiversity and its management" (ICMM, 2006, p. 15).

7.3 LAND ACQUISITION AND INVOLUNTARY RESETTLEMENT

When companies seek to acquire land for their business activities, it can lead to relocation and loss of shelter or livelihoods for communities or individual households. Involuntary resettlement occurs when affected people do not have the right to refuse land acquisition and are displaced, which may result in long-term hardship and impoverishment, as well as social stress (IFC, 2012). Despite the clear global standards around resettlement and land acquisition, notably the IFC's Performance Standard 5, in practice, this remains a particularly challenging area for mining companies.

> "Many projects do not begin planning resettlement activities early enough. Nor do they invest enough human or financial resources in ensuring impacts are assessed and mitigated, and that benefits are shared in a sustainable way. Consequently, grievances from resettled and host communities can result in conflict and mine closures. Nearby communities can also disrupt project activities if they do not see benefits accruing to them, even though they may not be directly affected by resettlement. However, projects that do invest in planning resettlement appropriately, with well-managed engagement of relevant stakeholders, have been shown to gain the trust of local communities, form more collaborative relationships with governments, and minimize disruptions to the business" (ICMM, n.d., p.6).

In its *Handbook for preparing a resettlement action plan*, IFC highlights that "involuntary resettlement may entail both the physical displacement of people and the disruption of their livelihoods [...]. Resettlement is involuntary when it occurs without the informed consent of the displaced persons or if they give their consent without having the power to refuse resettlement". Economic displacement means the "loss of income streams or means of livelihood resulting from land acquisition or obstructed access to resources (land, water, or forest) resulting from the construction or operation of a project or its associated facilities" (IFC, n.d., p. iii and ix). In this *Handbook IFC* also underscore that:

> "Without proper planning and management, involuntary resettlement may result in long-term hardship for affected people and environmental damage to the locations in which they are resettled. Such potentially negative consequences diminish the developmental impact of the project, and tarnish the reputation of the project sponsor [...]. Conversely, through proper resettlement planning, a sponsor can enhance the development impact

of a project, thereby improving the living standards of affected people. Investment in local economic and social development pays dividends to the sponsor in the form of enhanced good will within the host community, an enhanced national and international corporate reputation [...]. IFC urges sponsors to avoid involuntary resettlement wherever feasible, or to minimize it by exploring alternative project designs and sites. Where involuntary resettlement is unavoidable, IFC sponsors must engage affected people in the planning, implementation, and monitoring of the resettlement process. IFC encourages project sponsors to plan and execute involuntary resettlement as a development initiative to ensure that the livelihoods and living standards of affected people prevailing before their displacement are improved" (IFC, n.d., p.1).

Within the ICMM's human rights performance expectations of company members, it is stated that involuntary physical or economic displacement of families and communities should be avoided. Where this is not possible, the company is required to apply the mitigation hierarchy, and implement actions or remedies that address residual adverse effects to restore or improve livelihoods and standards of living of displaced people (ICMM, 2020). In this case, the key issue is in approaching resettlement as an opportunity for promoting sustainable development through improvements to the economic and social well-being of affected people.

Several involuntary resettlements recently occurred in the West-African mining sector (Guinea, Mali, Senegal, Ghana, Burkina Faso, etc.) and almost all sponsors claimed to be following the IFC guidelines and standards. Nevertheless, on the field, the results are sometimes very mixed, resulting sometimes in civil unrest, intervention of security forces, and inadequate restoration of livelihoods, or the creation of expectations that could not be met by the project. The responsibility for this mixed result is generally shared among the different stakeholders. Thus, the mining companies and their consultants sometimes arrive with resettlement options, ideas for restoring livelihoods, a schedule, and a pre-established budget. Sometimes even pre-established deadlines are communicated to investors as part of the fundraising process. Such an approach gives little chance for active listening and negotiation, and is therefore limited to the strict minimum required to obtain permits ("ticking the box" process). This shows that some people forget that the management of non-technical risks is often overly complex, and that the deadlines of social projects are often more difficult to meet than those of technical engineering projects. Also, although it is an excellent practice to benchmark the implementation of similar projects, trying to replicate success stories from elsewhere can fail if not adapted to the local socio-economic context. When working in Africa, one must learn to "tropicalize" certain processes and approaches drawn from Western experience, including putting in place culturally appropriate approaches to community engagement and consultation with local communities, where appropriate. Otherwise, by using culturally unappropriated engagement practices, there is a risk of deeply disturbing the harmony and traditional social organization, particularly through intergenerational conflicts or interethnic tensions.

Local administrative authorities and technical services have a crucial role to play in this process as a guarantor of compliance with procedures and agreements, but it sometimes happens that due to the scale of the economic, social, and political issues, and a lack of experience in the field of major resettlement projects, State representatives can be caught between the hammer of social pressure and the anvil of economic and political issues. As a result, State agents can end up behaving like helpless spectators of a process that overtakes them.

IFC Performance Standard 5 is the main guideline used within the mining industry for involuntary resettlement projects in West-Africa. During the stakeholder engagement process, project sponsors and their consultants like to remind local authorities and populations that the process will be conducted in accordance with IFC's world-class standards. Although local government officials are often not fully aware of the details of Standard 5, mentioning the IFC is usually a reassuring factor for stakeholders.

Performance Standard 5 applies to physical and/or economic displacement resulting from the following types of land-related transactions (IFC, 2012):

- Land rights or land use rights acquired through expropriation or other compulsory procedures in accordance with the legal system of the host country,
- Land rights or land use rights acquired through negotiated settlements with property owners or those with legal rights to the land, if failure to reach settlement would have resulted in expropriation or other compulsory procedures,
- Project situations where involuntary restrictions on land use and access to natural resources cause a community or groups within a community to lose access to resource usage where they have traditional or recognizable usage rights,
- Certain project situations requiring evictions of people occupying land without formal, traditional, or recognizable usage rights,
- Restriction on access to land or use of other resources including communal property and natural resources such as marine and aquatic resources, timber and non-timber forest products, freshwater, medicinal plants, hunting and gathering grounds, and grazing and cropping areas.

The objectives of this Performance Standard 5 aim to:

- Avoid, and when avoidance is not possible, minimize displacement by exploring alternative project designs,
- Avoid forced eviction,
- Anticipate and avoid, or where avoidance is not possible, minimize adverse social and economic impacts from land acquisition or restrictions on land use by providing compensation for loss of assets at replacement cost and ensuring that resettlement activities are implemented with appropriate disclosure of information, consultation, and the informed participation of those affected,

- Improve, or restore, the livelihoods and standards of living of displaced persons,
- Improve living conditions among physically displaced persons through the provision of adequate housing with security of tenure at resettlement sites.

All other details can be found in the IFC documents. However, it is important to emphasize here the crucial role of stakeholder engagement as a key factor in the success or failure of the land acquisition and involuntary resettlement processes. In its report entitled *"Land acquisition and resettlement—Lessons learned"* ICMM (n.d., p.24) provides relevant golden rules for a successful stakeholder engagement during this critical process:

Recommendations:

- It is important to develop a formal life-of-project stakeholder engagement plan to ensure a comprehensive and consistent approach to engaging with stakeholders,
- Encourage active community participation in project planning from the outset, and throughout the project life cycle,
- Engage early and in a sustained way through all stages of the project,
- […] always keep engaging. Where there is silence from the project, this will be replaced by rumor and speculation,

Who to engage:

- Focus the consultation process on households that will be affected by displacement. Use separate engagement mechanisms to involve the broader community or other communities as appropriate,
- Find ways to communicate directly with communities and key,
- stakeholders. Do not rely on just one communication source,
- Early and effective involvement of government and local leadership is critical. Understand local government capacity and complexities. Resource and plan the resettlement process accordingly,

- Take steps to determine if community leaders are truly representative, for example by creating space for vulnerable people, women, and other groups that may not typically claim leadership. Make sure community leaders adequately represent all community factions,
- Employees are key "internal and external" stakeholders. Good internal engagement is a prerequisite for successful external stakeholder engagement and managing expectations.

How to engage:

- Manage expectations—be realistic about project benefits,
- Be consistent with communication messages. Agree on key messages across the project, and who will deliver these,
- Process is as important as outcome.

Figure 27 shows the importance of stakeholder engagement through all stages of the land acquisition and resettlement process.

Negotiations with displaced people on how displacement impacts will be addressed should be central to the process. Stakeholder engagement is a two-way process of communication, and interaction within and between a project team and each of its stakeholders. It involves meaningful and multifaceted engagement with both external and internal stakeholders. It is an ongoing process throughout the life of a project (ICMM, s.d).

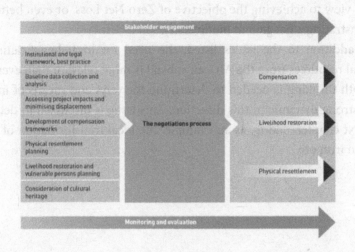

Figure 27: The land acquisition and resettlement process (Reddy et al., 2015). With permission.

Issues related to land acquisition, involuntary displacement of populations, and protection of their cultural heritage are particularly sensitive and delicate for the mining industry at the global level. In West Africa, where these issues are even more sensitive due to the vulnerability of local populations, the mining industry must, therefore, redouble its efforts by implementing the best international standards governing these issues. It must also mobilize the human and material resources required to carry out the processes, and ensure a satisfactory outcome for all stakeholders. Of course, one of the most important success factors will be the quality of the stakeholder engagement process, which must be culturally appropriate, and in a mindset of listening, inclusive dialogue, respect, trust, and commitment.

In addition to climate change, discussed in Chapter 9, biodiversity conservation is one of the greatest environmental challenges of our time and the expectations of stakeholders and society at large are increasingly high for the mining industry. The West African mining industry must therefore demonstrate, through concrete and verifiable results in the field, that it is determined and capable of reconciling its operations with biodiversity conservation; it must use a participatory approach that values the TEK, with a view to achieving the objective of Zero Net Loss, or even better, by demonstrating a net gain of biodiversity.

In addition to the issues listed, the need for local beneficiation of mineral resources from the African subsoil is more relevant than ever, and in-depth thinking is needed to determine the ways and means of initiating a strong dynamic in this direction. This issue is discussed in detail in the next chapter, taking, as an example, the local transformation of West African iron ore.

8. MINERAL BENEFICIATION: WEST AFRICA, THE NEXT IRON ORE, AND STEEL HUB?

"The calls for the wider implementation of mineral beneficiation have become louder across many developing countries. The calls emanate from a consensus that there is an inherent advantage for mineral rich countries to establish internal capacity to process their minerals into semi-finished or finished materials" (Zhuwarara, 2019). As emphasized by the United Nations, despite available opportunities, little value is added to Africa's mineral products. On the contrary, the increased commodity demand has led to an increase in exports of ores and concentrates. This has led to increased calls for development-oriented mineral policies which include instruments to increase value-addition. There is also increased awareness that value addition encompasses more than mineral processing, and includes all aspects of the mineral value chain, such as local inputs and services into the mineral sector. Further, there is the realization that research and development, and technological information are the basis for creating added value to the mineral sector (United Nations, 2009).

As Cheikhna Cissé eloquently stated in one of his chronicles on Financial Afrique:

"We develop by creating value, wealth. And to create wealth,
you must produce. And to produce well, you need, among other
things, efficient infrastructure, a robust local financial system,
virtuous governance, and (above all) a strong, diversified, and
competitive industrial sector. In short, Africa's future lies in

industrialization. There is a need to add more value to local raw materials through greater processing, with a view to retaining more of the value added of finished products for domestic consumption and export. If the distribution of the wealth thus created is equitable, poverty reduction becomes an almost obvious result" (Financial Afrique, 2020).

Based on this premise, in which we strongly believe, we discuss in this chapter West Africa's potential to position itself as a future global hub, both in the production of high-quality iron ore, and in the local production of steel to supply the African continent and the global market. As China's economic growth drove demand for iron ore, West Africa is being described as iron ore's new frontier, with deposits that could lead the region to account for about 10% of the world's supply (M'cleod, 2013; Steinweg & Römgens, 2015).

With this in mind, we begin by presenting the concept of mineral beneficiation and its potential for creating greater local value-added. Then the example of steel is used to present the value chain and the global market for a product that can play a leading role in the transition to a green economy, and on which West Africa could further position itself. Following an overview of the concepts of resources and reserves, this chapter presents some of the major West African iron ore deposits, with a view to recalling its sub-soil wealth and its potential as a hub for the production and local processing of this ore. Finally, given that the mining and metallurgy industry is energy-intensive and requires heavy investment in infrastructure, this chapter concludes with a presentation of the sub-region's energy potential, as well as the need to develop mining infrastructure with a view to regional integration and infrastructures sharing among the various stakeholders.

8.1 MINERAL BENEFICIATION AS A DRIVER FOR LOCAL VALUE CREATION—AN OVERVIEW

The value extraction of the ore and mineral can be broken down into four generic stages (Figure 28). A large proportion of the value extraction process has traditionally taken place outside of resource-rich countries.

The majority of the value that is extracted occurs after the ore has been developed into a highly concentrated product and sold to the consumer. This part of the process is mineral beneficiation. According to Deloitte (2011), the four stages of mineral beneficiation are:

1. This involves the extraction of the ore, the concentration of the particular mineral into concentrates, and the further beneficiation of the mineral into a saleable product, typically defined by industry standards; examples include gold doré (22+ carats) and platinum bars (99,99% Pt),
2. The mineral is enhanced by the addition of other metals to create a metal alloy. This is usually also done to meet defined industry standards,
3. This involves including the mineral in the production process for a saleable product; examples include the production of vehicle exhaust systems, and jewelry design and manufacturing. There may be more than one value enhancing step in this stage,
4. The last step is the sale of the product to the consumer for a margin.

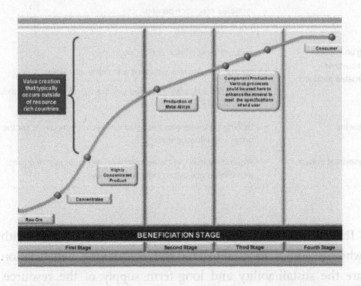

Figure 28: Stages of mineral beneficiation (Deloitte, 2011). With permission.

The beneficiation of minerals to finished consumer goods not only increases the revenue gained from the exploitation of the mineral resource, but also significantly increases the labor absorptive capacity of the industry. In accordance with the government's industrialization policy and mineral development, beneficiation aims to enhance the value of exports, and increase sources of consumption for local content and opportunities for sustainable employment. The strategy contributes to strengthening the knowledge economy in support of the overall competitiveness of the economy (Deloitte, 2011). Table 8 highlights the macroeconomics benefits of mineral beneficiation for mineral resource-rich countries.

Table 8 Macroeconomics benefits of mineral beneficiation
(Deloitte, 2011). With permission.

Potential job creation/ Sustainable employment	• Take advantage of governments NGP for employment creation • Creation of sustainable employment through the creation of long term projects • Increased industrialisation will facilitate access to skills, increased expertise and improved technology
Revenue potential	• Increase tax revenue for government through business creation • Increased integration benefits • Potential cost cutting
Saving on import/ export costs of beneficiated products	• Reduced transportation costs of raw material • Reduce costs and fees associated with import and export • Reduce the delay costs associated with the lack of infrastructure around import/export hubs
Tax benefits	• Utilising the tax benefits associated with each commodity as per the mineral beneficiation strategy
Environmental impact	• Possibility of reducing the environmental impact through improved technologies and carbon reduction initiatives

"The main challenges that developing countries are faced with when it comes to establishing and broadening beneficiation are the sustainability and long-term supply of the resource, availability of demand, access to markets, lack of domestic markets, infrastructural deficiencies, energy constraints, technological deficiencies, poor economic environments, and skills deficits. [...] In order to overcome these challenges, countries can look at regional capacity rather than national capacity. Therefore, sharing infrastructure, resources, skills, technology, and markets between countries can become a viable means of approaching the beneficiation initiative" (Zhuwarara, 2019).

Some Western countries are strongly advocating the local transformation of their mineral resources, and are putting in place legislative tools and incentives to support their strategic positioning. Thus, in Quebec, the Mining Act states:

"its purpose is to promote, in a perspective of sustainable development, prospecting, research, exploration and exploitation of mineral substances, while ensuring that the citizens of Quebec receive a fair share of the wealth created by the exploitation of these resources and considering the other possible uses of the territory. It also aims to ensure that the exploitation of non-renewable resources is carried out for the benefit of future generations, and to develop Quebec expertise in the exploration, exploitation, and processing of mineral resources in Québec. It is therefore in this logic of promoting the local processing of its mineral resources that the government of Quebec requires applicants for mining leases to provide, in addition to the extent and probable value of the deposit, a project feasibility study and an economic and market opportunity study for processing locally" (Gouvernement du Québec, 2020).

Deloitte's report on the 2010 financial year indicated that South Africa achieved gross revenue of $24.5 billion from export in crude forms of all minerals, but would have generated twice the revenue if they had been refined and processed as finished products locally for purposes of deriving full benefit of these resources.

By so doing, South Africans will benefit from the abundance of their mineral resources, leading to sustainable economic growth, increased employment, and poverty alleviation (Kgoale and Odeku, 2019). The "*South African Minerals Policy White Paper*" of 1998 defines beneficiation as "the successive process of adding value to raw minerals from their extraction through to the sale of finished products to consumers". Indeed, the South Africa government has taken a policy decision to use its vast mineral resources for beneficiation as a top priority for achieving inclusive economic participation; black entrepreneurships; increased job opportunities; economic growth and development; improved standard of living, particularly for the black majority; and poverty alleviation. To this end, the government has urged that the mineral resources beneficiation should be intensified and accelerated in order to achieve these desired outcomes (Naidoo, 2012). One of the legal tools that have been promulgated to drive and accelerate mineral resources beneficiation is the South African Mineral and Petroleum Resources Development Act (MPRDA) 2002, which brought structural change to the mining industry. The state is currently entrusted with the sole prerogative to decide when, where, and which minerals will be mined, and by whom. Therefore, the promulgation of MPRDA was the first step towards socio-economic beneficiation and transformation in the mining industry (Kgoale and Odeku, 2019). Zimbabwe has adopted various local content and beneficiation initiatives over the last few years. These initiatives generally include the imposition of levies on the export of unprocessed minerals, the compulsory setting aside of product for domestic processing, the selective restriction of mining consumables that can be imported, and the application of fiscal rewards for actions and strategies that support beneficiation and the use of local services and goods. Talking about diamond producers within the Southern African Development Community region, Selina Zhuwarara suggested that,

> "[...] instead of individually approaching this task, countries such as Botswana, South Africa, Zimbabwe, Namibia, DRC, Angola, Lesotho, and Tanzania can combine their capacities to establish and supply stones to a regional diamond manufacturing

hub. Not only does this create a sustainable supply of diamonds for beneficiation, it also establishes a wider market reach, both regionally and internationally. Each country can reserve a portion of their diamond production for this regional benefi- ciation hub. The model can be applied across different mineral sectors, and the location for each respective hub can be selected based on which country in the region has the best condi- tions and capacity to sustain hosting the beneficiation center" (Zhuwarara, 2019).

The same strategy could be used by West-African iron ore-rich coun- tries to implement a regional iron ore and steel hub within this region.

Of course, a competitive strategy for local transformation cannot just be the result of a spontaneous, emotional, and passionate nationalism. Thus, any winning mineral beneficiation policy will need to be based on strong and clear-headed assessment of its economic feasibility and sustainability, in collaboration with the mining industry. The latter must have the flexibility to adjust their production capacity and level of local mineral beneficiation according to the market trends and by considering the value chain profit split analysis. Obviously, a mine and its value chain must be profitable in order to be sustainable. Managers will need to generate profit responsibly for as long as possible by keeping costs to a minimum while maximizing revenue.

According to Crowson, the development of local downstream indus- tries requires the satisfaction of several pre-conditions if they are to be internationally competitive. He added that not all minerals can support extensive labor-intensive local processing. Depending on the minerals concerned, the requirements include political and social stability, adequate transport links to markets, a suitably flexible and educated labor force, the availability of risk capital, and competent management. Industries are unlikely to flourish and grow, however, unless they can compete in interna- tional markets. Local markets will seldom be large enough to absorb their output, except in a few relatively large countries with sizable populations. Mining is primarily an economic activity, and will only create wealth, yield profits, and earn economic rents if it supplies products for which there is a demand, at a price that exceeds their cost of production (Crowson, 2020). Without financial sustainability, there will be no social nor environmental sustainability, and therefore no shared value creation for shareholders, local communities, host countries, and other stakeholders.

8.2 STEEL: A MATERIAL OF CHOICE FOR A SUSTAINABLE WORLD

Steel is an alloy of iron and carbon containing less than 2% carbon and 1% manganese and small amounts of silicon, phosphorus, sulphur, and oxygen. Steel is the world's most important engineering and construction material. It is used in every aspect of our lives, in cars and construction products, refrigerators and washing machines, cargo ships and surgical scalpels (Figure 29) (World Steel Association, 2020).

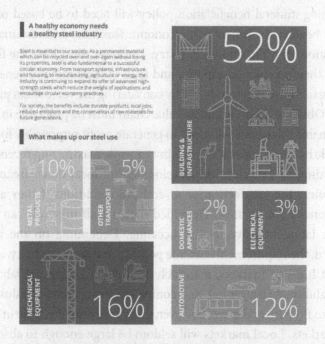

Figure 29: Steel usage (World Steel Association, 2020).

Steel is essential to our society. As a permanent material that can be recycled over and over again without losing its properties, steel is also fundamental to a successful circular economy (World Steel Association, 2020). Recycling produces significant savings in energy and raw materials. Each recycled ton of scrap steel saves more than 1,400 kilograms of iron ore, 740 kilograms of coking coal, and 120 kilograms of limestone (Government of Canada, 2019). From transport systems, infrastructure, and housing, to manufacturing, agriculture or energy, the industry is continuing to expand its offer of advanced high strength steels that reduce the weight of applications and encourage circular economy practices. For society, the benefits include durable products, local jobs, reduced emissions, and the conservation of raw materials for future generations. Innovative lightweight steels (such as those used in in automobiles and buildings) help to save energy and resources. The steel industry has made immense efforts to limit environmental pollution in the last decades. Producing one ton of steel today requires just 40% of the energy it did in 1960 (World Steel Association, 2020).

8.2.1   HOW IS STEEL MADE?

Steel is produced using one of two main routes: the blast furnace/basic oxygen furnace (BF-BOF) route and the electric arc furnace (EAF) route. Variations and combinations of production routes also exist. The key difference between the routes is the type of raw materials they consume. For the BF-BOF route, these are predominantly iron ore, coal, and recycled steel, while the EAF route produces steel using mainly recycled steel and electricity. Depending on the plant configuration and the availability of recycled steel, other sources of metallic iron such as direct-reduced iron (DRI) or hot metal can also be used in the EAF route (World Steel Association, 2020).

As outlined by the World Steel Association, a total of 70.7% of steel is produced using the BF-BOF route. First, iron ores are reduced to iron, also called hot metal or pig iron. Then the iron is converted to steel in the BOF. After casting and rolling, the steel is delivered as coil, plate, sections, or bars. Steel made in an EAF uses electricity to melt recycled steel. Additives, such as alloys, are used to adjust to the desired chemical composition. Electrical energy can be supplemented with oxygen injected into the EAF. Downstream process stages, such as casting, reheating, and rolling, are similar to those found in the BF-BOF route. About 28.9% of steel is produced via the EAF route. Another steelmaking technology, the open-hearth furnace (OHF), makes up about 0.4% of global steel production. The OHF process is very energy intensive, and is in decline owing to its environmental and economic disadvantages.

Most steel products remain in use for decades before they can be recycled. Therefore, there is not enough recycled steel to meet the growing demand using the EAF steelmaking method alone. Demand is met through a combined use of the BF-BOF and EAF production methods. All these production methods can use recycled steel scrap as an input. Most new steel contains recycled steel. Obviously, steel is not a single product. There are more than 3,500 different grades of steel, with many different physical, chemical, and environmental properties. Modern cars are built with new steels that are stronger, but up to 35% lighter than in the past (World Steel Association, 2020).

8.2.2 WORLD IRON ORE AND STEEL PRODUCTION AND CONSUMPTION

Iron and steel are so important that a steel company in the Republic of South Korea has this inscription on its entrance: "A nation that controls Iron controls the world" (Ajayi et al., n.d.). World crude steel production reached 1868 million tons (Mt) for the year 2019 (Figure 30). This world production is largely dominated by China, with 53.3% of the total produced in 2019.

Top steel-producing companies 2019

million tonnes, crude steel production

Rank	Company	Tonnage	Rank	Company	Tonnage
1	ArcelorMittal[1]	97.31	26	Rizhao Steel	14.20
2	China Baowu Group[2]	95.47	27	U. S. Steel Corporation	13.89
3	Nippon Steel Corporation[3]	51.68	28	EVRAZ	13.81
4	HBIS Group[4]	46.56	29	CITIC Pacific	13.55
5	POSCO	43.12	30	Gerdau	13.13
6	Shagang Group	41.10	31	Jingye Steel	12.58
7	Ansteel Group	39.20	32	MMK	12.46
8	Jianlong Group	31.19	33	Shaanxi Steel	12.45
9	Tata Steel Group	30.15	34	Sanming Steel	12.40
10	Shougang Group	29.34	35	thyssenkrupp	12.25
11	Shandong Steel Group	27.58	36	Zenith Steel	11.93
12	JFE Steel	27.35	37	Severstal	11.85
13	Valin Group	24.31	38	Tsingshan Stainless[e]	11.40
14	Nucor Corporation	23.09	39	Nanjing Steel	10.97
15	Hyundai Steel	21.56	40	Taiyuan Steel	10.86
16	IMIDRO[5]	16.79	41	Anyang Steel	10.54
17	JSW Steel	16.26	42	Metinvest Holding	9.58
18	SAIL	16.18	43	Xinyu Steel	9.47
19	Benxi Steel	16.18	44	Donghai Special Steel	8.90
20	Fangda Steel	15.66	45	Jinxi Steel	8.73
21	NLMK	15.61	46	Erdemir Group	8.61
22	Baotou Steel	15.46	47	Steel Dynamics, Inc.	8.59
23	China Steel Corporation	15.23	48	Kunming Steel	7.73
24	Techint Group	14.44	49	SSAB	7.62
25	Liuzhou Steel	14.40	50	Jiuquan Steel	7.48

[e] = estimate

[1] Includes shares in AM/NS India and China Oriental
[2] Includes tonnage of Maanshan Steel and Chongqing Steel
[3] Includes tonnage of Nippon Steel Stainless Steel Corporation, Sanyo Special Steel, Ovako AB, and shares in AM/NS India and USIMINAS
[4] Includes tonnage of Serbia Iron & Steel d.o.o. Beograd and MAKSTIL A.D. in Macedonia
[5] Combined tonnage of Mobarakeh Steel, Esfahan Steel, Khuzestan Steel and NISCO

Notes on company ownership and tonnage calculations:
For worldsteel members, the data was sourced from their official tonnage declarations. For Chinese companies, the official CISA tonnage publication was used, unless especially noted. Figures represent consolidated tonnage ending 31 December 2019, including interests in subsidiaries and joint ventures.

For an extended company listing go to [illegible]

8

Major steel-producing countries 2018 and 2019

million tonnes, crude steel production

Country	2019		2018	
	Rank	Tonnage	Rank	Tonnage
China	1	996.3	1	920.0
India	2	111.2	2	109.3
Japan	3	99.3	3	104.3
United States	4	87.8	4	86.6
Russia	5	71.9	6	72.1
South Korea	6	71.4	5	72.5
Germany	7	39.7	7	42.4
Turkey	8	33.7	8	37.3
Brazil	9	32.2	9	35.4
Iran	10	25.6	10	24.5
Italy	11	23.2	11	24.5
Taiwan, China	12	22.0	12	23.2
Ukraine	13	20.8	13	21.1
Vietnam	14	20.1	15	15.5
Mexico	15	18.5	14	20.2
France	16	14.4	16	15.4
Spain	17	13.6	17	14.3
Canada	18	12.9	18	13.4
Poland	19	9.0	19	10.2
Saudi Arabia	20	8.2	20	8.2
Belgium	21	7.8	21	8.0
Austria	22	7.4	24	6.9
Egypt	23	7.3	22	7.8
United Kingdom	24	7.2	23	7.3
Netherlands	25	6.7	25	6.8
Indonesia[e]	26	6.4	28	6.2
South Africa	27	5.7	27	6.3
Australia	28	5.5	29	5.7
Slovak Republic[e]	29	5.3	30	5.2
Sweden	30	4.7	34	4.7
Argentina	31	4.6	31	5.2
Malaysia[e]	32	4.5	35	4.1
Czech Republic	33	4.4	32	4.9
Thailand	34	4.2	26	6.4
Kazakhstan	35	4.1	37	4.0
Finland	36	3.5	36	4.1
Romania	37	3.4	38	3.5
United Arab Emirates	38	3.3	39	3.2
Pakistan	39	3.3	33	4.7
Byelorussia	40	2.6	41	2.5
Qatar	41	2.6	40	2.6
Algeria[e]	42	2.4	42	2.3
Luxembourg	43	2.1	43	2.2
Portugal	44	2.0	44	2.2
Oman[e]	45	2.0	45	2.0
Serbia	46	1.9	47	2.0
Hungary	47	1.8	46	2.0
Switzerland[e]	48	1.5	48	1.5
Philippines[e]	49	1.4	49	1.5
Greece	50	1.4	50	1.5
Others		15.9		15.9
[illegible]	[illegible]	[illegible]	[illegible]	[illegible]

[e] = estimate

9

Figure 30: Top steel-producing companies 2019 and Major steel-producing countries 2018-2019 in million tons (World Steel Association, 2020).

Except for Arab countries north of the Sahara and South Africa, the steel industry in most African countries is still in a state of slumber. At best, the industry can be described as in its infancy (MeSteel, 2002). Thus, in 2019, Africa made a very modest contribution of 0.9% of world steel production (World Steel Association, 2020).

> "The potential for the development of the iron and steel industry in African countries is nevertheless significant, and can be analyzed by considering their existing natural resources, including iron ores and alloying metal ores, fuels, reductants, energy, water, and additives. Africa has large reserves of iron ore, manganese ore, chromite, cobalt, and nickel ores, as well as substantial reserves of coal, natural gas, and oil, together with

huge water reserves and hydropower potential for electricity production, as well as availability of fluxes, clays, and refractories. Despite Africa's extensive resource base, only a few of its iron ore deposits are being commercially exploited. Most of Africa's iron ore resources remain largely undeveloped, owing to such constraints as non-availability of the necessary investment resources from both domestic and international sources, the general sluggishness of the world iron ore market, the relative inaccessibility of many reserves (necessitating large investment in transportation and other infrastructure), and civil and political strife that hampers development" (MeSteel, 2002).

In 2018, African iron ore production (82.6 Mt) was driven mainly by South Africa (61.7 Mt), Mauritania (10.8 Mt), and Liberia (4.6 Mt) (World Steel Association, 2020).

In addition to being a leader in production, China dominates the apparent steel use (finished steel products) with 51.3%, while all of Africa accounts for just 2.1%. Inequalities are also glaring when one compares the apparent steel use per capita around the world (table 9).

Table 9: Apparent steel use in kg per capita from 2013 to 2019
(Adapted from World Steel Association, 2020)

	Apparent steel consumption per capita						
	2013	2014	2015	2016	2017	2018	2019
European Union (28)	281.1	293.5	303.4	310.2	321.1	328.3	309.6
Other Europe	337.1	333.8	357.2	356.9	368.8	326.8	293.8
CIS	210.7	201.0	181.7	176.1	186.8	190.3	200.3
NAFTA	278.6	308.0	279.8	270.8	284.2	286.7	273.2
Central and South America	105.7	99.7	92.4	79.9	83.1	85.8	81.7
Africa	32.4	32.5	32.7	31.0	27.8	28.4	27.9
Middle East	228.1	231.5	224.3	217.4	214.1	197.3	189.6
Asia	259.6	253.8	243.1	246.5	267.8	283.0	299.2
Oceania	178.6	195.4	188.6	173.9	161.8	160.7	157.5
World	214.3	212.8	204.2	203.8	216.5	224.0	229.3

While the European Union steel consumption reached 309 kg per capita in 2019, and the world average was 229, the African consumption was just around 28 kg per capita. African consumption is heterogeneous, and is pulled up by Egypt (103.1 kg per capita) and South Africa (76.4 kg per capita). For the rest of the African continent, the average consumption per capita was 18.8 kg in 2019, which demonstrates the extremely low level of industrialization on the continent. The gradual industrialization of the continent should open new sustainable markets for the local steel industry, and thus become a lever for the local transformation of the continent's raw mineral resources.

In addition, the African Continental Free Trade Area (AfCFTA) is emerging, and should be a powerful additional lever for the market of products resulting from the local transformation of natural resources, including steel.

The AfCFTA agreement will create the largest free trade area in the world, measured by the number of countries participating. The pact connects 1.3 billion people across 55 countries, with a combined gross domestic product (GDP) valued at US$3.4 trillion. It has the potential to lift 30 million people out of extreme poverty, but achieving its full potential will depend on putting in place significant policy reforms and trade facilitation measures. The agreement will reduce tariffs among member countries, and cover policy areas such as trade facilitation and services, and regulatory measures such as sanitary standards and technical barriers to trade. Full implementation of AfCFTA will reshape markets and economies across the region, and boost output in the services, manufacturing, and natural resources sectors (World Bank, 2020).

Figure 31 shows the world trade in iron ore and steel by area, and hopefully by unlocking its real potential, the African continent, and especially West Africa, should gradually and resolutely take their rightful place in the concert of iron ore and steel producing nations, and thus have more weight in the continental market, as well as on a global scale.

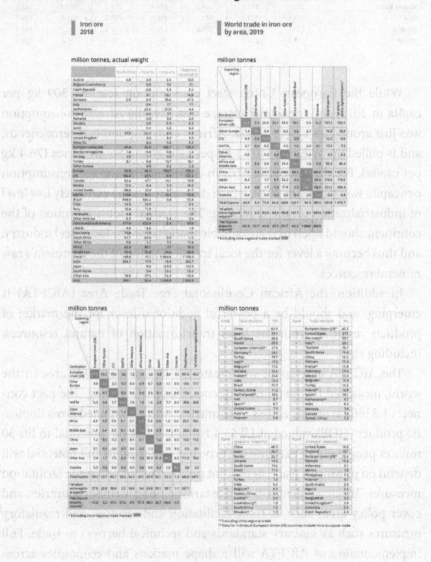

Figure 31: World trade in iron ore (top) and steel (bottom) by area in 2019 (Mt)
(World Steel Association, 2020)

8.3   RESOURCES AND RESERVES—DEFINITIONS

"[…] The main distinguishing feature of the mining industry is that it extracts mineral products from individual ore deposits that are essentially finite. It exploits non-renewable resources that are eventually depleted, even if the products made from the extracted materials are recyclable many times over. The nature of these underlying resources is basic to any understanding of the economics of the mineral industries, and of mineral policy" (Crowson, 2020, p.28).

Based on the Canadian Institute of Mining, Metallurgy, and Petroleum (CIM) Definition Standards:

"Mineral resources are sub-divided, in order of increasing geological confidence, into Inferred, Indicated, and Measured categories, based on a combination of the number of samples used in the interpolation, the distance from the block and finally, the type of samples used. An Inferred Mineral Resource has a lower level of confidence than the one applied to an Indicated Mineral Resource, and an Indicated Mineral Resource has a lower level of confidence than a Measured Mineral Resource (Figure 32). […] Mineral reserves are sub-divided in order of increasing confidence into Probable Mineral Reserves and Proven Mineral Reserves. A Probable Mineral Reserve has a lower level of confidence than a Proven Mineral Reserve" (CIM, 2014, p.4 and 6).

Ore deposits are three-dimensional according to Crowson, and they are largely hidden below the earth's surface. Their extent can only be properly determined by drilling, which is expensive. Mining companies only need to prove the existence of sufficient ore to justify their investments. They will merely measure enough ore to keep their operations running smoothly and cover the lives of their capital equipment. Companies may know that there is additional ore, but they do not need to measure it exactly, until they plan the next few years of mining (Crowson, 2020).

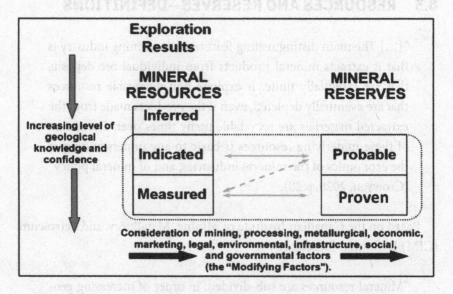

Figure 32: Relationship between Mineral Reserves and Mineral Resources, published in CIM Definition Standards for Mineral Resources & Mineral Reserves (CIM, 2014). Reprinted with permission of the Canadian Institute of Mining, Metallurgy and Petroleum.

The CIM Definition Standards require the completion of a Pre-Feasibility Study as the minimum prerequisite for the conversion of Mineral Resources to Mineral Reserves. A Pre-Feasibility Study is a comprehensive study of a range of options for the technical and economic viability of a mineral project that has advanced to a stage where a preferred mining method (underground mining, or the pit configuration, in the case of an open pit), is established and an effective method of mineral processing is determined. It includes a financial analysis based on reasonable assumptions on the Modifying Factors and the evaluation of any other relevant factors which are sufficient for a Qualified Person, acting reasonably, to determine if all or part of the Mineral Resource may be converted to a Mineral Reserve at the time of reporting (CIM, 2014).

A Pre-Feasibility Study is at a lower confidence level than a Feasibility Study. A Feasibility Study is a comprehensive technical and economic study of the selected development option for a mineral project that includes appropriately detailed assessments of applicable Modifying Factors, together with any other relevant operational factors and detailed financial analysis that are necessary to demonstrate, at the time of reporting, that extraction is reasonably justified (economically mineable). The results of the study may reasonably serve as the basis for a final decision by a proponent or financial institution to proceed with, or finance, the development of the project. The confidence level of the study will be higher than that of a Pre-Feasibility Study (CIM, 2014).

The third dimension of reserves is the accessibility of resources for economic exploitation (Figure 33). As highlighted by Crowson, accessibility may be restricted for a variety of reasons such as wars, civil unrest, restrictions on the export of unprocessed minerals, which inhibit exploration and mine development, prohibition of mining in national parks and wilderness areas in order to preserve the environment, and failure to obtain a social license to operate because of objections by local communities. It is therefore critical to keep in mind that reserves have several dimensions, which means that they are effectively variable. Even the estimates of the resources on which calculations of reserves are based can change with improved knowledge of the earth's crust and more sophisticated understanding of the way in which ore is created (Crowson, 2020).

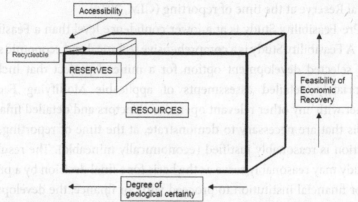

Source: After Peter Cook in. *The Role of the Earth Sciences in Sustaining our Life Support System*. British Geological Survey, Technical report WQ/91/1.

Figure 33: Extended classification of reserves and resources. Permit Number CP21/011 BGS © UKRI. All Rights Reserved. Sourced: BGS Publication, Technical Report Ref WQ/97/1 "The role of the earth science in sustaining our life support system," Peter Cook https://shop.bgs.ac.uk/Shop/Department/Bookshop

The cost curve in Figure 34 shows an analysis for iron ore supply to China. It indicates the dominance of the four largest iron ore producers: Fortescue (Australia), Rio Tinto (Australia), Vale (Brazil) and BHP Billiton (Australia). These four producers not only account for the largest share of world production, but also have the lowest-cost operations. Fortescue Metals Group (FMG) is shown as lowest cost provider of seaborne iron ore to China (FMG, 2018). The cost curve is a graph that plots the production capacity and costs of the entire industry; see the case below. On the X-Axis, cumulative production is ranked. Producers (or projects) are laid out from low to high cost, and bars are used to indicate their output—the wider the bar the more they churn out. On the Y-Axis is the cost of production. It provides a quick snapshot of the industry. Investors can overlay the current price of a commodity onto the cost curve to judge which producers are economically viable—and which are not. Generally, producers want their operations to be in the lowest quartile. That is especially true in a falling price environment. Cost curves can also be used to estimate price support levels, and where the high-cost producer sits in a given industry (FT, 2015).

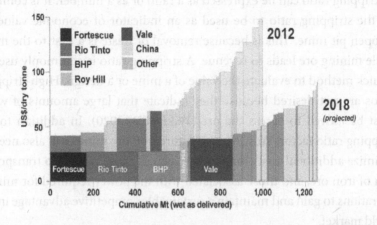

Figure 34: Cost curve for iron ore supply to China (imported and domestic). Costs are identified as CFR (cost & freight) that include royalties and ocean freight (Source: Metalytics, October 2017). With permission.

In addition to low production costs, Australia also enjoys a strong competitive advantage due to its geographical position close to China, which is its main export market. Nevertheless, with the gradual decline of high-grade iron ore mines in both Australia and Brazil, West Africa, with its high-grade, world-class deposits, is increasingly positioning itself as a new hub for iron ore production. The future West African iron mines will nevertheless have the double challenge of meeting the legitimate expectations of countries in terms of strategic infrastructure development (railways, ports, and roads, etc.) while ensuring competitive production costs in the global market, especially when prices are at the bottom of the cycle.

Usually, low strip ratios will ensure that most operations have low mining costs per ton. Indeed, strip ratios are often the determinant for whether an iron ore deposit is economically feasible. In surface mining, "stripping ratio" or "strip ratio" refers to the amount of waste (or overburden) that must be removed to release a given ore quantity. It is a number or ratio that expresses how much waste is mined per unit of ore. The units of a stripping ratio can vary between mines' types. For example, in coal mining, the stripping ratio is commonly referred to as volume/weight, whereas in metal mining, stripping ratio is unitless and is expressed as weight/weight.

A stripping ratio can be expressed as a ratio or as a number. It is common for the stripping ratio to be used as an indicator of economic value for an open pit mine. This is because removal of waste is a cost to the mine, while mining ore leads to revenue. A stripping ratio is commonly used as a quick method to evaluate the value of a mine or a design. High stripping ratios are not desired because they indicate that large amounts of waste must be moved to access the ore (Wikipedia, 2020). In addition to the stripping ratio factor, West African future iron ore mines will also need to optimize additional cost components such as those related to transportation of iron ore, and those associated with the power required for mining operations to gain and maintain a sustainable competitive advantage in the world market.

8.4 WEST AFRICAN IRON ORE RESERVES AND RESOURCES—AN OVERVIEW

Several West African countries have favorable geology and important iron ore reserves to support the required supply for sustainable and competitive production of iron ore concentrate, pellets, or sinter, and for local steel to supply the African and worldwide markets. The sections below highlight examples of the world-class iron ore deposits within the West African region.

8.4.1 SIMANDOU IRON ORE DEPOSIT (GUINEA)

Guinea is host to the famed Simandou project (Blocks 1, 2, 3 and 4), however, this country has never exported a ton and has struggled for decades to extract money from its iron ore, which has been left undeveloped because of protracted legal disputes and the cost of infrastructure to transport the ore to local ports (Mining Intelligence, 2020). Therefore, the main challenge is logistics (Jeune Afrique, 2019). In June 2019, Guinea signed an agreement with a consortium representing Chinese, French, and Singaporean interests for the development of its giant Simandou iron ore reserve, another step towards the realization of a project that it hopes will bring a $15 billion windfall over the 25-year lifespan. The

158

consortium—which includes Société Minière de Boké (SMB), Singapore's Winning Shipping, and Guinean government interests—won a $14 billion tender last November 2020 to develop blocks 1 and 2 of the largest known deposit of its kind, holding more than 2 billion tons of high-grade ore. The West African nation has sought to develop the Simandou deposit for decades, but the project was mired in protracted legal disputes, and high costs curbed interest. The government required bidders to build a 650 km (400 mile) railway and a deep-water port to transport the ore from the remote southeastern corner of Guinea to the coast for export (Mining Intelligence, 2020). In the framework of the exploitation of the Simandou Block I and II deposits, the SMB-Winning Consortium is committed to exporting its ore via the Guinean territory, notably by building a 650-kilometer railroad and a multimodal port platform in Matakang in the Forécariah prefecture on the Guinean coast. At the same time, the SMB-Winning Consortium also plans to create an agricultural growth corridor along the railway line and to build a steel mill in partnership with other operators once the feasibility studies have been validated. In total, the Consortium's investment is estimated at US$15 billion for the entire project. According to the explanatory memorandum for the adoption of a law ratifying the basic convention, the Ministry of Mines and Geology estimates that the Guinean State should receive US$15.5 billion in revenues from the operation of the Simandou Blocks I and II mining site during the 25-year term of the convention. In terms of employment, the project will create more than 30,000 direct jobs during the construction phase. Indirect employment could reach 65,000 during the construction phase and 20,000 during the operation phase. At the same time, the Consortium is committed to implementing a major training and skills transfer program for Guineans (SMB, 2019).

Rio Tinto owns 45.05% of Blocks 3 and 4, with China's Chinalco holding 39.95%, and the Guinean government 15%. Rio Tinto has done very little work on its block three and four tenements in the Simandou region since writing $1.8bn off the value of the project in 2016, and allowing a non-binding agreement to sell its 44.05 % controlling stake to China's Chinalco to lapse in 2018. But with iron ore prices above $100/t during the last quarter of 2020, and a trend towards increased demand for higher-grade ores like those held at Simandou, the firm is restarting work on project, including looking at a joint venture with SMB-Winning to fund the infrastructure required (Argus, 2020; Rio Tinto, 2018). Guinea would rank among the top producers if it mined its iron ore deposits (Mining Intelligence, 2020).

8.4.2   NIMBA IRON ORE DEPOSIT (GUINEA)

The Nimba iron ore project is located in the south-eastern part of Guinea, near the border with Liberia and Cote d'Ivoire. It is situated approximately 800 km from the country's capital, Conakry, and 26 km from the existing railway at Tokadeh in Liberia. The iron ore deposit is located at the base of the 1,000 meter-tall Mount Nimba, which is one of the highest iron ore peaks in Africa (Mining Intelligence, 2020). On September 5, 2019, High Power Exploration received consent from the Government of the Republic of Guinea to acquire a 95% interest in the Nimba iron ore deposit held by BHP, Newmont Goldcorp, and Orano, formerly known as Areva, the French Government nuclear utility. In a 2015 review completed by the United States Geological Survey, the Nimba deposit, which is located in the Forestry region of south-eastern Guinea, is estimated to comprise around a billion tons of high-grade iron ore containing very low levels of impurities. Iron ore of this quality is essential for reducing energy use, greenhouse gas emissions, and slag production during the steel-making process (HPX, 2019). The High Power Exploration plans to produce between one and five million tons in a first phase, with a view to increasing output to at least 20 million tons. Under the deal, Guinea's government will receive a 15% stake in Société des Mines de Fer de Guinée (SMFG), the company that owns Nimba. The government will also get two seats on SMFG's board (HPX, 2019). The logistics of transporting tons of raw materials to port from mining sites in remote parts of Guinea has been a major hurdle for prospective developers of the country's vast mineral wealth. Guinea and Liberia finally signed a deal to allow several mines in Guinea, including the giant Nimba iron ore project, to export through Liberia (Reuters, 2019).

8.4.3   YEKEPA MINE (LIBERIA)

ArcelorMittal currently has mining operations in 10 countries: Algeria, Bosnia and Herzegovina, Brazil, Canada, Kazakhstan, Liberia, Mexico, Russia, Ukraine, and the U.S.A. Liberia is currently the 5th largest mining operation of those sites, and had a production target of 4.5 million tons of iron ore in 2018. Liberia represented the first Greenfield mining project undertaken by ArcelorMittal, which was established in 2006 following the merger of Arcelor and Mittal Steel. ArcelorMittal mines iron ore in Yekepa, Nimba County, and transport it to the iron ore quay in Buchanan, Grand Bassa County. Liberian operations were initially scheduled in two phases (ArcelorMittal, 2018):

- Phase one (2011 to 2015): ore is mined and shipped to ArcelorMittal's European steel plants or to the open market in Asia,
- Phase two (2015 to ± 2030): the capacity of the iron ore mine was planned to be increased to 15 million tons a year. ArcelorMittal planned to invest in and construct a new fixed ship loader at the Buchanan port and a concentrator at the Yekepa concession to produce iron ore pellets.

Finally, the phase 2 project to invest $1.7 billion to construct 15 million tons of concentrate capacity and associated infrastructure has been delayed. This follows the contractor's declaration of force majeure on August 8, 2014 due to the Ebola virus outbreak in West Africa. Phase One operations are continuing as normal (ArcelorMittal, 2018). Recently in Q3 2020, ArcelorMittal announced that the decision has been taken to start the implementation of the phase 2. It will begin construction in 2021 and plans to produce the first concentrate in the fourth quarter of 2023 (Agence Ecofin, 2021).

8.4.4   TONKOLILI IRON ORE PROJECT (SIERRA LEONE)

The Tonkolili iron ore deposit is located within the Sula Mountain range, and forms part of a banded iron formation (BIF) featuring a north-east/

south-west trending magnetic anomaly. The mine contains four contiguous ore bodies, Simbili, Marampon, Numbara and Kasafoni. The mine contains 12.8 billion tons of Joint Ore Reserves Committee (JORC)-compliant iron ore resources (11.5 billion tons of magnetite ore). It is considered to be one of the world's largest magnetite deposits. The project, involving a fully integrated mine, rail, and port infrastructure, is planned to be developed in three phases. The first phase of development included the establishment of a mine, reconstruction of the Pepel Port and 74 km of existing railway, and the construction of a new 126 km narrow-gauge railroad. First phase direct shipping hematite iron ore production increased up to 20 million metric tons per annum (Mtpa) in 2013. The second phase is expected to produce 23 Mtpa of high-grade hematite concentrate. It includes the construction of a concentrator facility, at the mine site, with a capacity to process 30 Mtpa, and the development of a new purpose-built port at Tagrin Point. A proposed third phase will focus on the production of magnetite concentrate using a series of large-scale magnetite concentrators (Mining technology, n.d.).

Tonkolili mine is expected to have an operational period of more than 60 years. Initially, the UK-based African Minerals owned a 75% stake in the mine, while Shandong Iron and Steel Group (SISG) owned the remaining 25%. Unfortunately, Sierra Leone has lost hundreds of millions of dollars in export revenue, following the collapse of iron ore mining with the closure of African Minerals and Shandong iron mining Ltd. over four years ago. The country's economy is yet to fully recover from the twin shock of the Ebola crisis and the fall in global market price of iron ore in 2013-2016 (*The Sierra Leone Telegraph*, 2019). Until recently, Shandong had 100 equity in Tonkolili, after the acquisition of the remaining 75 stake in the Tonkolili mine from African Minerals, purchased for over $170 million, and will also own the associated infrastructure company, African Port and Railway Services. African Minerals has been battered by a rout in iron ore prices and costs related to the Ebola outbreak in West Africa (*Yahoo Finance*, 2015). In September 2020, the Government of Sierra Leone, through the Ministry of Mines and Mineral Resources, has handed over the Tonkolili Iron Ore Project to Chinese-owned Kingho Mining Company Limited, after Shandong Steel, which previously operated the mines, disengaged from mining in Sierra Leone (Sierra Express Media, 2020).

8.4.5 MARAMPA PROJECT (SIERRA LEONE)

The Marampa mine is a brownfield hematite iron ore mine located approximately 150 km north-east of Freetown in Sierra Leone. The project includes a 319 km² exploration license that borders the Marampa mining lease, which was mined extensively between 1933 and 1975 by the Development Corporation of Sierra Leone (DELCO). The property was acquired by London Mining in 2006 (Mining Technology, n.d.).

In March 2017, Gerald Group was awarded a renewable Cale Mining License granted under the Mines and Minerals Act, 2009, for a term of 25 years, and the National Parliament of Sierra Leone unanimously ratified SL Mining's Mining License Agreement, emphasizing the strong support for the Marampa project locally, and reflecting its significant importance to the national economy.

Gerald Group is one of the world's largest independent and employee-owned metal trading houses. Founded in 1962 in the United States, Gerald moved headquarters to London in 2017. SL Mining, a limited liability company incorporated in Sierra Leone, is a wholly owned subsidiary of Gerald Group, engaged in the exploration, development, and production of iron ore concentrate at Marampa in the Port Loko District, the northern province of Sierra Leone. SL Mining estimates resources at about one billion tons of iron ore grading 32% Fe, with potential to expand the resource, for production over the next 30 years (SL Mining, 2019). SL Mining has completed construction ahead of schedule, and is now ramping up production of "Marampa Blue," a high-grade iron ore with over 65% Fe concentrate, one of the highest grades in the world, and a first by any mining company in Sierra Leone (*The Sierra Leone Telegraph*, 2019).

8.4.6 FALEME PROJECT (SENEGAL)

Senegal, one of the most stable African countries according to the World Bank, is a major exporter of phosphate, but it is also looking to develop its iron ore, gold, and oil industries (Mining.com, 2014). The Société des Mines de Fer du Sénégal Oriental (MIFERSO), created in 1975, is responsible for the promotion, development, and valorization of the iron deposits of the Faleme. It is 76% owned by the Senegalese State, and the remaining 24% of the shares are owned by the BRGM/SERTEM association. The concession is in the extreme south-east of Senegal, approximately 750 km from Dakar and 110 km from Kedougou, the main city in this area. The Faleme iron deposit is one of the largest Paleo-Proterozoic iron deposits in the West African Craton. It is composed of several clusters of altered ore enriched in martite and iron hydroxide. Proven reserves are estimated at more than 630 million tons including 372 million tons of hematite (oxidized ore) and 258 million tons of magnetite (magnetic ore). The ores are of excellent quality, with average hematite grades 59% Fe in-situ and 62 to 65% Fe after treatment, and magnetite grades 43% Fe in-situ and 67% after treatment. Total reserves are estimated to be well over 750 million tons, as several studies on the concession are not well researched (ITIE Senegal, 2020a).

The planned production rate is between 12 and 25 million tons of iron ore, of which 50% is lump ore (65.6% Fe) and 50% agglomeration fines (62.7% Fe). The planned industrial facilities at the mine mainly include primary crushing, treatment plant, power and water production, technical services, and ore train handling and loading facilities. According to information provided by MIFERSO, the cost of the project is US$2.9 billion. The project, which expects an annual production of 15 to 25 million tons of iron, consists of an open pit mine at an estimated cost of US$700 million, a mineral port at Bargny for the same cost, and a steelmaking unit that would enable part of the ore to be transformed into steel for local and sub-regional consumption. After the withdrawal of ArcelorMittal from this project and the resulting legal battle, Senegal is currently working with the Turkish company Tosyali to launch the long-awaited project (ITIE Senegal, 2020a,b).

8.4.7   SNIM IRON ORE MINES (MAURITANIA)

The Société Nationale Industrielle et Minière (SNIM) mines mainly two types of iron ore, hematite, and magnetite, in the Tiris Zemmour region in northern Mauritania. The main hematite deposits currently in operation are T014 (Kédia) and M'Haoudatt. They provide 60% of SNIM's total production. Other small satellite mines along the Kédia River provide additional production when needed (SNIM, 2013a). Guelb El Rhein contains several hundred million tons of proven reserves. The average iron content of SNIM magnetites is approximately 37%. They are currently enriched by dry magnetic separation to produce a concentrate grading 66% Fe. SNIM owns and operates its own railway line linking the deposits to the mineral port over 700 km away. SNIM also has a modern communication system thanks to a project carried out between 2009 and 2011, with the installation of a fiber optic cable between Nouadhibou and Zouerate (SNIM, 2013b). This system now makes it possible to monitor train traffic in real time via a control station installed in Nouadhibou (SNIM, 2013b). The SNIM now has a new mineral port that can eventually receive ships of 250,000 tons with a loading rate of 1,0000 t/h (SNIM, 2013c).

SNIM's products have been on the market for 50 years, and SNIM is the second largest African iron ore producer with an annual capacity of 12 million tons. The Company's main customers are located in China and Europe. SNIM offers its customers naturally rich fines (65% Fe), very rich concentrates (66% Fe) and siliceous grades (52% Fe). SNIM's vision is to become one of the world's leading iron ore exporters by 2025, with an annual production of 40 million tons (SNIM, 2013d).

8.5 POWER SUPPLY OPPORTUNITIES FOR WEST AFRICAN IRON ORE AND STEEL LOCAL BENEFICIATION

As Africa's population rapidly expands and urbanizes, its need for reliable and sustainable energy supplies will continue to increase. This energy is needed, not only to drive the continent's economic development, but also to provide modern energy services to the large numbers of Africans currently living without them. Africa is set to emerge as a key driver of global energy demand growth, and is home to abundant reserves of fossil fuels, solar power, and minerals that will be vital for clean energy transitions worldwide. And even though Africa has produced just 2% of global

energy-related carbon dioxide (CO_2) emissions, the continent is dispro-
portionately on the front line when it comes to the effects of the world's
changing climate (IEA, 2019).

Mining is a power-dependent industry, and this power is one of the key
components of the production cost, especially in West Africa where the
mining industry is often not supplied by the public power grid. Securing
and sustaining enough power for heavy industry needs is obviously a key
driver for the development of a competitive mining industry including
local beneficiation of the extractive industry value chain. As highlighted by
the United Nations Economic Commission for Africa (UNECA):

"Modern energy is vital to sustainable human development. The
services that energy makes possible—from heating and lighting,
to manufacturing, agriculture, and mobility—are omnipres-
ent in developed countries, and commonly taken for granted.
Not everyone, however, enjoys the benefits that modern forms
of energy can provide. This is because energy resources are
unevenly distributed around the world, and more so in the sub-
regions of Africa, which accounts for almost 17 % of the world's
population, but only 4.5% of global primary energy demand.
Access to electricity is vital for all aspects of socio-economic
development. However, for most of Africa, the transformative
power of electricity remains unharnessed due to limited production and access. The continent has experienced a slow but
steady increase in access to electricity, rising from 39.7% in 2008
to 45.9% in 2014, and 53% in 2016 (covering some 660 million
people). Despite progress, access remains much lower than the
global average, and is less than half the corresponding figures
for East Asia and the Pacific. Moreover, rural / urban disparities
in access are stark in Africa, (excluding North Africa), where
the electrification rate in the rural areas averaged 17% in 2014,
compared with 70% in urban areas" (UNECA, 2018).

As stated in the African Mining Vision (AMV), nation states cannot
deliver the Vision alone. African states need to rally together to secure the

policy space required for the Vision. Regional cooperation and integration are essential to reduce transaction costs, establish intra-regional synergies, enhance the continent's competitiveness, and realize economies of scale that would catalyze minerals cluster development. However, for goods, services, capital, and other factors to flow freely in regional spaces, there is a need to expedite intra-regional alignment of laws, regulations, and fiscal regimes, among other critical factors (Antonio, 2012). According to UNECA:

"There are wide energy efficiency variations by sub region. Overall, North Africa has the lowest energy-intensity levels due to the adoption of energy efficiency strategies with ambitious goals and targets, regulatory framework, and specific programs that are supported by incentive measures. On the other hand, East Africa is the most energy-intensive sub-region (10.4 mJ per unit of output), followed by Southern Africa (9.7 mJ per unit of output), West Africa (8.6 mJ per unit of output) and Central Africa (7.5 mJ per unit of output). Energy inefficiency can mostly be attributed to inadequate infrastructure, poorly designed buildings, lack of enforceable policy on energy-efficient appliances and technologies (i.e., persistent use of incandescent lightbulbs or inefficient cooking stoves), and inefficient generation and transmission processes" (UNECA, 2018).

Africa is home to five regional power pools: Eastern Africa Power Pool (EAPP); Central African Power Pool (CAPP); Southern African Power Pool (SAPP); West African Power Pool (WAPP); and Maghreb Electricity Committee (COMELEC) (Comité Maghrébin de l'Électricité) (Figure 35) (IEA, 2019). These pools vary greatly in terms of scale, governance, and effectiveness. These ambitious regional grid integration projects help to connect power generation sources across Africa and have the potential to significantly transform Africa's energy landscape. Sustained investments and inclusive policy reforms are required to sustain progress.

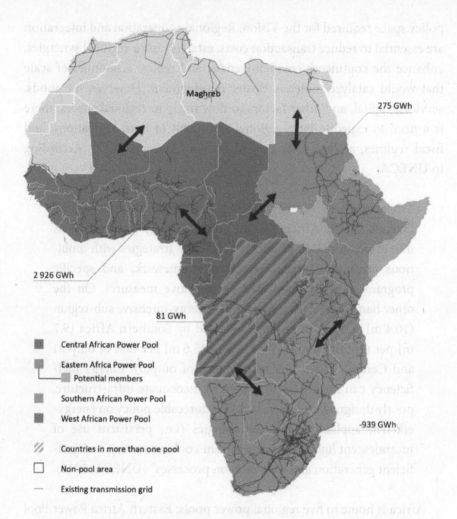

Maghreb

275 GWh

2 926 GWh

81 GWh

■ Central African Power Pool

■ Eastern Africa Power Pool
  ■ Potential members

■ Southern African Power Pool

■ West African Power Pool

// Countries in more than one pool

☐ Non-pool area

— Existing transmission grid

-939 GWh

Figure 35: Electricity trade between sub-Saharan states in 2018 (IEA, 2019)

The WAPP was created by Decision A/DEC.5/12/99 of the
Twenty-Second Summit of the Economic Commission of West Africa
(ECOWAS) Authority of Heads of State and Government. By Decision
A/DEC.18/01/06, the Twenty-Ninth Summit of the ECOWAS Authority
of Heads of State and Government held in Niamey adopted the Articles
of Agreement for WAPP organization and functions. The Headquarters
of the WAPP is based in Cotonou (Benin) further to the signing of the
Headquarter Agreement in 2006 with the Republic of Benin. The WAPP

vision is to integrate the national power systems into a unified regional electricity market with the ultimate goal of providing, in the medium and long term, a regular and reliable energy at competitive cost to the citizenry of the ECOWAS region. Its mission is to promote and develop power generation and transmission infrastructure as well as to coordinate power exchange among the ECOWAS Member states (WAPP, 2020).

As stated by the International Energy Agency in its last Africa Energy Outlook report, Africa stands on the cusp of a unique opportunity: the possibility of becoming the first continent to develop its economy primarily by using energy efficiency, renewables, and natural gas—all of which offer huge untapped potential and economic benefits (IEA, 2019). Compared to most fossil fuel-dependent industrialized countries, the energy transition in Africa presents an unprecedented advantage. Except for a few, most African countries have not exploited their fossil fuel reserves and are therefore well-positioned to meet their energy needs through alternative renewable and cleaner sources (AfDB, 2019). Clean, productive, and affordable renewable energy solutions offer the continent a chance to achieve its economic growth objectives in a sustainable manner. Africa's massive biomass, geothermal, hydropower, solar and wind power have the potential to rapidly shift the current economic reality, and offer the chance to leapfrog to a sustainable and prosperous future for all (AfDB, 2019). From this perspective, the energy sector could be seen as a strong driver for extractive industries development, with a key focus on the local beneficiation of the whole iron ore-to-steel industry value chain with more sustainable and cleaner energies.

Electricity demand in Africa today is 700 terawatt-hours (TWh), with the North African economies and South Africa accounting for over 70% of the total. Yet it is the other sub-Saharan Africa countries that see the fastest growth, as we approach 2040. Electricity demand more than doubles in the Stated Policies Scenario to over 1600 TWh in 2040, and reaches 2300 TWh in the Africa Case, with most of the additional demand stemming from productive uses and emerging middle and higher-income households. Renewables play a leading role in meeting this demand (IEA, 2019).

As stressed by the International Energy Agency (2019), to date, Africa has the richest solar resources on the planet, but has installed only five gigawatts of solar photovoltaics, accounting for less than 1% of global capacity. With the right policies, solar could become one of the continent's top energy sources. Natural gas, meanwhile, is likely to correspond well with Africa's industrial growth drive and need for reliable electricity supply. Today, the share of natural gas in sub-Saharan Africa's energy mix is among the lowest in the world. But that could be about to change, especially considering the supplies the continent has at its disposal: it is home to more than 40% of global gas discoveries so far this decade. The future could be different. There have been a series of major discoveries in recent years, in Egypt, East Africa (Mozambique and Tanzania), West Africa (Senegal and Mauritania) and South Africa, which collectively accounted for over 40% of global gas discoveries between 2011 and 2018. These developments could fit well with Africa's push for industrial growth and its need for reliable electricity supply (constraining the expansion of more polluting fossil fuels).

Data shown in Figures 36 and 37 will be critical for asset managers and investors within the extractive industry, as they will need to quickly start their transition to be able to operate their assets with LNG and renewables such as solar power, hydroelectricity, and wind power.

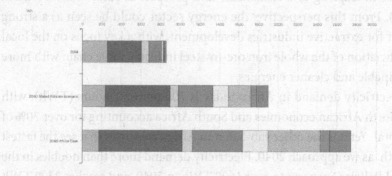

Figure 36: Electricity generation in Africa by scenario, 2018-2040
(IEA, 2019. Africa Energy Outlook. All rights reserved.)

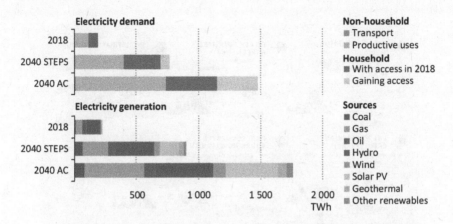

Figure 37: Electricity demand and generation in sub-Saharan Africa (excluding South Africa) by scenario 2018-2040 (IEA, 2019. Africa Energy Outlook. All rights reserved).

Considering the recent decarbonization wave around the world, mining companies operating in West-Africa will also need to have energy transition strategies that will lead to a continuous reduction of their carbon footprint and mitigate their impact on climate change. They will need to also improve their energy efficiency and initiate the use of renewable energy supplies for their operations. They have to define clear targets for this purpose and adopt corporate climate change, carbon management and disclosure policies using best-in-class GHG accounting standards (GHG Protocol, ISO 14064…), while initiating carbon offsetting programs through rural forestry initiatives, for example. These transitions must be made in collaboration with local communities, and must support national strategies and research related to climate change. Figures 38 and 39 present a few options for renewable energy sourcing and sale arrangements for the mining industry.

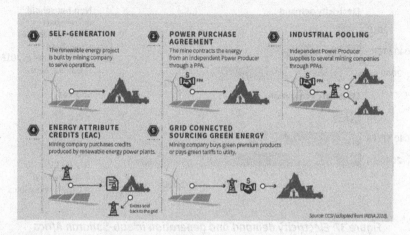

Figure 38: Renewable Energy Sourcing Arrangement for the mining industry (Columbia Center on Sustainable Investment, 2018). With permission.

Figure 39: Renewable Energy Sale Arrangement (Columbia Center on Sustainable Investment, 2018). With permission.

These figures summarize the fact that, apart from reducing operating costs, renewable energy solutions have the potential to help mining companies to (Columbia Center on Sustainable Investment, 2018):

- hedge against volatile commodity prices when the energy source is fossil fuel-based, and diversify energy sourcing risk
- reduce greenhouse gas emissions, thereby mitigating carbon tax risks, and complying with industry certification schemes

- secure the social license to operate by reducing local noise and air pollution, and improving energy access in remote regions when the mining project is off-grid and can be leveraged to electrify surrounding communities
- build a competitive advantage with ESG investors and clients by selling premium low-carbon products, and installing renewable energy projects on reclaimed mine sites to earn land leasing fees and support the region after mine-closure.

8.6 INFRASTRUCTURES FOR LOCAL MINERAL BENEFICIATION—A SHARING PERSPECTIVE

"Infrastructure development's impact on economic growth and poverty reduction cannot be overstated. The World Economic Forum estimates that every dollar spent on a capital project generates an economic return of between 5% and 25% per annum. Conversely, the lack of infrastructure affects productivity and raises production and transaction costs, which hinders growth by reducing the competitiveness of businesses and the ability of governments to pursue economic and social development policies" (PricewaterhouseCoopers (PwC), 2015. P.4).

For many countries in sub-Saharan Africa, the effective exploitation of natural resource wealth is vital to their future economic development, but a lack of available rail, port, and other critical infrastructure has long represented a major obstacle to developing many of Africa's world-class mineral deposits. Encouragingly, China has over the last decade demonstrated a strong willingness to fund and construct major infrastructure projects on the continent, including using "resource-for-infrastructure" deals (Collier & Ireland, 2015). However, the African continent has still an estimated annual infrastructure financing deficit (financing needed for infrastructure but not yet available) of $60 billion-$90 billion, according to African Union officials (Reuters, 2021). This situation constitutes one of the greatest constraints inhibiting the exploitation and development of the continent's immense mineral resources. In fact, as widely known and documented in several studies and reports, the high-grade iron ore deposits in Western and Central Africa need major rail and port infrastructure investments to transport the ore from mine to market. This infrastructure is needed to make these projects viable, especially since many of sub-Saharan Africa's large, undeveloped bulk mineral deposits are in remote, poorly explored, and highly prospective regions. Mining such deposits requires major investment in rail, port, power, and other infrastructure. When completed, this infrastructure could also be used to support other economic activities, including exploitation of yet-to-be-discovered mineral deposits, agribusiness, freight transportation, and passenger services. With the limited financial capacity of host governments, mining investors are expected to fund the infrastructure, which can be as much as three times more expensive than the costs associated with the development of the mining project itself (Toledano et al., 2014; Collier & Ireland, 2015). It is therefore increasingly critical to find mechanisms and strategies that enable the financing of host countries' infrastructure needs, while ensuring that mining projects demonstrate financial robustness and competitiveness that are attractive to investors. Among the proposed strategies, infrastructure sharing among projects and with the public sector seems to be the most popular and the most adapted to the West African context.

As highlighted by Aurecon, the ratio of infrastructure costs versus equipment costs has dramatically shifted in the last decade. Transportation costs make up some of the biggest outlays for a mining company. Choosing the right options can, therefore, have a big impact on a mine's operation. The costs of transportation are already high, and they are set to grow higher in the future. One factor is the rising distance mines are getting from the coast, and from buyers. Other factors include more challenging terrain, and difficult political and environmental conditions. Trends in the mining industry mean that transportation infrastructure and operational costs are becoming increasingly vital to the viability of resource projects (Aurecon, n.d.).

Deutsche Bank has estimated that more than 4,000 km of greenfield railway, costing in excess of US$50 billion, will need to be financed and constructed to unlock Africa's iron ore deposits alone. In most affected states, it is not practicable for host governments to fund this infrastructure to any meaningful degree (CAPEX represents multiples of their annual national budgets). This implies that funding must come from foreign (and perhaps domestic) private capital (IFC & Latham & Watkins, 2014). Mining companies are no longer able or willing to fund entire cost of mining infrastructure from their own financial resources (can be multiples of mine cost). Therefore, sharing has significant potential to facilitate broad-based economic development in a sustainable commercial structure through the multiplier effect (cf. downstream value-added businesses). Sharing mining infrastructure can (IFC & Latham & Watkins, 2014):

- reduce political risk by "linking" mining investment with local communities/economy
- facilitate development of smaller deposits/mines, thus avoiding stranded deposits

As outlined by Thomashausen and Ireland in their paper entitled "Shared-use mining infrastructure in sub-Saharan Africa: challenges and opportunities":

> "sharing of essential infrastructure is one of the most viable ways that mining activity can support the establishment of industries that will survive long after a country's mineral resources are fully exhausted. For example, a railway corridor and port facility can support large-scale and sustainable investments in agriculture and forestry by providing reliable access to foreign markets. A power plant constructed for a mine can be used to supply low-cost electricity to local communities or the nation's grid, improving living standards and supporting the development of small and medium enterprises. Similarly, a national or regional power or water utility that is upgraded and its transmission and distribution network extended to service mining demand will benefit other users with more extensive and reliable supply" (Thomashausen & Ireland 2015, p 9 and 10).

Host governments should, to maximize resource rents and promote broad-based economic growth, impose regulation requiring open access to such infrastructure. Such regulation will enable effective competition for mineral resources and support economic growth by ensuring that third parties can gain access to infrastructure on fair and non-discriminatory terms (Collier & Ireland, 2015). As has been well-documented, Chinese mining and other firms have been actively pursuing "resource for infrastructure" (R4I) transactions on the African Continent. This represents a competitive threat to Western mining groups. Mining groups are, therefore, increasingly open to participating in well-structured shared infrastructure solutions (Thomashausen & Ireland, 2015).

West Africa, as highlighted by PwC, is increasingly identified as an attractive destination for investors across all economic sectors. Its growing population of over 300 million and its abundant resources continue to drive steady economic growth, as seen by a 6% average annual growth rate over the past decade. This region has similar or more challenging infrastructure development statistics as compared to the rest of sub-Saharan Africa. Against the backdrop of continued economic growth in the region, the need for enabling infrastructure development is clearly evident (PwC, 2015). As stated by PwC in a paper published in 2015 (p.2):

> "A prominent view is that limited access to funding is perceived as the most significant challenge in delivering large complex infrastructure projects within the region. However, interestingly, our examination of projects indicates inadequate project preparation / planning as the most significant factor in failed project delivery in the West African region [...]. Several West African countries also have historically had challenges in taking projects through public procurement. Capacity / expertise issues in the public sector, a perceived lack of transparency or sound governance practices and protracted bureaucratic processes effectively reduce investor appetite and risk tolerance."

For its part, McKinsey emphasizes that:

"Africa's track record in moving projects to financial close is poor: 80 percent of infrastructure projects fail at the feasibility and business-plan stage. This is Africa's infrastructure paradox—there is need and availability of funding, together with a large pipeline of potential projects, but not enough money is being spent [...]. There is no shortage of private-sector finance, but investors struggle to match these funds against viable projects in Africa. Governments and their institutional partners can take decisive action to improve the commercial viability of projects, including by helping to mitigate political, currency, and regulatory risks, and by increasing the deal flow of bankable projects [...]. The right interventions could unlock up to $550 billion to invest in African infrastructure" (McKinsey, 2020).

In the light of the wave of major infrastructure projects underway in almost all West African countries, thanks to financing under public-private partnerships, it can be considered that a great deal of effort has been put in by governments to improve the way projects are put together and the governance of their implementation. These new infrastructure projects (ports, airports, hydroelectric dams, railways, telecommunications, roads, and highways, etc.) that are flourishing in West Africa are, in addition to those already existing, assets for the positioning of this sub-region as a future world-class mining hub.

This chapter confirms a real potential for West Africa to position itself as a hub in the production and local transformation of iron ore, with a view to benefiting more from the added value arising from the valorization of raw resources from its subsoil. Iron ore is used as an example here, but other ores such as bauxite, for example, can be valorized locally following the same logic as for iron, and Guinea is making interesting efforts in this perspective. Of course, any winning mineral beneficiation policy will be based on strong and clear-headed assessment of its economic feasibility and sustainability, in collaboration with the mining industry. From this perspective, policymakers could focus more on a multi-country approach in their strategies to promote local processing of mineral resources, through optimized sharing of existing infrastructure, or even the construction of heavy industries with a West-African purpose rather than getting lost in micro-nationalist projects that are unconvincing for investors and uncompetitive, in a global market that is increasingly emphasizing resource optimization and the decarbonization of the world economy. Accelerating the implementation of West African energy integration through the WAPP will also be a key factor in unlocking sub-regional industrial potential, particularly through a focus on green or lower carbon energy in order to tackle global climate change. The latter is the subject of the last, and perhaps most important, chapter.

9. CLIMATE CHANGE & DECARBONIZATION

In the coming decades, climate change is set to disrupt national economies and adversely affect people's livelihoods through changing weather patterns, rising sea levels, and more extreme weather events (UNDP et al., 2016). The United Nations SDG 13, which focus on Climate Action, is a strong global call to take urgent action to combat climate change and its impacts. The impacts of climate change touch on nearly all the SDGs, but the relationship between SDG13 and SDG7 (Affordable and Clean Energy) is fundamental. While climate change affects nearly all economic sectors, the level of exposure and the impact of climate-related risks differ by sector, industry, geography, and organization. The landmark 2015 Paris Agreement, signed by almost 200 countries, sets a global framework for stemming greenhouse gas emissions and adapting to the effects of climate change (UNDP et al., 2016).

This chapter provides an overview of the global challenges and opportunities related with climate change, with a main focus on the West African region and its mining industry, which recognizes the urgency of climate change. The mining reality is presented in this critical context, while providing drivers and levers for a progressive decarbonization of this industry, and giving some outlook for miners and the West African zone.

9.1   9.1 CLIMATE CHANGE – GLOBAL CHALLENGES, RISKS & OPPORTUNITIES

Until recently, there has not been a framework companies could use to disclose climate risk to investors in a consistent and comparable manner. With this in mind, the private sector-led Task Force on Climate-related Financial Disclosures (TCFD) was formed, and in June 2017, it released its recommendations for "voluntary, consistent climate related financial risk disclosures for use by companies in providing information to investors, lenders, insurers, and other stakeholders." These recommendations are structured around four key themes: governance, strategy, risk management, and metrics and targets (TCFD, 2017). The TCFD, a coalition with support from more than 300 investors with nearly $34 trillion in assets under management, recommends that companies report their "transition risks" under a 2°C decarbonization scenario (McKinsey, 2020). TCFD reports are the global standard for helping investors understand the most material climate-related risks (Figure 39) that companies face, and how companies are managing them. Several mining companies are already signatories to the recommendations (RMI, 2018).

Fundamentally, the financial impacts of climate-related issues on an organization are driven by the specific climate-related risks and opportunities to which the organization is exposed, and its strategic and risk management decisions about seizing those opportunities and managing those risks (i.e., through mitigation, transfer, acceptance, or control). Figure 40 outlines the main climate-related risks (transition and physical) and opportunities organizations should consider as part of their strategic planning or risk management to determine potential financial implications (TCFD, 2017). Transition risks (policy, legal, technology, market, reputation) relate to the economy's transition to using less carbon, such as new climate policies or technologies, and physical risks (acute and chronic) relate to those produced by the physical impacts of climate change, like rising sea levels or extreme weather events (Bloomberg, 2020; TCFD, 2017).

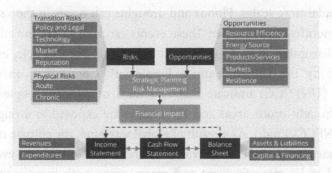

Figure 40: Climate-related risks, Opportunities and Financial Impacts (TCFD, 2017). With permission.

Climate-related issues can affect several important aspects of an organization's financial position, both now and in the future. For example, climate-related issues may have implications for an organization's businesses and capital expenditures. In turn, capital expenditures will determine the nature and amount of long-lived assets and the proportion of debt and equity to be funded on an organization's balance sheet. Climate-related issues may also carry implications for future cash flows (operating, investing, and financing activities). Therefore, investors and other stakeholders need to understand how climate-related issues may affect an organization's businesses, strategy, and financial planning over the short, medium, and long term. This information is used to inform expectations about the future performance of an organization. Investors and stakeholders also need to understand how an organization's climate-related risks are identified, assessed, and managed, and whether those processes are integrated in existing risk management processes (TCFD, 2017).

9.1.1 CLIMATE CHANGE REALITY IN WEST-AFRICA

Developing countries are already suffering from the impacts of climate change and are the most vulnerable to future change. Africa is a continent already under pressure from climate stresses, and is highly vulnerable to the impacts of climate change. Many areas in Africa are recognized as having climates that are among the most variable in the world on seasonal and decadal time scales. Floods and droughts can occur in the same area within months of each other. These events can lead to famine and widespread disruption of socio-economic well-being. For example, estimates reported by the United Nations Framework Convention on Climate Change (UNFCCC) indicate that one third of African people already live in drought-prone areas and 220 million are exposed to drought each year (UNFCCC, n.d.). As a result of global warming, the climate in Africa is predicted to become more variable, and extreme weather events are expected to be more frequent and more severe, with increasing risk to health and life. This includes increasing risk of drought and flooding in new areas (Few et al., 2004, Christensen et al. 2007) and inundation due to sea-level rise in the continent's coastal areas (Nicholls, 2004; McMichael et al., 2006). Africa will face increasing water scarcity and stress with a subsequent potential increase of water conflicts because almost all of the 50 river basins in Africa are transboundary (Ashton 2002, De Wit and Jacek, 2006). Climate change is an added stress to already threatened habitats, ecosystems, and species in Africa, and is likely to trigger species migration and lead to habitat reduction. Up to 50 percent of Africa's total biodiversity is at risk due to reduced habitat and other human-induced pressures (Boko et al., 2007). It is also highlighted that future sea level rise has the potential to cause huge impacts on the African coastlines. Coastal infrastructure in 30 percent of Africa's coastal countries, including the Gulf of Guinea, Senegal, Gambia, Egypt, and along the East-Southern African coast, is at risk of partial or complete inundation due to accelerated sea level rise.

Africa is one of the most vulnerable regions to the adverse effects of climate change. Countries that are already poor and under-developed lack the financial, technological, and human resource capabilities needed to cope with climate change. The countries in West Africa also have a high direct dependence on their natural resources, both for food, and in economic terms (Robinson & Brooks, 2010). An increase in the frequency of extreme rainfall events has been observed over the past 50 years and is likely to continue in this region. Soil suitability for major crops is expected to be affected by climate change, in particular, beans, maize, and banana production might face declines and require cropping system transformations (Rippke et al., 2016). The coastal countries of West Africa are also vulnerable to sea level rise resulting from global warming, leading to flooding and coastal erosion. Climate variability and change have affected, and are continuing to affect, land cover in West Africa by changing the amount and timing of water availability to vegetation cover (Figure 41). Land use decision-making responds to these changes in ways that further alter the land cover, from slight modifications of the quality of the land cover to outright transformations of the land cover type (USGS, n.d.).

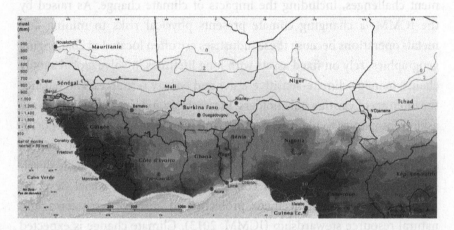

Figure 41: Mean annual rainfall 1981–2014, with number of months of 50 mm or more of rainfall (USGC, n.d.). With permission.

At a glance, in West Africa, the disastrous consequences of climate variability are not just projections. They are also combined with past and the present observations, which show that the living conditions of populations whose subsistence is highly dependent on nature (subsistence agriculture, livestock, fishing, agro forestry, etc.) are becoming more difficult. The repetition of extreme climatic events such as chronic droughts and devastating and deadly floods, the advance of the desert into the Sahelian zone, and the rise in sea level that causes salinization of agricultural land have all contributed to this situation. This context calls for a strong, concerted response between the governments of the countries concerned, the partners, and the private sector, particularly the sector exploiting local natural resource. This approach will make it possible to put in place the measures required to ensure adaptation and resilience to the impacts of climate change.

9.1.2   MINING REALITY IN A CHANGING CLIMATE CONTEXT

The mining industry is beginning to recognize the urgency of climate change (RMI, 2018). This sector faces a number of sustainable development challenges, including the impacts of climate change. As raised by the ICMM, a changing climate presents physical risks to mining and metals operations because these industries are often located in challenging geographies, rely on fixed assets with long lifetimes, involve global supply chains, manage climate-sensitive water and energy resources, and balance the interests of various stakeholders. Increasingly, external stakeholders are asking companies to identify, disclose, and plan for the risks and opportunities presented by a changing climate. By taking steps to adapt, mining and metals companies can also achieve complementary sustainable development goals related to local community engagement, social development, biodiversity enhancement, protection of sensitive ecosystems, and natural resource stewardship (ICMM, 2013). Climate change is expected to cause more frequent droughts and floods, altering the supply of water to mining sites and disrupting operations. A recent analysis by McKinsey on the impacts of water-stress and flooding on copper, gold, iron ore, and zinc found that today, 30 to 50 percent of production of these four commodities is concentrated in areas where water stress is already high. In 2017, these sites accounted for roughly $150 billion in total annual revenues and were clustered into seven water-stress hot spots for mining. Mining regions not accustomed to water stress are projected to become increasingly vulnerable. By 2040, 5 percent of current gold production will likely shift from low-medium water stress to medium-high, 7 percent of zinc production could move from medium-high to high water stress, and 6 percent of copper production could shift from high to extremely high-water stress. Depending on the water intensiveness of the processing approach, such changes, while seemingly minor in percentage terms, could be critical to a mine's operations or license to operate (McKinsey, 2020).

A Business for Social Responsibility (BSR) report emphasized that climatic conditions will affect the stability and effectiveness of infrastructure and equipment, environmental protection and site closure practices, and the availability of transportation routes. Climate change may also impact the stability and cost of water and energy supplies. Warming temperatures will increase water scarcity in some locations, inhibiting water-dependent operations, complicating site rehabilitation and bringing companies into direct conflict with communities for water resources (Business for Social Responsibility, n.d.). This BSR report stated that the mining industry should take a proactive approach to climate adaptation, and highlighted six key issues raised as the top ones within the mining industry: *Disturbance to mine infrastructure and operations, Changing access to supply chains and distribution routes, Challenges to worker health and safety conditions, Challenges to environmental management and mitigation, More pressure points with community relations, and Exploration and future growth.*

A changing climate has also the potential to affect hydroelectric power production through water availability if the estimated basis for design river flow ranges is no longer valid because of shifts in seasonal precipitation patterns. This may indirectly affect the availability and reliability of electricity provided to mining and metals operations (ICMM, 2013). As stated in an IFC and ICMM joint report on this subject, access to water remains one of the biggest global challenges of the 21st century. Growing population, water consumption, pollution, and climate variability are resulting in greater water scarcity, driving competition over water resources and increased conflicts amongst water users. Therefore, many industries face water-related operating risks and capital expenditures that threaten financial performance and even license-to-operate.

9.2 DECARBONIZING THE MINING INDUSTRY

To prevent severe climate change we need to rapidly reduce global greenhouse gas (GHG) emissions. The world emits around 50 billion tonnes of greenhouse gases each year. Figure 42 shows the breakdown of global greenhouse gas emissions in 2016 and highlights that global GHG emissions can be roughly traced back to four broad categories: energy, agriculture, industry, and waste. Almost three-quarters of GHG emissions come from energy consumption (Ritchie, 2020).

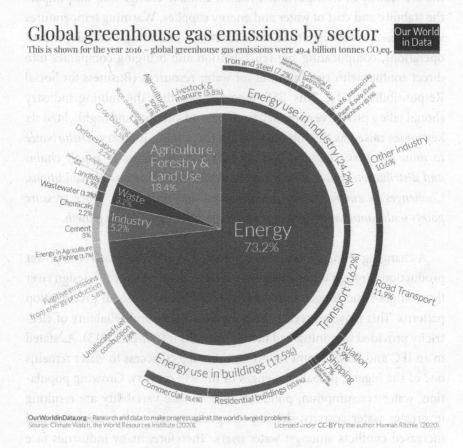

Figure 42: Global greenhouse gas emission by sector (Hanna Ritchie - Our World in Data, 2020).

Under the 2015 Paris Agreement, almost 200 countries pledged to limit global warming to well below 2.0°C, and ideally not more than 1.5°C above preindustrial levels. A report from consultancy McKinsey has raised concerns about the mining industry's climate change and decarbonization strategy, arguing it may not go far enough in reducing emissions in the face of pressure from governments, investors, and activists (IM, 2020).

9.2.1 DRIVERS FOR DECARBONIZING THE MINING INDUSTRY

According to Mckinsey the mining industry generates between 1.9 and 5.1 gigatons of CO_2 equivalent (CO_2eq) of GHG emissions annually. Most emissions in this sector originate from fugitive coal-bed methane that is released during coal mining (1.5 to 4.6 gigatons), mainly at underground operations. Power consumption in the mining industry contributes 0.4 gigaton of CO_2e. Further down the value chain—what could be considered Scope 3 emissions—the metal industry contributes roughly 4.2 gigatons, mainly through steel and aluminum production. Coal combustion for the power sector contributes up to roughly ten gigatons of CO_2. External pressure to decarbonize depends on a mix of factors, including involvement by investors, regulators, and customers. Decarbonization will also vary by geography, segment, and executives' own priorities (McKinsey, 2020).

Although the main drivers for adaptation in mining and metals companies are understanding and managing the implications of a changing climate for their businesses, companies are also responding to the changing expectations of external financial stakeholders in relation to climate risks and other corporate social responsibility and sustainable development considerations. Shareholders and investors are beginning to consider the implications of climate risks for the long-term financial performance of investment companies. Norway's sovereign wealth fund, which manages US\$582.7 billion in assets, offers an example of a large institutional investor assessing the risks of investing in climate-sensitive assets (ICMM, 2013). In his 2021 letter to CEOs, Larry Fink (BlackRock's Chairman and CEO) highlighted that there is no company whose business model will not be profoundly affected by the transition to a net zero economy—one that emits no more carbon dioxide than it removes from the atmosphere—by 2050. He added that "climate risk is investment risk, but we also believe the climate transition presents a historic investment opportunity." BlackRock pushes companies to adopt a 2050 net zero emissions goal and Fink said:

> "Given how central the energy transition will be to every company's growth prospects, we are asking companies to disclose a plan for how their business model will be compatible with a net

zero economy—that is, one where global warming is limited to well below 2°C, consistent with a global aspiration of net zero greenhouse gas emissions by 2050. We are asking you to disclose how this plan is incorporated into your long-term strategy and reviewed by your board of directors" (BlackRock, 2021).

"Any serious effort to implement Paris Agreement goals would require a major contribution from the entire value chain. To stay on track for a global 2°C scenario, all sectors would need to reduce CO_2 emissions from 2010 levels by at least 50 percent by 2050. To limit warming to 1.5°C, a reduction of at least 85 percent would likely be needed" (McKinsey, 2020).

Other authoritative voices from diverse backgrounds have been raised for the cause of climate change and environmental preservation. Among these voices, Pope Francis' encyclical *Laudato Si* (Praise be to you), published in 2015, is a strong challenge to us on the environmental and social issues of our time. With the subtitle "on the safeguarding of the common house," this encyclical is dedicated to environmental and social issues, to integral ecology, and in a general way, to the safeguarding of Creation. The Pope addresses it "to all people of good will," but also "to every person who inhabits this planet," calling them to act quickly and globally. In this encyclical, the Pope insists on the fact that climate change "constitutes one of the main current challenges for humanity" and will primarily affect the poorest and most fragile populations, who will not be able to protect themselves from its consequences. He adds that "the increase in the number of migrants fleeing poverty, increased by environmental degradation, is tragic" (Wikipedia, 2020). Pope Francis advocacy efforts in 2015 anticipated critical convocations of world leaders, including the UN General Assembly's ratification of the Sustainable Development Goals in September 2015, and the UN Climate Change Conference in Paris in December 2015 (Burke, 2016).

9.2.2 DECARBONIZATION LEVERS

As shown in Figure 43, there are several options to reduce on-site emissions from mines. A large proportion of mining industry emissions are driven by electricity supply. For many mining companies, a good first step for carbon reduction is cleaning up their electricity supply. While this may be harder in some regions than others due to regulatory barriers, it is a particularly excellent option for those mines currently powered by on-site diesel generators. It is important for mines to understand their energy security risks and to consider renewables as a possible mitigation (RMI, 2018).

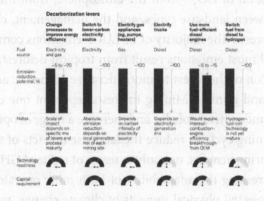

Figure 43: Decarbonization levers for mining (International Council on Clean Energy & McKinsey, 2020). With permission.

Renewable energy, especially achieved through large scale systems, is attractive not just for active mines, but for legacy mines as well. These sites typically have a large amount of unused land that has limited direct economic value, but the mining company must stay engaged with the site during the reclamation process and—assuming the site is grid connected—there is excess transmission capacity to help wheel power away, for which the mine can be compensated. The development of renewable resources offers value in asset conversion by providing a second productive life to a closing mine site (RMI, 2018).

Deforestation and forest degradation account for approximately 11 percent of carbon emissions, more than the entire global transportation sector and second only to the energy sector. It is now clear that in order to constrain the impacts of climate change within limits that society will reasonably be able to tolerate, global average temperatures must be stabilized within two degrees Celsius. This will be practically impossible to achieve without reducing emissions from the forest sector, in addition to other mitigation actions (UN-REDD, 2020). In other words, the reduction of GHG emissions from land use, land-use change, and forestry (LULUCF) need to be fully integrated in any sustainable climate change mitigation strategy, especially in developing countries. LULUCF relates to all emissions, and removal of CO_2—from the atmosphere, from the use of land conversion between land-use types, and the management, clearance and replanting of forests. The majority of LULUCF emissions come from land-use change and most emissions result from tropical deforestation, largely due to conversion of the forest to more lucrative economic activities such as agriculture and mining. Mining interests represent one of the largest private sector landowners globally, and there are a range of options at every stage of the mining cycle to reduce the land-use impacts of this industry. These options bring benefits, not only in terms of reduced GHG emissions, but also in increasing the adaptability of both mine operators and local areas to the projected physical impacts of climate change, reducing environmental impacts on water and biodiversity, and increasing benefits to local communities (ICMM, 2011). For example, Reducing Emissions from Deforestation and forest Degradation (REDD+), developed by Parties to the UNFCCC, is a climate change mitigation mechanism that puts a value on carbon in tropical forests, and is expected to provide Africa with a range of environmental and socio-economic benefits (Gizachew, 2017). The "+" refers to the inclusion of a provision for protection and enhancement of standing carbon stocks (ICMM, 2013). REDD+ creates a financial value for the carbon stored in forests by offering incentives for developing countries to reduce emissions from forested lands, and to invest in low-carbon paths to sustainable development. Developing countries would receive results-based payments for results-based actions. REDD+ goes beyond simply deforestation and forest degradation and includes the role of conservation, sustainable management of forests, and enhancement of forest carbon stocks (UN-REDD, 2020).

9.2.3 DECARBONIZATION OUTLOOK

For the global fight against climate change, China's commitment (September 2020) to achieving carbon neutrality by 2060 provides strong momentum for the world decarbonization journey. This strong commitment also aligns China with a global target of limiting global warming to 1.5°C over this period. China's decarbonization initiatives provide major opportunities to accelerate technology innovation and industrial upgrading, further strengthening its economy. Moreover, the health, quality of life, and well-being of its people are strongly linked with reducing emissions and pollution, securing greater crop yields, avoiding natural disasters, and increasing energy independence. In addition, China is setting an example for others. In the weeks following the announcement, Japan and Korea committed to net zero greenhouse gas (GHG) goals, putting additional pressure on other large carbon emitters to follow suit (BCG, 2020).

In the USA, the Massachusetts Governor Charlie Baker released a plan that mandates all new cars sold in the state be electric by 2035, in addition to other measures to reduce greenhouse gas emissions. The governor's action follows a similar one announced by California governor, which sets the same deadline. Massachusetts' commitment is among the most ambitious pledges by states in the U.S. and the rest of the world. It would bring the state on track to reach net zero fossil-fuel emissions by 2050. "The people of Massachusetts are experiencing record droughts, increased risk of wildfire, severe weather, and flooding in our coastal communities," Baker said in a news release. "The costly impacts of climate change are on display in the Commonwealth, making it critical that we take action" (The Fourth Revolution, 2020).

The recent return of the USA to the Paris Agreements following the election of President Biden opens a new era and adds powerful momentum to the process of decarbonization of the world economy. In Canada, the government released in December 2020 its strategy to dramatically reduce greenhouse gas emissions by 2030, and its centrepiece is a gradual hike in the federal carbon tax on fuels to $170 a ton by that year. Beyond the carbon tax hike, the government is promising $15 billion in new spending on climate initiatives over the next 10 years—money earmarked for improvements to the country's electric vehicle charging infrastructure, rebates and tax write-offs for zero-emissions vehicles, and funding for home retrofits, among dozens of proposed policies. The current $30 tax was already expected to hit $50 a ton in 2022. With this new initiative, the tax will increase by $15 a ton each year for the next eight years in order to wean consumers off fossil fuels in favor of cleaner energy sources (Canadian Broadcasting Corporation, 2020).

The World Gold Council (WGC) has urged the gold mining sector to embrace decarbonization, including switching to renewable electricity generation, in order to meet the Paris Agreement's 1.5°C global warming target. According to WGC, Gold sector emissions need to be reduced by 80% by 2050 to be aligned with the "well-below" 2°C scenario, or 92% by 2040 to align with a 1.5°C scenario outlined in the climate accord (Reuters, 2020). Replacing 45% of both grid power and direct fossil fuel-generated electricity would place the industry on track for the 1.5°C climate target, the WGC found (Reuters, 2020).

- Newmont mining recently committed to meeting an industry-leading climate target of 30% reduction in greenhouse gas (GHG) emissions by 2030, with a goal of becoming net zero carbon by 2050. As a part of this commitment, Newmont will be investing $500 million in climate change initiatives over the next five years, from 2021 through 2025 (Newmont, 2020).
- In its 2020 annual climate change report, Fortescue Metals Group (FMG) announced an industry-leading emissions reduction goal to achieve net zero operational emissions by 2040. This goal is core to FMG's Climate Change Strategy and is underpinned by a pathway to decarbonization, including the reduction of Scope 1 and Scope 2 emissions from existing operations by 26% from 2020 levels, by 2030. FMG has already announced investments and made progress on energy infrastructure projects that support its journey towards reaching its emissions reductions goal by increasing the use of renewable energy. FMG is also working towards decarbonizing its

mining fleet, which generates over 50 percent of its operational emissions, using the next phase of hydrogen and battery electric energy solutions. In addition, green hydrogen production, storage, and use is a key focus for FMG (Fortescue, 2020).

- ArcelorMittal has announced a group-wide commitment to being carbon neutral by 2050, building on the commitment made in 2019 for its European business to reduce emissions by 30% by 2030, and be carbon neutral by 2050. In its Climate Action Report and Europe Climate Action Report, ArcelorMittal refers to three clean energy vectors: clean electricity, circular carbon, and Carbon Capture and Storage. ArcelorMittal is the world's leading steel and mining company, with a presence in 60 countries and primary steelmaking facilities in 18 countries. In 2019, ArcelorMittal had revenues of $70.6 billion and crude steel production of 89.8 million metric tons, while iron ore production reached 57.1 million metric tons (ArcelorMittal, 2019 & 2020).

- On May 2021 the Mining Association of Canada released a new Towards Sustainable Mining (TSM) Climate Change Protocol designed to minimize the mining sector's carbon footprint, while enhancing climate change disclosure and strengthening the sector's ability to adapt to climate change. This Protocol is supported by the publication of the new *"Guide to Climate Change Adaptation for the Mining Sector"*, a comprehensive, first-of-its-kind guidance for the mining sector focused on assessing and identifying potential physical climate impacts, considering these risks in decision-making, and implementing corresponding adaptation measures (Mining Association of Canada, 2021).

- In May 2021, Judge Larisa Alwin, from a court in the Hague has ordered Royal Dutch Shell to cut its global carbon emissions by 45% by 2030 from 2019 levels, in a landmark case brought by Friends of the Earth and over 17,000 co-plaintiffs. The court also ruled that Shell is responsible for emissions from its customers and suppliers, known as scope 3 emissions, and further that Shell's activities constituted a threat to the "right to life" and "undisturbed family life," as set out in the European Convention on Human Rights. According to the Friends of the Earth "This is a turning point in the history. This case is unique because it is the first time a judge has ordered a large polluting corporation to comply with the Paris agreement. This ruling may also have major consequences for other big polluters" (Forbes, 2021; The Guardian, 2021).

- According to a report by the World Bank published in 2020, the energy transition to a low-carbon economy will cause a sharp increase in the demand for minerals (critical and strategic minerals) such as nickel, vanadium, iridium, cobalt, lithium, and graphite. Figure 44 shows anticipated growth, from 2018 to 2050, in the demand for minerals required for the use of technologies with low greenhouse gas (GHG) emissions (World Bank Group, 2020).

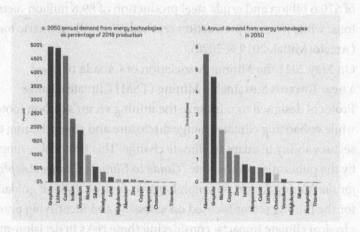

Figure 44: Projected annual mineral demand under 2DS only from energy technologies in 2050, compared to 2018 production levels (World Bank Group, 2020).

In its "Plan for the development of critical and strategic minerals (CSMs)," the Gouvernement du Québec highlights that:

"[...] smart devices and equipment, aerospace, telecommunications, renewable energy, energy storage, the medical sector, and transportation electrification are all high-growth sectors in which the supply of CSMs is vital. CSMs play an important role in our daily lives. They are found in many everyday objects: consider the graphite, lithium, cobalt, and nickel necessary to make batteries for laptop computers, smartphones, and electric vehicles; platinum group elements are used in computer hard drives; rare earth elements are found in electric motors. The demand for CSMs is growing strongly and supply is becoming a strategic issue for many companies and states." (Gouvernement du Québec, 2020).

The Gouvernement du Québec considers that critical minerals, which have economic importance in key sectors of our economy today, present a high supply risk, and have no commercially available substitutes. It also defines strategic minerals as those necessary to implement Québec's various economic policies. The accessibility and availability of these mineral resources thus have a growing impact on political, commercial, and economic relations between the major world powers.

For the same strategic and geopolitical reasons set out by Quebec, West Africa will have to make the exploitation and local valorization of its critical and strategic minerals a regional priority, and a lever for its transition towards green energies and technologies. Such an approach will be an incubator for a new green industry with high added value, thanks to the local production of finished or semi-finished products resulting from the enhanced valuation of critical and strategic minerals of the sub-region.

Obviously, this global transition towards green energy and rapid decarbonization holds significant potential for Africa's extractive sector. One of these opportunities lies in the growing demand globally for lithium, which is used in batteries for electric vehicles, smartphones, and off-grid energy storage. Therefore, African mining companies will need to lead the way in decarbonization of their operations and transition to clean energy to attract "green funds" (African Review, 2020). This is all the truer since African mineral resources are still under-explored and the industrialization of a large part of the continent is still embryonic compared to its immense potential. Consequently, Africa's contribution to global GHG emissions is still marginal, and the decarbonization of the local mining industry should come from the development of the immense renewable energy potential of the continent (solar, wind, hydroelectricity...). The continent's other challenge will be to prevent an increase in its GHG emissions with the upcoming acceleration of the exploitation of mining resources and progressive local industrialization. In order not to copy the model of Western economies whose industrial development has been based mainly on the use of fossil fuels, Africa must resolutely position itself as the new Eldorado of the green economy and adopt a neutral or low-carbon industrial strategy. Momentum is currently good, the technologies exist, and progressive innovation and optimization of existing precedents will make them more efficient and affordable.

As highlighted by the Task Force on Climate-related Financial Disclosures (TCDF), Mining is a carbon intensive industry. For CEOs in the mining industry who have not yet initiated a deep assessment of their climate-related risks, it might be the right time to include climate issues within the sustainability journey of their companies. They might start by initiating a Climate Change Focus Group with C-Level executives, including the chief sustainability officer, the chief finance officer, the chief operating officer, and the corporate's Enterprise Risk Management (ERM) owner, to not only assess material climate risks, but also to capture the significant opportunities that are arising with the beginning of the world decarbonization era. The results of such an approach could be particularly fruitful, and will likely point to the need for a corporate energy strategy that will serve as a frame of reference that points toward an unavoidable and profound transition towards green, or lower, carbon footprint energy as compared to the status quo. Such an energy transition seems to be a crucial prerequisite for the mining industry to meet the Paris targets.

The decarbonization of the developing countries must be prevented from translating into the transfer of polluting technologies to Africa. Such an approach would improve the carbon footprint of one part of the world but would not have a positive impact on the global effort to meet the Paris targets. A trend of pollution transfer is increasingly seen with the shipment to Africa of the used car fleets from some Western countries, because of the gradual arrival of electric vehicles in Western markets. To avoid a drift like this, it would be relevant to ensure that new mines and other upcoming industrial projects in Africa use the Best Green Technologies

Economically Available. The world, Africa and the mining industry cannot afford for this continent, which is facing the full impact of climate change, to miss the global decarbonization's wave and the green economy boom.

Let us not be afraid to face the challenges of climate change and capitalize on the new opportunities associated with it. Indeed, by focusing only on the risks and constraints that inhibit us and make us wear blinders, we often miss great business opportunities. It is therefore important to constantly keep in mind that next to each risk, there is an opportunity that is just waiting to be exploited.

CONCLUSION

As highlighted in this book, it is now obvious that challenges related to sustainable development are nowhere more relevant than in the natural resource sector, especially in Africa. From Guinea to Burkina Faso and Nigeria, from Democratic Republic of Congo to Mali, Angola, Ivory Coast, and Senegal, the African continent is rich in mineral resources, and the continent's potential remains under-explored. In this context, the continent's beautiful, serious, and pressing challenge is to ensure that the exploitation of its immense natural resources takes place in compliance with the best international standards in terms of sustainable development and transparent management, so that the wealth created can contribute to the significant improvement of living conditions for the populations of the host countries, while ensuring the attractiveness and competitiveness vis-à-vis other major mining regions. The mining industry obviously has a central role to play in this dynamic. The extractive industry has a more than unprecedented opportunity to contribute to achieving the Sustainable Development Goals through strong corporate sustainability strategies deeply embedded in corporate culture and the creation of shared value principles. Furthermore, the business case for sustainability has shown that only this approach can ensure long-term total shareholder returns while maximizing the total social impacts of the extractive industry.

One of the main challenges will be to avoid inequitable implementation of good sustainable development practices, with high standards for developed countries and second-hand standards, or even the absence of standards for some poor countries, which are often characterized by fragile institutions and embryonic governance. This is not desirable, acceptable, or fair, and would not be in the interest of host countries, nor

199

in the interest of investors, let alone the extractive industry. One of the best strategies to prevent or fill a potential North-South gap is to build the capacity of local human capital in all disciplines related to the mining value chain. This approach, which must include both mining employees and government officials in charge of the extractive industry, must be robust and cover disciplines as varied as governance, stakeholder management, community development, management, taxation, good practices in the extractive industry, and so on.

This document has been built around the notion of value creation, which is its main thread. And the value created can only be socially, ethically, and financially sustainable when it is shared in a respectful and equitable manner among stakeholders in the value chain, particularly with the most vulnerable stakeholders who are most affected by the direct impacts of mining operations. It is always within this logic of value creation that the question of local valorization of mining resources is increasingly raised from an international equity perspective. It is from this perspective that the author highlights the immense assets of the sub-region, particularly in terms of high-grade iron ore reserves, to envisage the future positioning of West Africa as a new continental and global hub in terms of production of high-grade iron ore and its local processing into steel to meet the continent's needs, as well as a part of the global demand. Of course, this transformation will have to be done in the context of progressive de-carbonization of the mining and steel industries in connection with the global problem of climate change, the negative consequences of which are already severely affecting vulnerable populations in West Africa. This new global movement towards the decarbonization of the world economy provides excellent momentum for the West African sub-region, which must take advantage of it to strongly position itself as a hub of the green economy, and thus attract the billions of dollars that will soon be invested in low-carbon projects. Once again, the sub-regional mining industry will have a crucial role to play in the success or failure of this positioning.

For interested corporate executives, operational managers, and sustainability practitioners, this essay could provide useful tools, strategies, best practices, and a roadmap to build, strengthen, or realign the sustainability journey of their organizations, while helping to give investors the whole picture of the risks and opportunities related to sustainability as they make their investment decisions. Therefore, my biggest hope is that this work will set a new level of corporate sustainability strategies within the extractive sector in West Africa, around Africa, and globally. Indeed, even though this work focuses mainly on the West African sub-region, most of the principles presented in this document are universal in scope, or at least can be adapted to all contexts.

Nevertheless, it must be acknowledged that the implementation of good sustainable development practices in the mining industry is an ongoing process, and its level of maturity varies across the globe. Thus, this process is improving, adjusting, readjusting itself, with visions and approaches that are sometimes different, and even contradictory depending on schools of thought.

An exciting and rich debate is therefore open on this subject, and this essay, which is far from being exhaustive, and which is open to criticism, is intended to be a modest contribution to this beautiful conversation that can be likened to a multicolored garden in which the cross-pollination of ideas forges robust and agile strategies that will enable the mining industry to position itself as a key pillar in the global transition to a green economy. Of course, from this perspective, no voice, however weak, should be ignored, as mining development can only be sustainable if it is fully inclusive. Therefore, the conversion about sustainable development in the mining industry will have to be a forum that serves as a resonant box for all voices that might be inaudible in the hubbub of dominant, and sometimes overwhelming, voices.

Hopefully, the extractive industry has a good understanding of the challenges and opportunities related to the new sustainability trends. With strong and high-level leadership and vision associated with available tools and skills, there is no doubt that the extractive industry will be able to face the challenges related to its sustainability journey and take advantage of the huge opportunities available to translate African resources into revenues, and those revenues into sustainable development outcomes and shared benefits, for both shareholders and stakeholders.

With that thought in mind, let us not forget that yesterday has already passed and tomorrow will be too late. The time for action is *here*, and *today*. Let us walk the talk. Let us unlock our shared value, for ourselves and for future generations!

REFERENCES

Accenture. (2013). "The UN Global Compact-Accenture CEO Study on Sustainability 2013." Accenture Sustainability Services. news events/8.1/ UNGC Accenture CEO Study 2013.pdf (d306pr3pise04h.cloudfront.net) (Accessed 7th May, 2019).

African Centre for Democracy and Human Rights Studies - ACDHR. (2017). "Resolution on the Protection of Sacred Natural Sites and Territories." https://www.acdhrs.org/wp-content/uploads/2017/07/Resolution-on-the-Protection-of-Sacred-Natural-Sites-and-Territories.pdf (Accessed 14th October, 2020).

Addison, T., and Roe, A. (2018). Extractive Industries: The Management of Resources as a Driver of Sustainable Development. WIDER Studies in Development Economics. Oxford University Press. Creative Commons license CCBYNCSA 3.0 IGO http://fdslive.oup.com/www.oup.com/academic/pdf/openaccess/9780198817369.pdf (Accessed 8th September, 2019).

African Development Bank (AfDB) & Bill & Melinda Gates Foundation (BMGF). (2015) "Creating local content for human development in Africa's new natural resource-rich countries." https://www.afdb.org/fileadmin/uploads/afdb/Documents/Publications/Creating local content for human development in Africa's new natural resource-rich countries.pdf (Accessed 24th June, 2020).

African Development Bank (AfDB) & Bill & Melinda Gates Foundation (BMGF). (2015b): "Leveraging extractive industries for skills development to maximize sustainable growth and employment." https://www.afdb.org/fileadmin/uploads/afdb/Documents/Publications/Leveraging extractive industries for skills development to maximize sustainable growth and employment.pdf Accessed 24th June, 2020).

Africa Intelligence. (2018). "OECD calls on Sahel Alliance to acknowledge artisanal mining in its programs to improve regional security." https://www.africaintelligence.com/ama/small-scale-mining/2018/10/23/oecd-calls-on-sahel-alliance-to-acknowledge-artisanal-mining-in-its-programs-to-improve-regional-security,108329112-bre (Accessed 15th September, 2019).

Africa Progress Panel. (2013). "Equity in Extractives—Africa Progress Report 2013: Stewarding Africa's natural resources for all." relatorio-africa-progress-report-2013-pdf-20130511-125153.pdf (reliefweb.int) (Accessed 10th November, 2018).

African Review. (2020, December 23). "Green energy and decarbonization: an opportunity for African Mining." https://www.africanreview.com/energy-a-power/oil-a-gas/green-energy-and-decarbonisation-an-opportunity-for-african-mining (Accessed 19th January, 2021).

Agence Ecofin. (2018, October 19). "L'orpaillage en Afrique de l'Ouest : des milliards de dollars incontrôlables." https://www.agenceecofin.com/hebdop2/1910-61006-l-orpaillage-en-afrique-de-l-ouest-des-milliards-de-dollars-incontrolables (Accessed 13th April, 2019).

Agence Ecofin. (2021). Emiliano Tossou. ArcelorMittal veut lancer l'extension de son projet de fer au Liberia, pour une entrée en production en 2023. ArcelorMittal veut lancer l'extension de son projet de fer au Liberia, pour une entrée en production en 2023 (agenceecofin.com).(Accessed 26th May, 2021).

Ajayi J. A., Adegbite M. A., Iyanda A. R. (n.d.). "Sustainable iron and steel production in Nigeria: the techno-economic backbone of the national development." (B1-1.MAINPAPER-Steel for Sustainable Development-AdeAjayi.pdf (midwestind.com) (Accessed 11th October, 2020).

Alo Advisors. (2020). https://www.aloadvisors.com/our-work/ (Accessed 17th November, 2020).

Angloamerican. (n.d.). "Our sustainability strategy FutureSmart Mining™: Our blueprint for the future of our business." https://www.angloamerican.com/~/media/Files/A/Anglo-American-PLC-V2/documents/approach-and-policies/our-blueprint-for-the-future-of-sustainable-mining.pdf (Accessed 13th November, 2020).

ArcelorMittal. (2018). "Our Operations." https://liberia.arcelormittal.com/who-we-are/our-operations.aspx (Accessed 10th September, 2020).

ArcelorMittal. (2019). "Climate Action Report." https://corporatemedia.arcelor-mittal.com/media/hs4nmyya/am_climateactionreport_1.pdf (Accessed 19th November, 2020).

ArcelorMittal. (2020, September 30). "ArcelorMittal sets 2050 group carbon emissions target of net zero." ArcelorMittal sets 2050 group carbon emissions target of net zero | ArcelorMittal (Accessed 10th May, 2021).

Argus. (2020, August 30). Rio Tinto restarts Simandou iron ore project. https://www.argusmedia.com/en/news/2136984-rio-tinto-restarts-simandou-iron-ore-project (Accessed 13th November, 2020).

Atteh, O. D. 1989. Indigenous Local Knowledge as Key to Local-Level Development: Possibilities, Constraints and Planning Issues in the Context of Africa. Seminar on reviving local self-reliance: challenges for rural/regional development in eastern and southern Africa. Unpublished.

Australia Mining. (2018, December 7). Ewen Hosie - "License to operate emerges as biggest concern for mining." https://www.australianmining.com.au/news/licence-to-operate-emerges-as-biggest-concern-for-mining/ (Accessed 17th January, 2019).

Boston Consulting Group - BCG. (2020, December 14). Baiping Chen, Lars Fæste, Rune Jacobsen, Ming Teck Kong, Dylan Lu, and Thomas Palme -"How China Can Achieve Carbon Neutrality by 2060." https://www.bcg.com/publications/2020/how-china-can-achieve-carbon-neutrality-by-2060 (Accessed 26th January, 2021).

BlackRock (2021). "Larry Fink's 2021 letter." Larry Fink CEO Letter | BlackRock (Accessed 14th April, 2021).

Bloomberg (2020, December 17). Jennifer Surane -"Citi Warns of 'Meaningful' Increase in Loan Losses on Carbon Tax." Citi Warns of 'Meaningful' Increase in Loan Losses on Carbon Tax - Bloomberg (Accessed 17th January, 2021).

Boko M., Niang I., Nyong A., Vogel C., Githeko A., Medany M., Osman-Elasha B., Tabo R., Yanda P. (2007). Africa. "Climate Change 2007: Impacts, Adaptation and Vulnerability." Contribution of Working Group II to the Fourth Assessment Report of the Intergovernmental Panel on Climate Change; Parry M. L., Canziani O. F., Palutikof J. P., van der Linden P. J., Hanson C. E. (eds). Cambridge University Press. Cambridge UK. pp. 433 – 467.

Bonini, S., Goerner, S. (2011). "The Business of Sustainability: McKinsey Global Survey Results." McKinsey & Company.

Bower, J. L., Paine, L. S. (2017). "Managing for the long term. The Error at the Heart of Corporate Leadership." Harvard Business Review - May–June 2017 issue (pp.50–60). https://hbr.org/2017/05/the-error-at-the-heart-of-corporate-leadership (Accessed 17th December, 2018).

Business for Social Responsibility - BSR. (2019). "Five-Step Approach to Stakeholder Engagement." https://www.bsr.org/en/our-insights/report-view/stakeholder-engagement-five-step-approach-toolkit (Accessed 5th August, 2020.

Business for Social Responsibility - BSR. (n.d.). "Adapting to Climate Change: A Guide for the Mining Industry." https://www.bsr.org/reports/BSR_Climate_Adaptation_Issue_Brief_Mining.pdf (Accessed 17th November, 2020).

Burke, I. (2016). "The Impact of Laudato Si' on the Paris Climate Agreement – White paper." LaudatoSi.org - Climate Change (Accessed 26th November, 2020).

Buxton A., Wilson, E. (2013). "FPIC and the Extractive Industries: A guide to applying the spirit of free, prior and informed consent in industrial projects". International Institute for Environment and Development, London. https://pubs.iied.org/sites/default/files/pdfs/migrate/16530IIED.pdf (Accessed 14th July, 2019).

Cameron, Peter D., Stanley, Michael C. (2017). Oil, Gas, and Mining: A Sourcebook for Understanding the Extractive Industries. Washington, DC: World Bank. doi:10.1596/978-0-8213-9658-2. License: Creative Commons Attribution CC BY 3.0 IGO

CECP. (2016). "Investing with Purpose—A Pilot Study." cecp_iwp_interactive_Final.pdf (Accessed 20th February, 2019).

Canadian Institute of Mining Metallurgy and Petroleum - CIM. (2014). "CIM Definition Standards for Mineral Resources & Mineral Reserves." https://mrmr.cim.org/media/1128/cim-definition-standards_2014.pdf (Accessed 13th November, 2020).

Bloomberg. (2020, December 17). Jennifer Surane "Citi Warns of 'Meaningful' Increase in Loan Losses on Carbon Tax." Citi Warns of 'Meaningful' Increase in Loan Losses on Carbon Tax - Bloomberg (Accessed 7th January, 2021).

Coller, P., Ireland, G. (2015). "Shared-Use Mining Infrastructure: Why It Matters and How to Achieve it." https://milkeninstitute.org/sites/default/files/reports-pdf/Shared-Use-Mining-Infrastrucure.pdf (Accessed 27th November, 2020).

Columbia Center for Sustainable Investment. (2014). "Local Content in Nigeria." http://ccsi.columbia.edu/files/2017/07/Local-Content_Nigeria_May2014.pdf (Accessed 8th March, 2020).

Columbia Center for Sustainable Investment. (2019). "Local Content in Burkina Faso Mining." http://ccsi.columbia.edu/files/2017/07/Local-Content-Burkina-Mining-CCSI-July-2019.pdf (Accessed 8th March, 2020).

Crowson, P. (2020). Mineral Economics and resources policy. Centre for Energy, Petroleum and Mineral Law and Policy. University of Dundee.

Davidson, A. (2016). "Why are corporations hoarding trillions?" Why Are Corporations Hoarding Trillions? - The New York Times (nytimes.com)

De Nederlandsche Bank (2020). "Indebted to nature." Indebted to nature (dnb.nl). (Accessed 10th April 2021).

De Haan, Jorden, Dales, Kirsten, McQuilken, James. (2020). "Mapping Artisanal and Small-Scale Mining to the Sustainable Development Goals." Newark DE: University of Delaware (Minerals, Materials and Society program in partnership with PACT). Available online via http://www.pactworld.org and https://sites.udel.edu/ceoe-mms/. (Accessed 10th January 2021)

Deloitte & Touche. (2011). "Positioning for mineral beneficiation. Opportunity knocks." http://deloitteblog.co.za/wp-content/uploads/2012/08/Positioning-for-mineral-beneficiation.pdf. (Accessed 5th January 2021)

Driving Sustainable Decisions. (2018). "Decomposition tools – workbook." https://www.moresustainabledecisions.com/decomposition (Accessed 15th November, 2018).

Eckerle, K., Whelan, T., DeNeve, B., Bhojani, S., Platko, J., Wisniewski, R. (2020). "Using the Return on Sustainability Investment (ROSI) Framework to Value Accelerated Decarbonization." JACF-ROSI-20202305843009215927245.pdf (aloadvisors.com) (Accessed 5th January 2021)

Ernst & Young. (2018). "Top 10 business risks facing mining and metals in 2019-2020." Metal Mining paper May2012 (ey.com) (Accessed 15th November, 2019).

European Commission. (2019). "Guidelines on reporting climate-related information". Guidelines on reporting climate-related information (europa.eu) (Accessed 10 June, 2021).

Extractive Industry Transparency Initiative. (2018). "EITI and opportunities for increasing local content transparency." https://eiti.org/files/documents/

brief on eiti and local content transparency - formatted.pdf. (Accessed 30th April, 2020)

Extractive Industry Transparency Initiative. (2020). "Burkina Faso." https://eiti. org/burkina-faso. https://eiti.org/burkina-faso. (Accessed 30th April, 2020)

F&C Asset Management. (2004). "Is biodiversity a material risk?" F&C BIODIVERSITY Report A-W-G (businessandbiodiversity.org) (Accessed 18th January 2021)

Few R., Ahern, M., Matthies, F., Kovats, S. (2004). "Floods, health and climate change: a strategic review." Working Paper No. 63. Tyndall Centre for Climate Change Research

Finance for Biodiversity (2021). Finance-for-Biodiversity Guide-on-biodiversity-measurement-approaches.pdf (Accessed 30th April, 2021)

Financial Afrique. (2020, November 21). Cheikhna Bounajim Cissé – Autopsie des programmes du FMI en Afrique (4) : la lutte contre la pauvreté, du rêve de chœur au crève-cœur. Autopsie des programmes du FMI en Afrique (4): la lutte contre la pauvreté, du rêve de chœur au crève-cœur | Financial Afrik (Accessed 23th January 2021. Translation by the author)

Financial Expats. (2017, May 11). "The benefits of taking an expat mining job in Africa." The benefits of taking an expat mining job in Africa https://expatfi-nancial.com/the-benefits-of-taking-expat-mining-job-in-africa/   (Accessed 16th April, 2020)

Financial Times. (2015, January 29). Neil Hume - "Cost curves." https://www. ft.com/content/678f78f8-a714-11e4-8a71-00144feab7de   (Accessed 27th September, 2020)

Forbes. (2018, September 17). Denis T. Whalen - "ESG Matters... Now What?" https://www.forbes.com/sites/kpmg/2018/09/17/esg-matters-now-what/#4923085f3989 (Accessed 6th October, 2019)

Forbes. (2021, May 26). David Vetter - 'Monumental Victory': Shell Oil Ordered To Limit Emissions In Historic Climate Court Case. https://www.forbes. com/sites/davidrvetter/2021/05/26/shell-oil-verdict-could-trigger-a-wave-of-climate-litigation-against-big-polluters/?sh=506058e61a79   (Accessed 28 June, 2021).

Fortescue Metals Group. (2020). "FY20 Climate Change Report." fy20-climate-change-report.pdf (fmgl.com.au) (Accessed 3rd March, 2021)

Fortescue Metals Group. (2018). "Fortescue Metals Group FY18 Results." Full Year Financial Results (FY2018) Corporate Presentation FINAL (fmgl.com. au) (Accessed 22nd November, 2020)

Forum intergouvernemental sur l'exploitation minière, les minéraux, les métaux et le développement durable (IGF). (2016). "Évaluation du cadre directif pour l'exploitation minière : Sénégal." Winnipeg: IISD. https://www.iisd.org/ system/files/publications/senegal-mining-policy-framework-assessment-fr. pdf (Accessed 14th November, 2020)

Franks, D. M. (2015). *Mountain Movers: Mining, Sustainability and the Agents of Change*. London: Routledge.

Freeman R.E.; Harrison J.E.; Hicks, A.; Parmar B.; and De Colle, S. (2010). The Stakeholder Theory – The State Of Art. Published in the United States of America by Cambridge University Press, New York

Gbaguidi, J. P. (2020). "Coaching. Module développement de stratégies de carrière. Expert formateur international certifie CEGOS. lecoleducoach.net." Unpublished. joelgbaguidi@gmail.com

Gizachew, B., Astrup, R., Vedeld, P., Zahabu, M. L., Duguma, L. A. (2017). "REDD+ in Africa: contexts and challenges." Natural Resources Forum 2017. DOI: 10.1111/1477-8947.12119. REDD+ in Africa: Contexts and Challenges: (cgiar.org) (Accessed 23th November, 2020)

Global Reporting Initiative. (2013a). "Sustainability topics for sectors: What do stakeholders want to know?" https://www.globalreporting.org/resourcelibrary/ sustainability-topics.pdf.

Reuter (2020, December 9). Jeff Lewis and Helen Reid - "Gold miners must ramp up renewable energy to meet climate goals: industry group"Gold miners must ramp up renewable energy to meet climate goals: industry group | Reuters (Accessed 16th February, 2021)

Clark, G., Feiner, A., Viehs, M. (2015). "From the stockholder to the stakeholder. How sustainability can drive financial outperformance." https://arabesque. com/research/From the stockholder to the stakeholder web.pdf (Accessed 13th September, 2019)

Gouvernement du Québec. (2020). "Critical and strategic minerals Québec plan for the development of critical and strategic minerals 2020-2025." Québec Plan for the Development of Critical and Strategic Minerals 2020-2025 (quebec.ca) (Accessed 27th February, 2021)

Gouvernement du Québec. (2020). "Loi sur les Mines." http://legisquebec.gouv.qc.ca/fr/pdf/cs/M-13.1.pdf (Accessed 27th February, 2021)

Government of Australia. (2016). "Community engagement and development Leading Practice Sustainable Development Program for the Mining Industry." https://www.industry.gov.au/sites/default/files/2019-04/lpsdp-community-engagement-and-development-handbook-english.pdf (Accessed 17th September, 2019)

Government of Canada. (2019). "Iron ore facts." https://www.nrcan.gc.ca/our-natural-resources/minerals-mining/iron-ore-facts/20517 (Accessed 18thNovember, 2020)

Government of British Columbia (2014, August 4). Mount Polley Mine Tailing Dam Breach. Mount Polley Mine Tailing Dam Breach - Province of British Columbia (gov.bc.ca) (Accessed 28 June, 2021).

Global Reporting Initiative. (2021). Materiality and topic boundary. Materiality and topic boundary (globalreporting.org) (Accessed 26 June, 2021).

The Guardian. (2021, May 26). Daniel Boffey – Court oderders Royal Dutch Shell to cut carbon emission by 45% by 2030. https://www.theguardian.com/business/2021/may/26/court-orders-royal-dutch-shell-to-cut-carbon-emissions-by-45-by-2030 (Accessed 28 June, 2021).

Harvard Kennedy School & Saudi Arabian General Investment Authority. (2008). Corporate Social Responsibility (CSR) in Saudi Arabia and globally: Key challenges, opportunities and best practices. SAGIA Leadership Dialogue Report 1.16.09 (harvard.edu) (Accessed 21 June, 2021).

Hazoume, Yann. (2020). "'Repats' : 7 conseils pour un retour réussi." https://yannhazoume.com/repats-7-conseils-pour-un-retour-reussi/. (Accessed 3rd April 2020)

Heifer International. (2014). Carol Moore – Corporate Social Responsibility and Creating Shared Value: What's the Difference? 20140529_154810_12047.pdf (ymaws.com) (Accessed 7 February, 2019).

Henisz, W.J., Dorobantu, S., Nartey, L. (2011). "Spinning Gold: The Financial Returns to External Stakeholder Engagement." January 2011. Strategic Management Journal 35(12) DOI:10.1002/smj.2180. https://business.illinois.edu/business-administration/wp-content/uploads/sites/39/2014/09/henisz_paper.pdf (Accessed 19th September, 2019)

REFERENCES

High Power Exploration - HPX. (2019). "Nimba." https://www.hpxploration.com/projects/nimba/ (Accessed 15th November, 2020)

Hocking, J., Michelle, B., Harzing, A. W. (2007). "Balancing global and local strategic contexts: Expatriate knowledge transfer, applications, and learning within a transnational organization." https://www.researchgate.net/publication/227561593_Balancing_global_and_local_strategic_contexts_Expatriate_knowledge_transfer_applications_and_learning_within_a_transnational_organization. (Accessed 17th March, 2020)

Hubbard, D. (2014). *How to Measure Anything: Finding the Value of Intangibles in Business, Third Edition.* Wiley, 3rd edition (March 17, 2014). https://www.howtomeasureanything.com/books-by-douglas-hubbard/ (Accessed 17th November, 2018)

International Association for Public Participation - IAP2 (2018). "IAP2 spectrum of public participation." Spectrum_8.5x11_Print_(ymaws.com) (Accessed 24th October, 2020)

International Council on Mining and Metals – ICMM. (2006). "Good Practice Guidance for Mining and Biodiversity." ICM0001 (icmm.com) (Accessed 2nd November, 2020).

International Council on Mining and Metals - ICMM. (2011). "The role of mining and metals in land use and adaptation." https://www.icmm.com/website/publications/pdfs/climate-change/land-use-and-adaptation (Accessed 2nd November, 2020).

International Council on Mining and Metals – ICMM. (2013). Adapting to a changing climate: implications for the mining and metals industry http://www.icmm.com/website/publications/pdfs/climate-change/adapting-to-climate-change (Accessed 2nd November, 2020).

International Council on Mining and Metals – ICMM. (n.d.). Land acquisition and resettlement: Lessons learned. ICMM-Resettlement-pr8-hi-res-links.pdf (commdev.org) (Accessed 16th September, 2020).

Inglis. J. (1993). Traditional ecological knowledge concepts and cases. Canadian Museum of Nature / IDRC. (PDF) Traditional Ecological Knowledge: Concepts and Cases (researchgate.net) (Accessed 17th September, 2020).

International Energy Agency (2019). "Africa Energy Outlook 2019." IEA, Paris https://www.iea.org/reports/africa-energy-outlook-2019. Africa Energy Outlook 2019 – Analysis - IEA (Accessed 16th September, 2020).

International Finance Corporation – IFC. (2006). "Performance Standard 6 Biodiversity Conservation and Sustainable Natural Resource." Management.https://www.ifc.org/wps/wcm/connect/992a4e23-304f-43cc-945c-8dd3326a95b5/PS_6_BiodivConservation.pdf?MOD=AJPERES&CVID=jqewQEI (Accessed 24th November, 2020).

International Finance Corporation – IFC. (2007). "Stakeholder's engagement. A Good Practice Handbook for Companies Doing Business in Emerging Markets." https://www.ifc.org/wps/wcm/connect/affbc005-2569-4e58-9962-280c483baa12/IFC_StakeholderEngagement.pdf?MOD=AJPERES&CVID=jkD13-p (Accessed 28th July, 2020).

International Finance Corporation – IFC. (2012). "Performance Standard 5 – Land acquisition and involuntary resettlement." https://www.ifc.org/wps/wcm/connect/75de96d4-ed36-4bdb-8050-400be02bf2d9/PS5_English_2012.pdf?MOD=AJPERES&CVID=jqex59b (Accessed 15th March, 2020).

International Finance Corporation – IFC. (2012a). IFC Performance Standard 8 - Cultural Heritage. Section 1: Purpose of this Policy (ifc.org) (Accessed 24th November, 2020).

International Finance Corporation – IFC. (2012b). "Guidance Note 8 – Cultural heritage." https://www.ifc.org/wps/wcm/connect/cce98f3d-f59e-488f-be59-6456c87d3366/Updated_GN8-2012.pdf?MOD=AJPERES&CVID=mRQk91V (Accessed 24th November, 2020).

International Finance Corporation – IFC. (2014). "Sustainable and Responsible Mining in Africa. A getting started guide." https://www.ifc.org/wps/wcm/connect/dfaac38043fea19b8f90bf869243d457/Sustainable+Mining+in+Africa.pdf?MOD=AJPERES (Accessed 17th June, 2020).

International Finance Corporation – IFC. (n.d.). "A Guide to Biodiversity for the Private Sector." Mining.cdr (ifc.org) (Accessed 24th November, 2020).

International Finance Corporation – IFC. (n.d.). "IFC Handbook for preparing a resettlement action plan." http://documents1.worldbank.org/curated/en/492791468153884773/pdf/246740PUB0REPL020020Box12600PUBLIC0.pdf (Accessed 18th June, 2020).

International Finance Corporation, ICMM, Brunswick. (2013). "Changing the game – Communication & Sustainability in the mining sector." https://www.commdev.org/pdf/publications/

Changing-the-game-communications-and-sustainability-in-the-mining-industry.pdf (Accessed 15th June, 2019).

International Finance Corporation – IFC. (2012). "Cultural Heritage." https://www.ifc.org/wps/wcm/connect/topics_ext_content/ifc_external_corporate_site/sustainability-at-ifc/policies-standards/performance-standards/ps8 (Accessed 24th November, 2020).

International Labor Organization. (2012). Current and future skills, human resources development and safety training for contractors in the oil and gas industry: Issues paper for discussion at the Global Dialogue Forum on Future Needs for Skills and Training in the Oil and Gas Industry, Geneva, 12–13 December 2012/International Labour Office, Sectoral Activities Department. Geneva, ILO, 2012. http://www.ilo.org/wcmsp5/groups/public/---ed_dialogue/---sector/documents/meetingdocument/wcms_190707.pdf (Accessed 20 June, 2021).

International Institute for Sustainable Development & Intergovernmental Forum. (2018). "Local content policies in mining - Stimulating direct local employment." https://www.iisd.org/sites/default/files/publications/local-content-policies-mining-direct-local-employment.pdf. (Accessed 17th May, 2019).

International Council on Mine and Metals - ICMM. (n.d.). "Working Together— How large scale mining can engage with artisanal and small-scale miners." Working together: How large-scale mining can engage with artisanal and small-scale miners - CommDev (Accessed 27th November, 2019).

International Finance Corporations - IFC. (2014). "Sustainable and Responsible Mining in Africa—A getting started." Sustainable+Mining+in+Africa.pdf (ifc.org) (Accessed 27th November, 2019).

International Mining. (2020, January 29). Daniel Gleeson - "Miners need to do more in climate change, decarbonization battle, McKinsey says". Miners need to do more in climate change, decarbonisation battle, McKinsey says - International Mining (im-mining.com) (Accessed 13th July, 2020).

International Council on Mining and Metals, IFC, World Bank, CommDev, and ASM. (2010). Working Together. How large-scale mining can engage with artisanal and small-scale miners. Working Together 8x11 (icmm.com) (Accessed 13 July, 2019).

International Petroleum Industry Environmental Conservation Association - IPIECA. (2017). "Creating successful, sustainable social investment. Guidance document for the oil and gas industry." Guide to successful, sustainable social investment for the oil and gas industry | IPIECA (Accessed 26th June, 2019).

Initiative for Responsible Mining Assurance - IRMA. (2018). "IRMA Standard for Responsible Mining." https://responsiblemining.net/wp-content/uploads/2018/07/IRMA_STANDARD_v.1.0_FINAL_2018-1.pdf (Accessed 18th July, 2020).

Initiative pour la transparence dans les industries extractives - ITIE Sénégal (2020a). "Aperçu du secteur." https://itie.sn/apercu-du-secteur/ (Accessed 14th December, 2020).

Initiative pour la transparence dans les industries extractives - ITIE Sénégal (2020b). Protocole d'accord entre le Gouvernement du Sénégal et la Société Tosyali Holding (Turquie) pour la réalisation d'un complexe minier et sidérurgique au Sénégal. Protocol-daccord-signé-avec-TOSYALI.pdf (itie.sn). (Accessed 26th May 2021).

International Work Group for Indigenous Affairs - IWGIA (2017). Extractive Industries, Land Rights and Indigenous Populations'/Communities' Rights. https://www.iwgia.org/images/documents/extractive-industries-africa-report.pdf

Jeune Afrique. (2019, December 11). Fadi Wazni - "SMB-Winning : Au Simandou le principal défi est logistique." https://www.jeuneafrique.com/mag/866722/economie/fadi-wazni-smb-winning-au-simandou-le-principal-defi-est-logis-tique/ (Accessed 28th August, 2020).

Kemp, D., Owen, J. R. (2013). Community relations and mining: Core to business but not "core business." Resource Policy - Volume 38, Issue 4, December 2013, Pages 523-531.

Kgoale, P. T., Odeku, K. O. (2019). "Transformative mineral resources ben-eficiation intervention fostering local entrepreneurship in south Africa." https://www.abacademies.org/articles/Transformative-mineral-resources-beneficiation-intervention-fostering-local-1528-2686-25-2-239.pdf (Accessed 17th October 2020).

Kirk, T., Lund, J. (2018) "Decarbonization Pathways for Mines: A Headlamp in the Darkness." Rocky Mountain Institute, 2018. https://info.rmi.org/path-ways_for_mines/ (Accessed 19th October 2020).

KPMG. (2021). "Climate related risks in financial statements." 21RU-002 Climate-related risks in financial statements (assets.kpmg). (Accessed 17th March 2021).

Latham & Watkins. (2014). "Shared Use of Mining Infrastructures." shared-use-mining-infrastructure-SSA-2014 (lw.com). (Accessed 14th December 2020).

Laszlo, C. (2008). Sustainable Value. Problems of sustainable Development, Vol. 3, No. 2, pp. 25-29, 2008, Available at SSRN: https://ssrn.com/abstract=1481164 (Accessed 28 June, 2021).

Laszlo, C. (2003). The sustainable company: How to Create Lasting Value Through Social and Environmental Performance (Island Press, Washington DC - October 8 2003, ISBN 1-55963-836-2).

Ireland, G. (2013). Latham & Watkins - "Financing Mining Infrastructure: Unlocking Africa's Resource Potential III." G20 Africa Infrastructure Investment Conference 17-19 July 2013. Microsoft PowerPoint - G20 Mining Seminar - Financing Mining Infrastructure - Glen Ireland - 19 July 2013(2942594_1_LO).PPTX [R (lw.com). (Accessed 14th December 2020).

Michael Matteson, M. and Metivier C. (2021). Understanding Friedman's thesis. In Busines Ethics. Understanding Friedman's thesis | Business Ethics (uncg.edu) (Accessed 20th June 2021).

M'cleod, H. (2013, December 13). "Sustainable development and iron ore production in Sierra Leone: The next 50 years. International Growth Center." https://www.theigc.org/blog/sustainable-development-and-iron-ore-production-in-sierra-leone-the-next-50-years/ (Accessed 14th September 2020).

Mining Association of Canada - MAC. (2019). "TSM 101: A Primer." https://mining.ca/wp-content/uploads/2019/07/TSM-Primer-English-Final-1.pdf (Accessed 10th December 2020).

Mining Association of Canada - MAC. (2020). "Biodiversity Conservation Management Protocol." https://mining.ca/wp-content/uploads/2020/03/FINAL-2020-Protocol-Biodiversity.pdf (Accessed 10th December, 2020).

Mining Association of Canada - MAC. (2021, May 5). Canada's Mining Industry Commits to Climate Change Action. Canada's Mining Industry Commits to Climate Change Action - The Mining Association of Canada (Accessed 10 May, 2021).

MACIG. (2019). "Global Business Report—West Africa." https://www.gbreports.com/files/pdf/_2018/MACIG-2019-prerelease-2-WestAfrica-v16-medres.pdf. (Accessed 17th December, 2020).

Manning, T. (2016). "Financing Mechanisms to support sustainable practices." Center for Sustainable Business, New York University Stern.

Manning, T. (2018). "Green Bonds: What's New, What's Next and Why does it Matter." Center for Sustainable Business, New York University Stern.

McKeeman, R., Brewer, L. (2012). "Non-technical risk leadership: Integration and execution. " Paper presented at the International Conference on Health, Safety and Environment in Oil and Gas Exploration and Production, Perth, Australia, September 2012. Paper Number: SPE-157575-MS. (Accessed 11th November, 2018).

McKinsey & Company. (2013). "Competitiveness and challenges in the steel industry." OECD Steel committee 74th session, Paris, July 1, 2013. http://www.oecd.org/sti/ind/Item%203.%20McKinsey%20-%20Competitveness%20in%20the%20steel%20industry%20(OECD)%20-%20final.pdf (Accessed 18th December, 2020).

McKinsey. (2020). "Climate risk and decarbonization: What every mining CEO needs to know." Climate risk and decarbonization: What every mining CEO needs to know (mckinsey.com) (Accessed 17th March, 2021).

Melca Ethiopia. (2017). New African Commission Resolution on the protection of Sacred Natural Sites.

Ministère de l'Énergie et des Ressources naturelles du Québec - MERN. (2017). "Analyse de risques et de vulnérabilités liés aux changements climatiques pour le secteur minier Québécois." analyse-changements-climatiques-secteur-minier.pdf (gouv.qc.ca). (Accessed 11th December 2020).

MeSteel (2002). Steel and trade in sub-saharan Africa. Paper presented at the 4th regional meeting on trade in steel products organised jointly by the arab iron and steel union and the Jordan steel company held at amman, jordan on 3rd to 5th june, 2002. Steel and trade in sub-saharan africa (mesteel.com) (Accessed 18th November, 2020).

Millennium Ecosystem Assessment. (2005). "Ecosystems and Human Well-Being: Opportunities and Challenges for Business and Industry." World Resources Institute.

Mining Intelligence. (2020). "China-backed JV set to start work at Simandou." https://www.mining.com/china-backed-jv-about-to-start-work-at-guineas-simandou/ (Accessed 17th January, 2021).

Mining Intelligence. (2020). "Friedland's Nimba iron ore project to get World Bank backing." https://www.mining.com/friedlands-nimba-iron-ore-project-to-get-world-bank-backing/ (Accessed 17th January, 2021).

Mining Intelligence. (2020). "Guinea approves SMB-Winning deal for Simandou." https://www.mining.com/web/guinea-approves-smb-winning-deal-for-simandou/ (Accessed 17th January, 2021).

Mining Technology. (n.d.). "Marampa Haematite Iron Ore Mine." https://www.mining-technology.com/projects/marampamine/ (Accessed 17th January, 2021).

Mining Technology. (n.d.). "Tonkolili Iron Ore Mine." https://www.mining-technology.com/projects/tonkolili-iron-ore-mine/ (Accessed 17th January, 2021).

Minor, D., Morgan, J. (2011). "CSR as Reputation Insurance." California Management Review, 53(3), 40-59.

Sy, M. and Hathie, I. (n.d.) "Institutional Forms of Philanthropy in West Africa. IDRC. PBDD." Microsoft Word - Institutional forms of Philanthropy SY HATHIE Formatted.doc (issuelab.org). (Accessed 7th October, 2020).

MSCI. (2013). "User Guide & Ratings Definition." MSCI ESG Stats.

Naidoo, S. (2012). "Nationalization taken off the table at mining indaba." Mail & Guardian, Accessed from: https://mg.co.za/article/2012-02-06-nationalisation-taken-off-the-table-at-mining-indaba (Accessed 18th October, 2019).

Narfeldt, S. (2017). "Opinion: How to invest responsibly in Africa's human capital." https://www.devex.com/news/opinion-how-to-invest-responsibly-in-africa-s-human-capital-91343 (Accessed 14th November, 2019)

National Resources Governance Institute. (2015). "Local content—Strengthening the Local Economy and Workforce." https://resourcegovernance.org/sites/default/files/nrgi_Local-Content.pdf. (Accessed 30th April, 2020)

Newmont (2020). "Investing $500 Million to Address Climate Change." Newmont Corporation - Sustainability - Climate Change (Accessed 15th January, 2021).

Niamey 2J. (2018). "Interférence des groupes terroristes dans la production et le commerce de l'or au Niger, au Burkina Faso et au Mali (rapport OCDE)." https://www.niameyetles2jours.com/l-economie/mines/0911-3087-interference-des-groupes-terroristes-dans-la-production-et-le-commerce-de-l-or-au-niger-au-burkina-faso-et-au-mali-rapport-ocde (Accessed 20th November, 2019)

Nicholls R J. (2004). "Coastal flooding and wetland loss in the 21st century: changes under the SRES climate and socio-economic scenarios." Global Environmental Change. 14: pp 69 – 86

Odon, A. (2015). "Why local content in Africa's extractive sector won't work without home grown human capital." http://theconversation.com/

why-local-content-in-africas-extractive-sector-wont-work-without-home-grown-human-capital-45133 (Accessed 24th October, 2019)

Organisation for Economic Co-operation and Development - OECD. (2019). "The Post-2020 Biodiversity Framework: Targets, indicators and measurability implications at global and national level." report-the-post-2020-biodiversity-framework-targets-indicators-and-measurability-implications-at-global-and-national-level.pdf (oecd.org) (Accessed 10th January, 2021).

Organisation for Economic Co-operation and Development - OECD. (2020). "The Post-2020 Biodiversity Framework: Targets, indicators and measurability implications at global and national level." The Post-2020 Biodiversity Framework: Targets, indicators and measurability implications at global and national level - OECD (Accessed 10th January, 2021).

Paydar. (2014). "Workforce Nationalization in Emerging Oil and Gas Markets" https://www.onepetro.org/conference-paper/SPE-172036-MS. (Accessed 6th May, 2019)

Porter, M. E., van der Linde, C. (1995). "Green and Competitive." Harvard Business Review (September October), 120-134.

Porter, M. E., van der Linde, C. (1995). "Toward a New Conception of the Environment-Competitiveness Relationship." Journal of Economic Perspectives, 9(4), 97118.

PricewaterhouseCoopers. (2015). Ian Aruofor - Understanding West Africa's Infrastructure Potential. understanding-was-infrastructure-potential.pdf (pwc.com). (Accessed 13th February 2021)

Reddy, G., Smyth, E., Steyn, M. (2015). Land Access and Resettlement: A Guide to Best Practice. Sheffield, Greenleaf Publishing

rePlan. (2014). "Teranga Development Strategy. Executive Summary." http://s1.q4cdn.com/851853033/files/doc_downloads/CSR/140318_TDS_SUMMARY_Eng_v001_n0cecn.pdf. (Accessed 15th March, 2019)

Reuters. (2019). "Guinea's Nimba iron ore project gets green light to export via Liberia." https://www.reuters.com/article/us-guinea-iron-idUSKBN1WQ2CL (Accessed 12th October, 2020)

Reuters. (2020). Jeff Lewis, Helen Reid. "Gold miners must ramp up renewable energy to meet climate goals: industry group." Gold miners must ramp up renewable energy to meet climate goals: industry group | Reuters. (Accessed 11th February 2021)

Reuters. (2021, February 19). Duncan Miriri. African Union to set up infrastructure fund for the continent | Reuters. (Accessed 16th March, 2021)

Ritchie, H. (2020, September 18). "Sector by sector: where do global greenhouse gas emissions come from." Sector by sector: where do global greenhouse gas emissions come from? - Our World in Data (Accessed 16th March, 2021)

Rio Tinto (2018, October 28). Rio Tinto update on Simandou. Rio Tinto update on Simandou (Accessed 26th May, 2021)

Rio Tinto. (2020, September 4). Rio Tinto provides additional information to Parliamentary Inquiry on Juukan Gorge. Rio Tinto provides additional information to Parliamentary Inquiry on Juukan Gorge (Accessed 26 June, 2021).

Robinson, R., Brooks, R. F. (2010). "West Africa: the climate of change Climate change impacts, awareness and preparedness across West Africa." University of Cambridge Programme for Sustainability Leadership." https://www.cisl.cam.ac.uk/resources/publication-pdfs/west-africa-final-report-v2. (Accessed 26th November, 2020)

Ruggie, J. (2011). "Managing human rights impact in a world of converging expectation." 60120 (ideaspaz.org) (Accessed 13th September, 2020)

Russell Investments (2018). Emily Steinbarth & Scott Bennet. "Targeting the ESG issues that impact performance—the material ESG score." Materiality Matters. http://images.engage.russellinvestments.com/Web/FrankRussellCompany/%7B1f483faf-a3d9-48d2-91ef43940d14c757%7D Materiality Matters EMEA V1D1 1801.pdf?ga=2.189515947.1063218450.1535615991-1603196335.1535615991 Accessed 13th April, 2019)

Scheible, D. (2017). "The role of expatriation in the context of managing diversity in international organizations."https://www.researchgate.net/publication/335321181 The Role of Expatriation in the Context of Managing Diversity in International Organizations. (Accessed 15th March, 2020)

Shared Value Initiative. (2014). "Extracting with Purpose—Creating Shared Value in the Oil and Gas and Mining Sector's Companies and Communities." Extracting-with-Purpose-FSG.pdf (sharedvalue.org.au) (Accessed 20th November, 2018)

Sierra Express Media. (2020, September 26). Abdul Malik Bangura "China Kingho Takes Over Tonkolili Iron Ore Mines In Sierra Leone." https://sierraexpressmedia.com/?p=88043 (Accessed 18th November, 2020)

African Arguments (2020, April 6). Sirleaf, E. J., Koroma, E. B. "When biodiversity fails, human health is on the line." When biodiversity fails, human health is on the line | African Arguments (Accessed 10th January, 2021).

SL Mining. (2019, August 14). « Government communications. » https://slmining. com/government-communication/ (Accessed 18th September, 2020)

Société Minière de Boké - SMB. (2020, June 27). "Guinée : l'Assemblée Nationale donne le feu vert à SMB-Winning pour exploiter Simandou, un projet à 15 milliards $." http://www.smb-guinee.com/guinee-lassemblee-nationale-donne-le-feu-vert-a-smb-winning-pour-exploiter-simandou-un-projet-a-15-milliards/ (Accessed 18th September, 2020)

Smith, H. (2008). "Using Traditional Ecological Knowledge to Develop Closure Criteria in Tropical Australia." https://papers.acg.uwa.edu.au/d/852_6_Smith/6 Smith.pdf. Northern Land Council, Australia. Mine Closure 2008 – A.B. Fourie, M. Tibbett, I.M. Weiersbye, P.J. Dye (eds) © 2008 Australian Centre for Geomechanics, Perth, ISBN 978-0-9804185-6-9. (Accessed 13th September, 2020)

Société Nationale Industrielle et Minière - SNIM. (2013a, March 3). "Mine." https://www.snim.com/index.php/operations/mines.html. (Accessed 15th January, 2021).

Société Nationale Industrielle et Minière - SNIM - SNIM. (2013b, March 3). "Train minéralier." https://www.snim.com/index.php/operations/train.html (Accessed 15th January, 2021).

Société Nationale Industrielle et Minière - SNIM - SNIM. (2013b, March 3). "Port." Port minéralier (snim.com) (Accessed 15th January, 2021).

Société Nationale Industrielle et Minière - SNIM - SNIM. (2013d, March 3). "Marché." Marchés (snim.com) (Accessed 15th January, 2021).

Steinweg, T., Römgens, I. (2015). SOMO. "African Minerals in Sierra Leone. How a controversial iron ore company went bankrupt and what that means for local communities." https://www.somo.nl/wp-content/uploads/2015/04/African-Minerals-in-Sierra-Leone.pdf (Accessed 10th September, 2020).

Stephenson, P. J., Carbone, G. (2021). "Guidelines for planning and monitoring corporate biodiversity performance." Gland, Switzerland: IUCN. https://portals.iucn.org/library/sites/library/files/documents/2021-009-En.pdf (Accessed 30th March, 2021).

Lydenberg, S., Rogers, J., Wood, D. (2012). "From Transparency to Performance. Industry-Based Sustainability Reporting on Key Issues." The Hauser Center for nonprofit organizations at Harvard University – Initiative for Responsible Investment. https://iri.hks.harvard.edu/files/iri/files/iri_transparency-to-performance.pdf (Accessed 16th January, 2019).

Sustainability Accounting Standards Board. (2013). "Conceptual Framework." http://www.sasb.org/approach/conceptualframework/ (Accessed 10th March, 2020).

Sustainability Accounting Standard Board. (2020). SASB, "Proposed Changes to the SASB Conceptual Framework and Rules of Procedure," August 2020. Invitation-to-Comment-SASB-CF-RoP.pdf (Accessed 26 June, 2021).

Sustainable Brands. (2018, November 6). Alissa Stevens, Aishwarya Chaturvedi, Cindy Mehallow, Aurora Dawn, Benton Mia Overall and Max Pinnola "Finance and Investment. Future Value, Submerged Value, ROP and other facets of ROI sustainability." Future Value, Submerged Value, 'ROP' & Other Facets of the ROI of Sustainability - Sustainable Brands (Accessed 17th May, 2019).

Task Force on Climate-related Financial Disclosures - TCDF. (2017). "Recommendations of the Task Force on Climate-related Financial Disclosures." https://assets.bbhub.io/company/sites/60/2020/10/FINAL-2017-TCFD-Report-11052018.pdf (Accessed 18th October, 2020).

Task Force on Climate-related Financial Disclosures - TCDF. (2017). "Implementing the Recommendations of the Task Force on Climate-related Financial Disclosures." FINAL-TCFD-Annex-Amended-121517.pdf (bbhub.io) (Accessed 18th October, 2020).

Teranga Gold Corporation. (2019). "Sustainability report 2018." https://s2.q4cdn.com/949220588/files/doc_downloads/responsibility_governance/responsibilityReports/Teranga_Gold_2018_Responsibility_Report_ENG.pdf (Accessed 7th February, 2020).

The Fourth Revolution (2020). "Massachusetts to require new cars sold to be electric by 2035". Massachusetts to require new cars sold to be electric by 2035 - The Fourth Revolution (thefourth-revolution.com). (Accessed 30th March, 2021).

The Sierra Leone Telegraph (2019, June 21). Abdul Rashid Thomas - "Sierra Leone resumes iron ore export after painfully long break. " https://www.thesierraleonetelegraph.com/

sierra-leone-resumes-iron-ore-export-after-painfully-long-break/ (Accessed 10th October, 2020).

Thomashausen, S., Glen, P., (2015). "Shared-use mining infrastructure in sub-Saharan Africa ". 7(1) Mining Law Committee News 9 (2015). https://scholarship.law.columbia.edu/sustainable_investment_staffpubs/128 (Accessed 5th October, 2020).

Thomashausen, S., Ireland, G. (2015). "Shared-use mining infrastructure in sub-Saharan Africa: challenges and opportunities." Mining Law Committee Newsletter – October 2015. Mining-Law-Shared-use-mining-infrastructure-in-sub-Saharan-Africa-Oct-2015.pdf (columbia.edu) (Accessed 5th October, 2020).

Toledano, P., Thomashausen, S., Maennling, N., Shah, A., (2014). "A Framework to Approach Shared Use of Mining-Related Infrastructure." Columbia Center on Sustainable Investment, Columbia University. A-Framework-for-Shared-use_March-2014.pdf (columbia.edu) (Accessed 5th October, 2020).

Mining Association of Canada - MAC. (2020). Toward Sustainable Mining - Biodiversity Conservation Management Protocol. https://mining.ca/wp-content/uploads/2020/03/FINAL-2020-Protocol-Biodiversity.pdf (Accessed 17th November, 2020).

UNDP, Columbia Center on Sustainable Development, Sustainable Development Network, and World Economic Forum (2016). "Mapping Mining to the Sustainable Development Goals: An Atlas."Mapping Mining to the SDGs: An Atlas | UNDP

Craterre-ENSAG / Convention France-UNESCO (2006). "Cultural heritage and local development. A guide for African local governments." https://whc.unesco.org/en/documents/116273

United Nations Framework Convention on Climate Change - UNFCCC. (n.d.). "Climate change: Impacts, vulnerabilities and adaption in developing countries." Climate change: impacts, vulnerabilities and adaptation in developing countries (unfccc.int) (Accessed 27th November, 2020).

United Nations. (2009). "Africa Review Report on Mining - Economic commission for Africa - Committee on Food Security and Sustainable Development." *Microsoft Word - CFSSD-6 African Review Report on Mining Summary-English (un.org) (Accessed 11th July, 2020).

United Nations. (2018). "Sustainable Development Goals." https://www.un.org/sustainabledevelopment/sustainable-development-goals/ (Accessed 19th March, 2019).

UN-REDD. (2020). "About REDD+." What is REDD+? - UN-REDD Programme Collaborative Online Workspace (Accessed 27th January, 2021).

United States Geological Survey - USGS. (n.d.). "West Africa: Land Use and Land Cover Dynamics." https://eros.usgs.gov/westafrica/node/157 (Accessed 14th October, 2020).

Vale. (2019, December 12). Vale informs on the release of the Report of the Expert Panel on the Technical Causes of the Failure of Feijão Dam I. Vale informs on the release of the Report of the Expert Panel on the Technical Causes of the Failure of Feijão Dam I (Accessed 26 June, 2021).

West Africa Biodiversity and Climate Change - WA BiCC (2020). Reducing Deforestation, Forest Degradation, And Biodiversity Loss – West Africa Biodiversity and Climate Change (WA BiCC).(Accessed 3rd March, 2021).

Whelan, T., Fink, C. (2016). "Is Sustainability Part of Your Employer Brand?" Harvard Business Review. https://www.cebglobal.com/talentdaily/sustainability-employer-brand/ (Accessed 18th November, 2018).

Whelan, T. and Fink, C. (2016, October 21). The Comprehensive Business Case for Sustainability. The Comprehensive Business Case for Sustainability (hbr.org) (Accessed 13 March 2019).

Wikipedia. (2020). "Laudato si." Laudato si' — Wikipédia (wikipedia.org) (Accessed 27th October, 2020).

Wikipedia. (2020). "Stripping ratio." Stripping ratio - Wikipedia (Accessed 14th October, 2020).

World Bank Group. (2012). "Increasing local procurement by the mining industry in West Africa : road-test version (English) ". Washington, D.C. : World Bank Group. http://documents.worldbank.org/curated/en/361611468338459156/Increasing-local-procurement-by-the-mining-industry-in-West-Africa-road-test-version (Accessed 14th March, 2020).

World Bank Group. (2020). Climate-Smart Mining Facility - Kirsten Hund, Daniele La Porta, Thao P. Fabregas, Tim Laing, John Drexhage "Minerals for Climate Action: The Mineral Intensity of the Clean Energy Transition." Minerals-for-Climate-Action-The-Mineral-Intensity-of-the-Clean-Energy-Transition.pdf (worldbank.org) (Accessed 19th January, 2021).

World Bank Group, IFC, UKaid. (2019). "A Guide to Community Engagement for Public-Private Partnerships. Draft for discussion." A Guide to Community Engagement for Public-Private Partnerships - Draft Discussion June 2019.pdf (worldbank.org) (Accessed 17th April, 2020).

West African Power Pool - WAPP. (2020). "Member countries of the WAPP. http://www.ecowapp.org/en/content/creation-wapp (Accessed 13th January, 2021).

World Bank Group. (2020, July 27). The African Continental Free Trade Area. The African Continental Free Trade Area (worldbank.org) (Accessed 16th December, 2020).

World Steel Association. (2020). "About steel." https://www.worldsteel.org/about-steel.html (Accessed 24th January, 2021).

World Steel Association. (2020). "World steel in figures." https://www.worldsteel.org/en/dam/jcr:f7982217-cfde-4fdc-8ba0-795ed807f513/World%2520Steel%2520in%2520Figures%25202020i.pdf (Accessed 24th January, 2021).

Yahoo Finance. (2015, April 21). Shivam Srivastava - "Shandong acquires Tonkolili iron ore mine from African Minerals." Shandong acquires Tonkolili iron ore mine from African Minerals (yahoo.com) (Accessed 13th September, 2020).

Zhuwarara, S. (2019, February 22). "Aligning beneficiation with sustainability in Zimbabwe." Mining Review online. https://www.miningreview.com/top-stories/beneficiation-sustainability-zimbabwe/ (Accessed 10th September, 2020).